Peter van Sommers is a distinguished Australian psychologist. He teaches at the School of Behavioural Sciences, Macquarie University. He has been involved in research and interviewing on jealousy for the past two decades. He is the author of *The Biology of Behaviour* and *Drawing and Cognition*.

PETER VAN SOMMERS

— Q —

JEALOUSY

PENGUIN BOOKS

PENGUIN BOOKS

Published by the Penguin Group
27 Wrights Lane, London W8 5TZ, England
Viking Penguin Inc., 40 West 23rd Street, New York, New York 10010, USA
Penguin Books Australia Ltd, Ringwood, Victoria, Australia
Penguin Books Canada Ltd, 2801 John Street, Markham, Ontario, Canada L3R 1B4
Penguin Books (NZ) Ltd, 182–190 Wairau Road, Auckland 10, New Zealand

Penguin Books Ltd, Registered Offices: Harmondsworth, Middlesex, England

First published 1988

Filmset in Linotron 202 Palatino

Typeset, printed and bound in Great Britain by
Hazell Watson & Viney Limited
Member of BPCC plc
Aylesbury Bucks

Contents

———————— Q ————————

To Robin Winkler

Preface

— Q —

This book deals chiefly with sexual jealousy. It has been written for ordinary readers including not only those who are jealous or have jealous partners, but also anyone with an intelligent curiosity about complex human emotions. I do not try to defend or celebrate jealousy, but I do try to counter the idea that it is intrinsically abnormal. Jealousy is not a sign of a weak, corrupt or immature mind. It ought to be acknowledged and understood, not denied, abused or brushed aside.

I have made generous use of first-hand accounts of jealousy from people I have interviewed, extracts from biographies and diaries, and case histories compiled by other authors. I dip into history and biology, into anthropology and psychoanalysis. There is a chapter on morbid or pathological jealousy and a short section on treatment for severe jealousy. My approach is also 'political': I am interested in how and why jealous people have been denigrated and abused, in the way infidelity and jealousy relate to freedom and duty, and in how modern feminism deals with the problems of sexual 'triangles'.

I can perhaps offer a brief 'reading guide'. Although I have tried to write simply throughout, I also wanted to treat the topic seriously so that students, academics and professionals could get something useful from the book. I wouldn't say that the chapters on anthropology, on the Mediterranean 'societies of honour and shame' and on biology are 'dry', but they are necessarily less personal. They try to struggle with the big question: how to comprehend jealousy and other complex emotions that seem to owe something to biology and a lot to culture. In this sense the book is a bit of a sandwich: there are many more interview extracts and case histories in the earlier and later chapters and a more 'straight' material in three central chapters.

I am not psychoanalytically oriented. Indeed I include a rather sceptical chapter on Freud's treatment of jealousy, and I completely neglect Melanie Klein. (At the time I write this another, somewhat bigger, book is available, which gives a sympathetic hearing to her views, so the topic is by no means an orphan.)

A second 'blind spot' is the topic of jealousy in homosexual relationships on which I lack adequate case material. An equally significant omission is the whole area of modern quantitative studies of sexual or romantic jealousy which were excluded for reasons of length. The reference list for Chapter 1 includes an excellent review by two pivotal contributors to this research, Robert Bringle and Bram Buunk, that will give the interested reader guidance.

People regularly ask me whether my interest in jealousy is personal. It isn't. Comparing notes with others suggests that I am probably somewhere about half-way down the jealousy spectrum. In the late 1960s, at the time when 'a thousand flowers' were trying to bloom in psychology, I began urging my senior students to break out and look at some new topics of real significance to people and society, and to adopt an approach more similar to that of natural history. One student, Jan Milton, chose to study embarrassment, which turned out to be very difficult, and another, Kathy Ernst, took up jealousy, which we found very productive for reasons I describe at the beginning of Chapter 1. I have kept an academic interest in the topic ever since.

It might seem obvious that some of the best material on jealousy should be in literature, so let me say a word about fiction. Readers may be disgusted to learn that I have never been a great fan of *Othello*, nor of the *Medea* of Euripides, at least in their written forms. Academically I find fiction to have distinct strengths and limitations, and I identify the split as lying between *theory* and *evocation*. Plots of novels and plays can be suggestive, but unless they are actually disguised biographies, they are doubtful sources of evidence. Take one of the great literary treatments of jealousy: Tolstoy's *Kreutzer Sonata*. From the point at which the narrator, Pozdnychev, awakes at night in the country with an overwhelming feeling of rage and dread, to the moment where he is trying to face the reality of having murdered his wife, the description is riveting. But the material in that same story about the relationship between youthful debauchery and later jealousy I found inauthentic, and a reading of Tolstoy's own Epilogue confirms that that part of the exercise is quite artificial and didactic. But to read Swann (I nearly said Proust) trying to extract information from Odette, or Anna Karenina's final struggle to rescue her relationship with Vronsky before she kills herself, or the introspective passages dealing with alienation and exclusion in Simone de Beauvoir's novel *L'Invitée* can't be passed over, any more than the eloquent letters and diaries that tell us how people like Bertrand Russell, Vita Sackville-West or Freud himself felt, day by day, about their passions.

I have many people to acknowledge. I must put Robin MacKenzie at the top of the list. I regard myself as a sort of brash student of Robin and of Gill Bottomley, as well as of Margie Jolly, Martha McIntyre, John Franklin, Daphne Hewson, Ailsa Burns, June Crawford, Julie Marcus, Rosemary Pringle, Nick Modjeska, Ian Bedford, Gill Cowlishaw, Les Hiatt, Carol Boland, Beverley Tulloch, Kay Bussey, Una Gault, Wendy Cowling, Jim Jupp, and Graeme Russell. Overseas, I must acknowledge Ayala Pines, Michael Shepherd and Annette Lawson who directed me to several of the writers discussed in the final chapter and whose book on adultery I eagerly await. Thanks are also due to Pauline Presland, Karen Neeley and Kerry Murray for research help.

I am indebted to the Penguin editor in Australia, Jackie Yowell, who first encouraged the project, and Andrew Franklin in London, who saw it on its way. I have had brave assistance from some excellent secretaries, Sharon Stephens, Robyn Price, Barbara Freeman and Di Jones. Finally the staff at Macquarie Library (Inter-library Loans in particular) and at the library at the Sorbonne provided me with excellent service.

Peter van Sommers
December 1986

CHAPTER 1

My Lover's Lover is My Enemy

———————— Q ————————

WHAT DEFINES JEALOUSY?

In psychological terms jealousy is not always easy to distinguish from envy, but the dictionary makes this separation: envy concerns what you would like to have but don't possess, jealousy (from the same origin as 'zealous') concerns what you have and do not wish to lose. Jealousy comes in many forms, but the particular variety I shall be dissecting here is sexual jealousy: reactions to intrusions upon a sexual attachment, what Tellenbach has inelegantly called 'venereal jealousy'.

Intermittently over a period of years I have been interviewing men and women from eighteen years old to their mid-forties about their experiences of jealousy. My informants come in response to an invitation posted on university bulletin boards. Occasionally they refer one another. I begin each interview with a simple definition of the topic of inquiry. I make it clear that I prefer to hear first-hand experiences rather than theory. It has not proved difficult to get informants launched on the topic and once started they exhibit an unnerving degree of 'total recall'.

Subjects in psychological inquiries are prone to bias their reactions towards what they feel the investigator is seeking. It would be foolish to claim that this hasn't happened to me, but it is perhaps not as great a problem as it might be, since my informants typically give detailed accounts of their experiences in very concrete terms and with a minimum of intervention on my part. Indeed I sometimes have difficulty in breaking in on their accounts long enough to ask that they slow the rate of delivery so that I can take notes.

A few people come because they need help with debilitating jealousy, but the majority feel that their jealousy, though distressing, is within the normal range. A minority of informants report long discussions with their partners about their jealousy, often in the course of a confrontation, but most report that they conceal their jealousy and have never before talked frankly to anyone about it at any length. They may express surprise at their present candour, and not uncommonly they report that exploring their experiences with a stranger who occasionally nods with (feigned?) understanding is something of a catharsis.

It is not hard to recognize why feelings of jealousy are a private agony for so many people. Jealous reactions are diverse, as we shall see, but they are uniformly unpleasant. Few people go out of their way to be made jealous, and it is for many the bitterest of their discontents. Many informants feel that revealing their jealousy to their partner is counterproductive, at least in the short term. If one is competing unsuccessfully for someone's affection and allegiance, trying to win them back by expressing anger, depression or humiliation and calling them to account is not the strategy of first choice. Laclos has one of his characters say to her hostile lover,

Either you have a rival or you have not. If you have one, you must please [me] if you wish to be preferred to him; if you do not have a rival, you must still please to avoid having one . . . All I can say in answer to your threatening letter, then, is that it has neither the gift of pleasing me nor the power of intimidating me, and that at the moment I could not be less disposed to grant your demands.

Jealousy is notorious for making us do things that even at the time we know are fatal. Aldous Huxley expresses this on the first page of *Point Counter Point* in a passage so telling that I suspect it discouraged many people from reading the rest of the novel:

It was two years now since they had begun to live together. Only two years; and now already, he had ceased to love her, he had begun to love someone else . . . 'Half past twelve,' she implored, though she knew that her importunity would only annoy him, only make him love her the less. But she could not prevent herself from speaking . . . It would have been better for her, and perhaps better for Walter too, if she had had fewer principles and given her feelings the violent expression they demanded . . . An imploring 'Half past twelve, Walter' was all that managed to break through her principles. Too weak to move him, the feeble outburst would only annoy. She knew it and yet she could not hold her tongue.

The passage brings out poignantly the forces carrying someone forward from their passion into the territory that in a spirit of cold rationality they would not enter, and the reaction when it comes is a product of a sort of unhapppy marriage, if I can use the phrase, between passion, calculation and gentility.

2

The jealous do not seem any more attractive to themselves than they appear to others, nor do they feel capable of remedying the situation. It is remarkable how often the people I interview have said that they cannot stop 'being jealous'. They can and often do control the more destructive expressions of their jealousy, although this suppression is rarely complete. (It isn't easy to act with spontaneous gaiety and effervescence when undergoing a jealous crisis.) But while such external management is often feasible, to shut off the internal emotional reaction is evidently not a simple feat. Yet these very same people who report that their own jealousy is intractable, in the next breath conform to popular opinion and say that jealousy in another person is a profitless and destructive thing that could be banished by the application of a little personal insight.

To this mixture of pain, ugliness and impotence can be added another ingredient: the acceptance of blame by the jealous. I shall describe later the strong moralistic tone adopted towards jealousy in most treatments of the topic in both popular and pastoral literature and the elaborate insults that are heaped on the jealous. Jealousy is widely regarded as a character fault. It is a symptom of defective affections, of a warped development. It is written about as though jealous persons were immediately responsible both for their reactions and for the unhealthy emotional relationships that are alleged to lie behind them.

Jealousy has acquired yet another taint. It is often held to be politically and ideologically illegitimate. In particular it is said to arise when we treat those we love as our property, so the jealous commit a double crime: treating people as objects and claiming private possession of them. Karen Durbin described this most recent addition to the sins of the jealous thus: 'To be jealous is to be the capitalist pig of the heart: you're being possessive . . . being politically incorrect.'

What this adds up to is that people are caught with emotions they don't like, that jeopardize the very relations they seek to protect, that are supposedly the products of unhealthy emotional traits, and that are a source of guilt because of their ideological impropriety and their poor fit with modern sexual mores. No wonder people so often try to keep all this under cover and express relief at being able to spill it out to an uncritical stranger!

Before I review some theories of jealousy I should like to make clear my attitude towards certain modern psychological treatments not just of jealousy, but of emotions in general.

Jealousy, when it is mentioned at all in standard psychological writing, is classified as a 'complex' emotion (by contrast with fear or anger, which are simple or primary emotions). Stanley Schachter conducted some influential psychological experiments on the physiological and cognitive bases of complex emotions. The view that he developed has become very popular in all branches of psychology, but I do not accept it. Briefly, Schachter stated that if a person is injected with the hormone adrenalin, which circulates in the bloodstream during many emotional states, it produces a relatively undifferentiated state of restlessness and arousal. Put in hilarious company the subjects of this treatment are supposed to report themselves amused; put in hostile company, they report themselves angry. What this purports to show is that the bodily (that is the physiological, organic, 'biological') aspect of emotion is diffuse and unstructured, and the fine tuning of the system is cognitive, social and learned.

I don't believe Schachter's experiment shows any such thing. There have been disputes about the outcome of Schachter's original experiment and some difficulty in reproducing it, but that is not my main concern. Even if Schachter's study had produced robust effects, I don't believe it tells us what we need to know about the structure of emotions or their origins. The fault with the argument was to equate 'physiological', or 'biological', with 'resulting from blood-borne chemicals', as though all the biological effects must operate from the neck down and everything that goes on in the brain is necessarily cognitive and learned.

We have some evidence on this from a rather unusual source, the split-brain patient – a person in whom the two halves of the brain have been disconnected for medical reasons by cutting the large bundles of nerve fibres that cross the mid-line. Although the right hemisphere of the brain cannot ordinarily produce speech, it can receive and respond to information, including material that provokes emotional reactions. If by careful experimental procedures the right hemisphere is given exclusive access to some event like a foul smell or an erotic picture, it will process this information and generate an emotional reaction. In certain cases this emotion seems to be restricted to one half-brain, so that the other half may hear a word produced by its isolated partner as part of an emotional reaction. Gordon and Sperry had subjects who would exclaim 'Ugh', 'Yuk' or 'Whew' in response to a strong or disgusting smell administered to the right half-brain, although the left seemed neither to experience the emotion itself nor to know what caused it. In other words, the particular emotion mechanism seemed to be controlled quite high up in the brain.

Michael Gazzaniga later reported that in some instances one half-brain *can* experience emotions generated in the other hemisphere. In such cases the nervous activity has evidently passed down through the lower parts of the brain that have not been split and across to the other hemisphere. The emotions may be quite distinctive. The person feels indignant or embarrassed by a suggestion of kissing the experimenter, is titillated by a nude picture, amused by old family photographs, made 'nice and calm' by a holiday picture of the ocean, or made scared and jumpy about the risk of fire. In each case the emotion is identified quite specifically, yet the semi-isolated half-brain that identifies it knows nothing whatever about the situation that provoked it. Hence one of Gazzaniga's split-brain patients, having seen with one half-brain a film of people being threatened by fire said:

I don't really know why, but I'm kind of scared. I feel jumpy. I think maybe I don't like this room, or maybe it's you. You're getting me nervous.

When shown a photograph of a nude person one subject chuckled, smiled and made a comment about 'that funny machine'.

As Gazzaniga says, the idea that we identify specific emotions only by our knowledge of the provocation is quite ruled out by these experiments, which show that the brain generates quite specific and recognizable emotions. This is of course what most of us would have believed in the first place. We don't necessarily need to look at the world to discover how we feel. We sense that we are tense or calm, buoyant or depressed, mischievous or apprehensive, sexy or irritable, without any obvious outside trigger that helps us identify the nature of our emotions, which are felt as individually distinct experiences. In a later chapter we shall see that strong jealousy itself can occasionally arise from some obscure inner cause with the result that pathologically jealous people actually have to search for reasons for the jealousy they feel.

Given that the brain may generate distinct emotions, is this a biological process or something entirely learned and social? Biology could well be expected to contribute, for the brain contains large

5

masses of tissue, specifically in the limbic system that handles emotional and motivational processes linked to sexuality, aggressivity, attachment and so on. The details of how such circuitry operates in humans is understood in only the most fragmentary way, but there is certainly no reason for disqualifying all biological factors from contributing to our experience of complex emotions simply because the presence of chemicals like adrenalin in the bloodstream do not have very specialized effects.

This excursion into physiological psychology I feel is necessary to clear the decks for what is called in the jargon an 'interactionist' view, a view that entertains the possibility that complex emotions, whether they be grief, love, loneliness, embarrassment, jealousy, panic or whatever, may result from some interweaving of a hereditary mechanism or predisposition, developmental history and social force. It would be profitless to try to parcel out fractions or components to one or other of these variables, but I think it would be unfortunate if any of the theories I am about to discuss were dismissed out of hand because they were or were not based on allegations about biological, cultural, social-developmental or any other type of influence. We may need them all.

ESSENTIALISM IS OUT

Jealousy arises when there is a challenge to a special relationship we have with someone, or when we think there is. The sexual, affectionate and contractual relationships we have with partners and lovers are very complex affairs. When they are challenged through infidelity or threaten to disintegrate we have very complex and variable reactions, which I shall be exploring throughout this book.

Most traditional writers on jealousy began from an intellectual tradition called 'essentialism'. Each tried to develop a single, powerful, systematic idea about jealousy. It was an approach that was applied not only to emotions like love or jealousy but to humour, aesthetics, curiosity or whatever else they were analysing. Each theorist picked up a certain legitimate observation about the topic and tried to expand it to cover all the cases. As a result we have separate, monolithic, 'jealousy-is-nothing-but' theories that see it as due to possessiveness, or selfish love, or vanity, or excessive tendencies to control a partner, and so on. No matter what the theory, exceptions invariably came to light. To take one example, if jealousy is essentially frustration at a reduction in sexual favours due to sharing, we run into theoretical difficulties with retrospective jealousy, that is jealousy of people who are no longer present. What do we then do? Discard the idea of loss of sexual services and affection altogether, like a hat that doesn't fit, and search for another? My answer is that we will never find the perfect hat, because we are trying to fit a creature with many heads. Once we recognize that virtually all the theorists picked up something useful, but then took the false step of trying to build it into an essentialist principle, we can begin to adopt a more constructive attitude to their work. If we were foresters and wanted to know why trees languish and die, we should not consider making a grand theory solely from impoverished soil, acid rain or the elm beetle. We would develop a more complex view of alternatives and combinations. We must do the same in the groves of passion. So in the section that follows we shall review some of the major theoretical ideas, examining example and counter example.

Some theorists, like Freud or the biologists, have proposed more internally elaborate theories that can't be dealt with simply by acknowledging their positive value, and to them I have devoted special chapters.

JEALOUSY AS AN ATAVISTIC DRIVE

The most venerable theory of jealousy regards it as an 'atavistic emotion'. This simply suggests that we have inherited it from our forebears (which these days usually means early humans or our primate ancestors). Boris Sokoloff provides us with a resoundingly unambiguous statement of the position:

To us, jealousy is not only inbred in human nature, but it is the most basic, all-pervasive emotion which touches man in all aspects of every human relationship. The origin of this emotion may be found in the past of mankind, when man was wild and primitive. And yet in jealousy, the intensity and force of this reaction does not diminish with the development of sophistication . . . we believe and we intend to prove that jealousy is autonomous to a great degree, an independent psychological unit of enormously variable manifestations . . .

For readers who do not have Sokoloff's book at hand but have had their curiosity aroused by his promise of proof, let me say that what he offers is a remarkable set of case studies of severe jealous reactions, in many cases amounting to obsession and madness and resulting to varying degrees in social manipulation, cruelty and

7

violence. He certainly sustains his claim that jealous behaviour can have great intensity and force, but I doubt whether that would cut any ice with those who want to deny evolutionary roots to the phenomenon of jealousy.

I chose the term 'atavistic' rather than simply 'instinctive' to bring out the implication that jealousy is not only an inherited tendency, but is also seen as irrational or, even more important, as barbaric and destructive. Davis comments, 'Jealousy is . . . regarded as an animal urge, and since biological nature and socio-logical nature are assumed to be eternally at odds, jealousy is denounced as anti-social.'

Modern students of biological contributions to behaviour and experience would have a much easier task if the contrast between the biological and the social were so clear. Our difficulties arise from our recognition that animal existence is above all social, and that instinctive behaviour was selected because of its usefulness in a social setting. For this reason the differences between the biologi-cal and the sociological are not those between the nonfunctional and functional or the irrational and the rational. Arguments now typically draw on speculative reconstructions of the environment and social life of early humans that attempt to establish what selection pressures might have been operating and what might have evolved as a result. Any element of 'irrationality' is hence based on a mismatch between tendencies developed in one social milieu (that in which humans evolved) and the needs of another (for example, some twentieth-century western culture).

Another reason for thinking jealousy might be 'instinctive' is that it can be so strong, so passionate. Let us consider the qualities that Weitman gives as the credentials of 'passions':

Passions are here defined as that class of sentiments which distinguish themselves by their extraordinary intensity, their automaticity, their capacity to overwhelm and their escalatory propensities.

There is some justification for believing that genetic mechanisms might have a clumsy, automatic character, because we can think of them as rough 'rules of thumb', useful across many generations. It may be generally adaptive for a bird to drive out all other animals from a nest site because of the strong likelihood that intruders will be predators or sexual competitors. It is presumably better from an evolutionary point of view *not* to ask that this discovery be made on the basis of experience by each succeeding generation, since unless there are complex guides to action being transmitted within the animal community from experienced to inexperienced animals, each generation of parent birds is likely to lose at least the first nestful of offspring in the process of becoming knowledgeable!

Unless there are facilities available to the animals to tune and refine their behaviour to take account of local conditions, we might expect the mechanism to have a blind, mechanical quality to them. As I shall mention later, there is in fact every reason to believe that genetic mechanisms *are* tuned and adapted in terms of experience, but let us accept the 'brute force' tag for the moment.

The remaining question is, why should all genetic mechanisms be thought of as characteristically intense, so overwhelming, so prone to escalation? The fact is that they aren't. There are many items of behaviour that have a well-attested genetic basis that are quite low-key. The question therefore becomes, if jealousy has a genetic basis, why has it evolved as a reaction of great intensity and force? Because the force that it is trying to combat is also powerful? Because the cost of failure is so high?

The suggestion that jealousy is instinctive or 'atavistic' does not absolve us from the responsibility of finding some logic to its presence, since functionalism is at the heart of instinct theory. Likewise finding a social logic to jealousy does not inevitably lead us to the conclusion that it is a product of culture. At this point I will not take the question of the possible biological contribution to jealousy any further, because later I devote a whole chapter to the issue. I simply want to note that throughout the history of the topic there has been a recurring belief that jealousy involved, at least in part, an inherited mechanism or predisposition. Although this book documents and emphasizes cultural contributions to jealous experiences and reactions, I do not feel able to reject this long-standing view.

JEALOUSY IN INFANCY

Certainly there is plenty of documentation of jealousy among young children, although it isn't easy to decide whether this is equivalent to sexual jealousy. Generations of children have invented jealousy for themselves if they didn't inherit it. It is not my intention to explore jealousy in childhood in much detail. A couple of first-rate books (by Dunn and by Dunn and Kendrick) have appeared recently, and I shall quickly mention a few of the matters their research has revealed. Even a brief glimpse shows that some of the 'received wisdom' on the subject has turned out not to be so wise, and that the topic has its own special intricacies. Back in 1927 Sybil Foster put the view that jealousy in children was a product simply of incitement by parents. Foster studied fifty children who had been referred to 'Habit Clinics' in Boston in the 1920s, partly at least because of a problem with strong jealousy. She reported numerous incidents in which parents drew pointed comparisons between the children to the detriment of the jealous child. I would not claim that this does not happen, but I find it impossible to believe that it is an essential cause of infantile jealousy. Foster herself quotes the case of a boy who showed no jealousy until one day his mother covered the baby with the boy's favourite blanket, and many of the incidents of incitement occur *after* the manifestation of jealousy rather than before.

Dunn emphasizes that (fortunately) absolute, unrelenting antagonism between brothers and sisters is rare, as most parents know. Along with vigilance, hostility, upset and naughtiness there is attachment, caring and interest. Next, not all the conflicts between siblings can be properly attributed to jealousy. This is important if we hope to establish links between childhood and adult jealousy by asking adults to recall their childhood experiences, because what they are likely to call up are memories of general friction and resentment rather than strife due specifically to jealousy over their brother's or sister's relations with adults. Children are in conflict over many things: over space ('Keep out of my room'); over possessions ('Leave my bike alone'). There is conflict over moral authority and discipline – children boss one another about, either self-righteously or with blatant self-interest. In larger families children may 'team up' and there may be conflicts over allegiance. There may be envy of qualities and achievements and competition between siblings. I am not claiming that these conflicts cannot be made worse by jealousy, but according to Dunn one can find children who rarely fight, who frequently share, but who none the less get very jealous over a brother's or sister's relationship with adults. In any event it is doubtful whether a global characterization of 'jealous' or 'not jealous' is always appropriate, because it is not uncommon for a child to be jealous of one of its siblings but not of another. Likewise there may be no clue in the relationships a child has with people outside the family to jealousy within it.

Jealousy, or at least upset, at the arrival of another child in a family certainly seems common enough. Parents with jealous children sometimes fail to recognize to what a large club they belong (just as they sometimes underestimate how many adults experience jealousy). In the first instance it is the older child who is likely to react badly. When a baby brother or sister arrived, 93 per cent of the Eng-

10

lish children that Dunn and Kendrick studied became more demanding and naughty. (Dunn describes a child who methodically sprinkled the sofa with milk from his cup as a reaction to an excess of mutual admiration between his mother and baby sister.) It was less common for children in Dunn's Cambridge group to attack a sibling directly, although it does happen. (I regard as classic the case of a toddler who reached into the cot, removed the bottle from the baby's mouth, drank the milk and hit the baby with the empty bottle.) Dunn and Kendrick's children seemed to restrict themselves largely to aggravating their siblings rather than assaulting them. Dunn points out that small children often achieve their most precocious intellectual feats in calculating what will most effectively annoy their parents and siblings in the context of jealousy.

Over half the children Dunn and Kendrick studied became more 'clinging and tearful', and returned to a more babyish way of acting. Over a quarter had greater sleeping problems. There is an interesting paper by Wisdom that suggests that the children's problems may sometimes be compounded by guilt about their own aggressive feelings. He relates the story of a child subject to nightmares who was actually comforted by being shown the baby before he went to sleep, which presumably reassured him that his secret desire to annihilate his little brother had not been fulfilled.

Much of the aggravation is directed at adults – not just at mothers, but also at fathers and grandparents. According to Dunn and Kendrick, '50 per cent were said to be jealous of the grandparents holding or playing with the baby'.

Classic theory would predict the greatest jealousy to be between children of the same sex, on the grounds that they are in direct competition for the love of the parent of the opposite sex, but Dunn quotes three independent studies showing just the reverse: cross-sex jealousy is more potent. According to Dunn, mothers pay more attention to their new babies if they are of a different sex from the preceding child, so when children are of different sexes there may be more provocation – more to be jealous about.

Classic theory would also predict that breastfeeding would be a particularly potent incitement to jealousy. Dr Spock evidently supported this idea, no doubt taking a lead from psychoanalysis, but this, too, is contradicted by the research findings. It is *bottle*-feeding that provokes more adverse reactions. Here too there seems to be a rather pragmatic explanation. According to Dunn, mothers who breastfeed recognize that they are going to be more completely out

11

of action and hence make more elaborate provisions to amuse or distract the older child.

What would we expect to accentuate jealousy, a background of attention, or a background of relative indifference? Mothers who played a lot with the older child before or around the time of the birth of the baby encountered more jealousy. Is this just because there is more to be lost by the older child? According to the research, mothers who play a lot with one child will do the same with the second, so once again there is an issue of increased provocation to jealousy. This may also explain the rather odd fact that when a mother experienced particular depression and fatigue after the birth of the second child, fourteen months later the children ended up on *better* terms with one another than the norm, according to Dunn and Kendrick.

We do not have a very clear understanding of the relationship, if any, between childhood jealousy and adult sexual jealousy, but I hope I have said enough about the situation in early childhood to discourage any 'potted' thinking on the topic. Jealousy in childhood is certainly pervasive. It appears early. But it isn't necessarily a simple, stable characteristic of particular children. With the possible exception of a tendency on the part of certain jealous children to be withdrawn and anxious, much of the effect seems to be related to how much change there is in the situation facing the child, how much attention he or she had previously received, how much the parent lays the groundwork for the new child's arrival, how much attention is paid to the new child, and how much care the parent takes to look after the immediate needs of the potentially jealous child (as in the breastfeeding case). These are largely situational matters, and although they may affect the relations between the two siblings in an enduring way, that is not to say they produce a generally jealous person, because as we have seen, a child may be jealous of one sibling and not of another. And in any case there is plenty of documentation of rivalry between children giving way at a later age to great affection and mutual support.

I think it would be surprising if jealousy between children had nothing in common with jealousy in adults. The same mechanisms may very well be involved. But I do not believe you have to have experienced pronounced jealousy in childhood in order to experience it later, and I know of no good evidence that adult jealousy is a replay of infantile emotions except that cited by theorists who want to see *all* adult emotions as based on childhood reactions, conscious or unconscious. (This is a theme to which we shall return in the chaper on Freudian theory.)

12

But childhood jealousy, particularly early jealousy, does have some relevance to the question of whether jealousy is 'natural', simply because it appears so early. It certainly creates difficulties for people who think that jealousy is the product of modern industrial society and years of conditioning to concepts of property. These things may shape and amplify jealousy, but whether they create it initially is another question entirely.

At one time I thought that the nature–nurture issue about jealousy was all-important. Now I feel that it is theoretically interesting but in practice perhaps rather beside the point, since if jealousy is a social construction it has been constructed so firmly for many people it might almost as well have been laid down in their genes! On the other hand, if it is biological, it is so dependent on social meaning and developmental history that it might as well be regarded basically as a product of society. As I said earlier, few individuals seem able to eradicate jealousy entirely. We may protect ourselves from it either by failing to commit ourselves to deep attachment or by engineering security from intrusion or unfaithfulness. Likewise we may more or less successfully curtail or manage the active expression of jealousy, but until someone discovers a reliable strategy to eradicate it at the core, it has to be accepted as a powerful phenomenon, irrespective of its biological or social origins.

THE ECONOMICS OF ACCESS

In speaking about jealousy in childhood, I observed that the child's behaviour is not without its economic point, even if the basic demand is extravagant and the reactions exaggerated. The appearance of another infant in the family inevitably means that there will be a sharing of attention, affection and care. Whether young children have fully formulated this in their minds or are following a genetic pre-scription based ultimately on that reality is not clear. As Dawkins comments, 'Survival machines do not do sums in their heads'. It is crediting a small child with considerable prescience to assume that jealousy of a freshly arrived first brother or sister is based on an immediate assessment of the future limitations of access, but it cannot be ruled out.

The model invoked here to account for jealousy is one of absolute deprivation in a situation of limited goods. An economic situation in which individuals have to compete for a fixed quantity of something – in which one person's gain is another's loss – is termed a 'zero-sum model' (pluses for one are cancelled by minuses for the other). When

13

someone intrudes upon a close emotional relationship, what is it that is being competed for? Time, emotional energy, sexual potency, tranquillity. (Biologists might add, access to reproductive opportunity.) In other words jealousy is seen not so much as a primary process in itself but as a predictable outcome to a contraction in the supply of emotional goods. The reaction, according to this view, is not unique or special; it is simply the anger or sorrow that one might expect if anything at all were to interrupt or threaten these. Hoyland asked himself why, as his unfaithful wife became happier, he felt 'so crushed, so left out, so insecure, so inadequate, so lonely, so paranoid':

Partly, and most obviously, her present gain is my present loss. Nearly all her sexual and emotional energy is going out to C— not me. Our sex life has pretty well come to a full stop. She is still too involved in her relationship with C— to be able to parcel out her emotions as she would like.

The issue of access can obviously be very real, but it may play different roles at different times. In the heat of the first collision with infidelity the jealous person may be supremely unreceptive to reassurances about access to the partner's attention. At a later stage demonstrations of love maintained may or may not soften the blow.

Perhaps one of the most civilized (and unlikely) exchanges on this issue of the economics of access was that between Voltaire and the highly intelligent Marquise du Châtelet. As Nancy Mitford tells the story, Voltaire walked in on his inamorata and a young aristocrat for whom she had developed a temporary passion 'at a moment when it is preferable not to be interrupted'. Voltaire exploded with indignation. There was an argument, during which Voltaire sensibly refused an invitation to a duel. He called for his carriage and prepared to leave. The Marquise managed by a subterfuge to delay his departure long enough for his temper to cool. Then they had the following conversation:

Mme du Châtelet: I still love you . . . but you must admit it's a long time now since you have been able to —. I have no wish to kill you, nobody is more concerned with your health than I. On the other hand, I have my own to consider. As you can do nothing for it any longer it is not very reasonable of you to be so angry when I find one of your friends who can.
Voltaire (laughing): Ah, Madame . . . of course you are in the right as usual. But you really should manage that these things do not take place before my eyes.

Voltaire was then fifty-four and had told the Marquise at the age of forty-six that he was too old to make love. It is difficult to know if the

14

recovery of his temper was due to his celebrated rationalism or to the cooling of his ardour. (Shortly afterwards his infirmities were remedied on the couch of his next and last lover, Mme Denis.)

Even if the infidelity is not known to the partner, the economics of access may still be invoked. Seeman reports how the women she was treating for pathological jealousy reconciled their own infidelities with their strong jealous feelings towards their husbands: 'It was never done in his time. I didn't take anything away from him.' The husbands, they claimed, stole real time by staying at work to be with their lovers. Furthermore the women said that they managed to be just as affectionate in spite of having lovers, while the husbands were incapable of maintaining two sexual relationships in parallel.

Spiteful and Retrospective Jealousy

There are at least two cases that don't fit with the theory of the economics of access. The first is that of 'spiteful' jealousy, where the jealous person is not at all interested in what a partner has to offer, yet resents intrusions upon it. This is common in long-established relationships from which sexual feelings and affection have largely departed. It certainly appears often enough in pathological jealousy, which seems to be precipitated in certain cases by a decline in sexual ability by the jealous person. Those sexual feelings and affections may exist of course in a mythical form. In other words, the parties may never have made it explicit to themselves or to one another that there is no real warmth or affection left in the relationship and so nothing to be lost.

The second exception is the familiar phenomenon of retrospective jealousy, where past history is called to account. One agonizes not over present or future deprivations arising from another's gains, but over events that can no longer affect the quantity and duration of access to one's partner. Quite irrationally one wants to rewrite history to make oneself the only object of real passion at *any* time.

Exclusivity

There is another emotional commodity involved that renders the 'zero-sum' game irrelevant. What many people value in emotional relations is *exclusivity*. Indeed the notion of exclusive or 'top priority' attachment is a very important one in both love and jealousy, and once exclusivity is involved, it does not matter whether an intruder reduces time, attention, potency or reproductive privileges; any intrusion is enough to prejudice the special relationship.

This may be seen in situations where a partner, for reasons either of guilt or of personal consideration, lavishes extra loving attention on a partner while developing an outside attachment. The discovery of such a relationship cannot be depended upon to pass with cosy tranquillity. Even if the total fund of emotional goods is expanded generously to accommodate both who share, the attack on exclusivity is likely to be most important. Many bouquets and chocolate boxes have been trampled and hurled when such expanded generosity has been 'unmasked' as a failure to maintain exclusivity.

It would be unwise, however, to leave the zero-sum theory itself too heavily trampled. Jon Wagner, trying to adopt a constructive attitude towards sexual sharing, describes how he survived and even in a limited sense benefited from the arrival of his lover's lover in his house. The situation was a precarious one, but it seems to have succeeded through a combination of two factors: first, a vague feeling that the situation was not permanent; and second, the well-advertised care taken by the girl in the triangle to ensure that neither of her lovers suffered rejection or loss of affectional privileges as a result of the presence of the other. That is, she tried her best to ensure that it was not a 'zero-sum' game.

Ideas of economic trade-off have featured more prominently in theories of envy than jealousy. The two major reviews of the subject by Schoeck and G. M. Foster are essentially economic. Foster, in particular, explores the idea of 'zero-sum societies', societies in which the assumption strongly prevails that benefits are always at another's expense.

THE THEORY OF PROPERTY

In explaining some of the current ideological hostility to the jealous, I referred to the links between property, possessiveness and attachment. The idea that jealousy is a reaction to trespass on property is clearly related to the economic notions we have just discussed, but it also introduces some new ideas. Kingsley Davis pointed out that we have not one but several relations to property, and these apply both to objects and to persons. We use property in satisfying needs: food and shelter in the case of objects, servants and prostitutes in the case of persons. Property also supports pride and vanity. The distinction between pride and vanity has an old-fashioned flavour but concerns the legitimacy of our claims to public regard: pride is a legitimately earned credit for what we own; vanity is based on the mere crude fact of possession. It is a little hard at first to see that anyone can justly claim credit for 'owning' a person. All public display and ego-boosting through association with an attractive individual seems obnoxious. But as we shall see when we consider society's attitude to the jealous and ask why certain jealousies call forth sympathy and others scorn and ridicule, we do have a calculus of legitimate and illegitimate claims to public regard connected with our personal associations. These public attitudes are not necessarily rational or attractive but they are compelling and real.

Davis points out that what makes the ownership of persons so precarious is the fact that the person we 'own' (love) controls the affection we seek, and the more deeply we care about that ownership, the more vulnerable we become. It is as though one were a collector in a world where each connoisseur can keep only one art object at a time (serial monogamy). The quality of the piece one collects represents a measure of one's worth as a collector. But what if the art object with which one has such success is itself capable not only of choice, but also of changes of preferences for collectors? It is not hard to see why initial choices may be tentative and the collectors and the collected may be inclined to make pacts and contracts to stabilize the trade!

This analysis emphasizes the public aspect of attachment and loss. When people are belittling jealousy it often suits their purposes to caricature affection and attachment as mere vanity about the outward show of possession. But consider Sally Vincent's description of her reactions when she walked in on her lover having breakfast with another girl: 'I would have killed her. Sitting there with *my* man, at *my* table, eating *my* egg with *my* spoon.' The language is that of possession, but the sentiment refers to the destruction of an image. Some of the most poignant experiences I have heard described by my informants were when they were suddenly confronted by the fact that their (ex) lovers had systematically exploited the whole of a private world they had constructed and shared together to impress another person.

It is unreasonable to dub this merely frustrated possessiveness. The problem is that shared private worlds are not to be held in easy contempt. Rightly or wrongly we have invested certain ways of treating one another sexually with special status. Many people in our society take great pains to emphasize that they value sexual relations most when they are embedded in a context of care and personal regard. They appreciate being treated as worthy of special attention

17

and invest sometimes quite trivial places and occasions with special significance. If we wish to attack this as a breeding ground of destructive emotions such as jealousy, I do not think it is honest to rewrite it as crude public possessiveness, like that of a man who struts before a band that went home two blocks back. This is an especially clear example of why it is important not to press too hard towards a monolithic theory of jealousy. We need an account of jealous anger at a loss of public prestige, but also a theory that accounts for some aspects of jealousy in terms of the destruction of a personal world.

LOSS OF CONTROL

Whitehurst describes the eruption of jealous anger of certain men into violence. The simplest explanation of this is simply to say that jealousy varies in intensity, and if strong enough expresses itself as violence. Whitehurst prefers to say that the violence gains some of its motivation from an attempt by the man to reassert his identity after a failure of control. This does not of course refer to the loss of control of his temper, but to the relationship that is threatened. There is an implication here that the need to control in such situations is greater in men than in women, and this is certainly consistent with the common view Whitehurst propounds, that within our society there has been less emphasis on autonomy, initiative and assertiveness for women than for men.

There are two aspects to control. The first concerns people who, even under stable, unthreatening conditions, need to maintain ascendancy and tight constraint in a relationship. Such people might react acutely to an intrusion because it challenges control. The most exaggerated instance I can give of this came from a male informant who had recurring disputes within his marriage about his wife's freedom. First he spoke as if he had done his wife a favour in marrying her. Then he went on: 'She is very limited in what she can do. She is more or less restricted to the house. I feel responsible for that. She would like a car. She wouldn't get past the driving test. She wears strong glasses. I would worry about her safety.' As the interview progressed a whole series of such statements emerged: 'There are problems of security. Too many things happen these days. She makes contacts very easily. You don't know people's motives for establishing contact. She is indiscriminate. She talks to strangers in the street.' And finally, 'She understands it [the control]. We talk about it, but fall back into it.' Of course the control and jealousy are tightly related, but one has the impression that the pervasive control is not entirely inspired by jealousy as it is in other cases.

The other notion of control concerns reactions to existing threats. Even a person who doesn't keep a firm ascendancy over another under normal circumstances may react to an intrusion by attempting to monitor and shape the ensuing events. Obviously many men and women have much to lose in such predicaments. Some seize the initiative in advance, and so it occasionally happens that partners stage-manage their partner's infidelity. The motives may be mixed but one seems to be 'If my partner is going to be unfaithful, at least I shall prescribe when and how'. Perhaps this allows the potentially jealous partner to construe the event differently. They tell themselves that their partners did not really prefer the other person sufficiently to initiate things themselves. The partner is becoming faithless only in a superficial, opportunistic way. It also places the jealous person in a superior position over the potential rival, by suggesting that he or she could not have become the lover without help. It marks the rival as someone who has been manipulated – a pawn in the hands of the partners, who act as a team.

There is also the possibility that the jealous partner sets up one rival in order to keep another out, as in the case of a woman who made all the arrangements for a liaison between her husband and a young girl he was becoming attracted to. She may have simply seen that a relationship was inevitable and wanted to convert it into an action on her part, but it is also possible that a young girl did not represent as deep a threat to the partnership as a sophisticated older woman might have done.

The process is not invariably successful, at least in the short term. In the case just mentioned the woman had a bad reaction to the liaison she had orchestrated. Another woman described to me how she arranged a meeting that she sensed was about to occur between her lover and an attractive female friend. She tried to neutralize the threat by suggesting sexual experimentation for 'clinical' reasons, but the matter got out of hand (from her point of view) almost immediately.

Again, to say that jealousy is an aspect of a need to control hardly does justice to the situation. In the case of the man who restricted his wife's mobility there is a complex blending of control with jealousy. In the latter instances control is a response to jealousy rather than jealousy being simply a failure to control.

Linton described the sexual relation of the Marquesans. These Poly-nesian people had two broad categories of sexual behaviour: 'gang' sexual activities, which were varied, public, vigorous and promiscu-ous; and 'private affairs' in which selection was important. Rebuffs in private affairs might lead to stereotyped and well-advertised suicides (self-poisoning by women, the men diving head first from high trees). Such suicides did not occur amongst all groups of men and women, but were restricted to married women (whose husbands were attend-ing to another woman) or unmarried men who had been rebuffed. According to Linton, 'The main factor seems to have been wounded pride . . . fear of ridicule was undoubtedly an important factor in the prevalence of suicide because of jilted love.'

The Marquesan culture allows us to separate the audience effect from a preoccupation with the emotional relationship between the couple. Linton reports that jealousy in the form of hostility towards intruders is unacceptable behaviour. It is rarely expressed except when people become drunk. So the suicides, which are acceptable public gestures, are not identified with jealousy in the sense of per-sonal hostility and resentment, for this cannot legitimately be expressed in public. It is the social significance of the jilting that counts.

Within our culture we use the term 'jealousy' as a relatively undif-ferentiated term that includes public humiliation, disappointment and hostility. Such fusing does make some sense, of course, because the shattering of an inner romantic image, the hostility to intrusion and the hurt from public loss of regard appear as an amalgam. It is not possible to make an absolute distinction between the shattering of private and of public images, since the private image is about social relationships.

My informants varied considerably in their preoccupation with the audience. One man reported a rather complicated emotional life with lovers who themselves had affairs. When I inquired how the personal attractiveness of his partners affected his jealous reactions he replied, 'To me internally, it's worse if she's attractive. To the audience, the less attractive one is worse.' It seems that some are so intent on their personal disappointment that the public significance of the event passes them by completely. At the other extreme is a young man who brought a girl to the city from an outlying town. He had no interest in her at a personal level. 'She was,' he said 'just a body.' But when the 'body' proved capable of exercising choice and began talking to other men in a bar the young man reacted with fury at what he experienced as a social insult. Another youth described how he telephoned a girl and was told that she 'had an appointment'. The youth told this to his friends and they went off together to the city. There they encountered the girl with another friend. The feeling of public humiliation was very powerful.

Public impact can compound private hurt. 'I was the last to know,' said a woman. 'At least he could have made some effort to be discrete.' In spite of the emphasis in this comment on public impact, the woman was very injured personally both by the infidelity and by the absence of diplomacy. The indiscretion not only exposed her to public comment, but conveyed a profound disregard for her feelings.

One woman informant received the first news of unfaithfulness within a long-term relationship by overhearing gossip in the supermarket. In another instance the news first reached the children, who kept it to themselves, and later the wife learned not only of the infidelity itself, but also of the public awareness *and* of the children's prior knowledge. The combination was devastating. It seems hardly reasonable to categorize this merely as 'concern for public appearances', on a par with the man whose sexual ornament from the country displayed indifference to him in a public bar.

We cannot deal with the role of the audience simply by saying that it is unhealthy to care about one's public image in emotional relations. Certainly nobody wastes much sympathy on the sexual show-off; but the person who is the last to know of the disintegration of an important emotional relationship surely warrants more compassion.

The 'public' may in some instances be a creation of the jealous person's imagination, as he or she rakes over inner rage and resentment. The privatization of jealousy – the social and personal process of driving it underground – may protect people from hurtful public opinion, but it may also prevent them from learning how unimportant or unthreatening it may actually be. One informant watched his wife at a dinner party joking with a man from the local swimming club. A woman seated beside him unwittingly referred to a long-standing flirtation between the two, assuming that the husband knew of it. The man was dismayed and upset and tried to terminate the conversation. His informant did not catch this message and pressed on. Fortunately her next comment, as he put it, 'demolished the whole thing. She said he [the intruder] was pathetic. It was just trivial. It obviously didn't reflect on me.'

An 18-year-old girl whose boyfriend was having an affair with another girl reported, 'It took me some time to realize what was going

21

on. My *male* friends noticed it. That made me feel better, because it made me feel not so crazy at getting upset.' Here the intensity of emotional expression seemed to be reduced by public legitimization of her feelings.

Of course, as I mentioned earlier, public disclosure can be very damaging, and many people know themselves well enough to try to avoid it and forestall unnecessary hurt: 'I don't want to know', is a common comment by mature informants.

LOVE AS ADDICTION, JEALOUSY AS WITHDRAWAL

There remains the question of whether jealousy is tied to a particular form of love. Peele and Brodsky suggest that love can take on the aspect of an addiction and rejection produces the symptoms of withdrawal. If we take this to mean that love and grieving over loss have an obsessive quality, I think it is a fair observation. But of course addiction and withdrawal have overtones of deviance and wilful self-abuse, and in this sense they are echoing in an extreme form the common view that jealousy is a product of faulty affections. Like many of the allegations about jealousy, this is not a carefully researched idea; it is a casual hunch that a bad thing like jealousy must spring from disreputable antecedents. Since love and jealousy are complex phenomena and they both justify a more thoughtful dissection, I shall devote the next chapter to an exploration of love and a review of the jealous reactions.

CHAPTER 2

Love and Jealous Reactions

───────── Q ─────────

JEALOUSY AND WRONG LOVING

That love and jealousy are related is hardly news, but writers have tried to tie jealousy to certain sorts of love, and, naturally enough, see it as a product of an inferior variety. This bad variety is variously called 'need-love' or 'deficiency-love' (Maslow). It is dependent, regressive (i.e. infantile) and is motivated by what one can get out of love. Its antithesis has a more ethereal quality. Lewis calls it 'gift-love', Maslow, 'being-love'. The theme is sharing, if not giving. I want to underline the implication that it is the 'bad' love that cultivates jealousy. The image is of a morbidly sucking child that screams or broods when the teat is removed – hardly the type of allegation to make jealous people more pleased with themselves.

Let me make a brief observation about this idea: there seems to be no hard evidence to suggest that jealousy *is* more pronounced in those whose passion is to take rather than to give. I do not believe this is as self-evident as some writers imply. The very first person I interviewed said, 'I am a giver. Occasionally I want for myself, but really I try to read what *he* wants.' This included sexuality, in which the man's enjoyment was the primary aim, and all aspects of her domestic and recreational relationships with men. Yet her sequence of affiliations and love affairs was punctuated by incidents of jealousy of one degree of severity or another.

I have no doubt that such cases could be discounted by saying that this isn't 'real' giving. I suspect, however, that the claim is not fundamentally one of fact, but arises from a need in the writers to discredit jealousy. Regrettably it also puts down the jealous. Nor should we easily assume that 'giving' love is on other grounds as delightful a thing as this literature would have us believe. In *The Second Sex* Simone de Beauvoir uses the example of Sonya Tolstoy to point up the destructive impact of total giving, and sees jealousy as one of the weapons to defend oneself in a disastrously impotent position.

LOVE AND SEXUALITY

Let me begin my discussion of love with an academic anecdote. A few years ago I was making a little speech on how neglected the topic of love was from the point of view of academic psychology (a situation that in the meantime has been partially rectified). The most usual rejoined would be, 'Why not leave love alone?' But on this occasion a colleague said, 'It is simply secondary reinforcement. What more do you need to know?' What does that mean? It means that love arises from sexual relief. It means that all the varieties and intricacies of love – the attraction, attachment, affection, the ache, the caring, the giving, the grooming, the dreaming and doubting, fears, fantasies, shared confidences, the blindnesses, the isolation from the world – all these are accidental encrustations on the final reward, the moment of sexual ecstasy, like someone who loves a vacuum cleaner that happens to fall under their gaze at the instant of orgasm. What can I say? Perhaps that it might simplify life if we made love to melons or cucumbers, bought gifts of fertilizer and wrote odes to the vegetable patch. My colleague's remark not only dismisses and trivializes the phenomenon of love but also alleges an identity between attachment and sexuality that is probably wrong. Attraction, attachment and sexuality may in practice coincide and closely interact, but they may none the less involve separate processes.

THE FUNCTIONS OF LOVE

Just as I feel that there may be some biological underpinnings to jealousy, so I suspect that certain core aspects of love, in the sense of attraction and attachment, are part of our emotional and motivational inheritance. It doesn't sound a very radical view, but it is probably a more popular idea among the general population than among academic thinkers. Sociologists, anthropologists and historians have difficulties with it because they are conscious of the mutability of desire. The emphasis on love and attachment varies so much from society to society and from one historical period to another. What is attractive seems culturally unpredictable and fickle. Psychologists, too, have doubts, partly because they find it difficult to conceive how a biological mechanism of love might work under such circumstances (van Sommers, 1986).

24

Since the same problem arises with grief and depression, hatred, the attachment of parents and children, and many social reactions found in lower animals, we have to find a way around the problem or convince ourselves that biology contributes nothing to feelings and conduct. I shall explain in Chapter 5 how these difficulties might be tackled, but for the present I shall side-step the problem and ask what love is and what biological functions it might serve.

At the very least love involves being attracted to a partner and 'bonding' to them for a time. This, combined with sexuality, serves rather obvious functions in promoting the survival of genes in the next generation. But presumably this could be achieved without the dramatic events we describe as 'falling in love' or 'infatuation', which are documented so eloquently by Tennov in her recent book on love: intrusive thinking about the loved person, acute longing for signs of acceptance, idealization, vivid imagining, mood swings from buoyancy to despair depending on reciprocation, and so on.

It is vital to recognize the social nature of the process. Let me start with a statement by Theodore Reik:

What is the aim of sex? We have already stated it: the disappearance of a *physical* tension, a discharge and a *release*. What is the aim of the desire we call love? Disappearance of a *psychical* tension, a *relief*. In this contrast between release and relief lies one of the most decisive differences . . . The sex urge hunts for lustful pleasures; love is in search of joy and happiness.

Reik is making the important distinction between sexuality and attachment that I mentioned earlier, but he is doing so in the language of romantic individualism. Love is defined from the viewpoint of one person. Reik talks of aims, but says nothing about functions. He makes contact with neither the social nor the biological aspects of love.

If we go back to evolutionary principles, we shall see that in pair formation in advanced animals, including humans, there is a very fundamental conflict. On the one hand there is a need for out-breeding, exogamy (the avoidance of mating with immediate genetic relatives, in particular parents and siblings). On the other there is a well-attested, biologically based shyness and reticence with strangers, described by Eibl-Eiblesfeldt. In other words, we need to be attracted to, to court, and ultimately to make the most intimate physical and emotional contact with outsiders whom we are naturally inclined to shun.

The process we call passionate love or infatuation can be seen as a mechanism well suited to resolving this paradox. It involves strong attraction, a rapid collapse of shyness, idealization and a sort of 'tunnel vision' – an intense preoccupation with the loved person. These processes are in fact most dramatic and intense when the object of love is a stranger. It is a universal theme in literature and folklore, but it also gains some support from research. There is the long-term effect of sexual attraction being weakened by the process of growing up together, as seems to happen in the Israeli kibbutz, and the shorter-term one of daily contact between mature individuals decreasing the likelihood of 'grand passions'. When students first started living together in university coeducational residences they reported that the most intense romantic infatuations tended to be those with outsiders.

In certain societies sexual contact outside the family or lineage group is achieved by social arrangement. Partners may simply be assigned to each other, usually the women to the men; the biological and cultural ends are met by a combination of sexuality, power and, where necessary, force. But in most societies, even those in which marriages are arranged, the process of attraction and attachment and the development of emotional intimacy will be found somewhere, either within the formal system or outside it (as when elopements occur, sometimes at the risk of severe punishment or death).

RECIPROCITY AND GIVING

Whether the process of falling in love is social, or a mixture of the social and the biological, there is another issue to be clarified. To form a partnership two processes are needed *within each member of the pair*. We must like the other person and want them to like us. We must be attracted and want to be attractive, love and want to be loved. The processes are separate but complementary. They are normal and necessary. When you ask people about the texture of their love they include both 'I want to look at the person' and 'I want the person to look at me'; 'I miss the person' and 'I hope they miss me'. They like to give gifts and to be given gifts.

Giving itself has a double edge. We may think of it as selfless, as generous, but the exploration of the subtleties of gift-giving by Mauss has made us aware that the act of giving ties the receiver into a web of obligation. Whatever we give – objects, advice, compliments – we alter the balance of the relationship in a significant way. It is for this reason that we are often at pains to decline gifts.

I have mentioned writers who want to characterize jealous love as somehow defective by contrasting healthy 'giving' love and unhealthy 'taking' love. Even Margaret Mead followed this theme:

26

The . . . distinction can be observed between the behaviour of the zealous suitor and the jealous one. He who is zealous studies his mistress's face to learn her pleasure, seeks out special gifts to please her, tries to arouse her interest and fulfil her slightest wish; all of his behaviour is positive, constructive, directed towards a goal. But the jealous suitor looks into her face only to read there his own dismissal or signs of his rival's triumph . . .

Her description of the jealous person can hardly be disputed, but the earlier remarks about the zealous giver are based on a superficial view of both love and giving. It may well be that we give the most when we care the most and will under such circumstances be most devastated by a loss of love. Giving is not necessarily a sign of an asymmetry in a relationship; it may also be a personal style. Occasionally both members of a new partnership make the rather comical discovery that both want to please more than be pleased.

INTENSITY, ASYMMETRY AND THE COCOON OF LOVE

In reviewing the properties of love that might be relevant to jealousy, intensity hardly needs listing. L'amour can be faible or fou, mild or mad. It can also be balanced or lopsided and the couple can be encapsulated, detached from the rest of the social world, or can stay in the open. Finally, love can vary in its quality. I cannot promise rigorously to relate all of these four qualities – intensity, symmetry, isolation, and variety of love – to jealousy, but they provide an agenda for inquiry. Popular belief would certainly maintain that jealousy would be most prominent when love is intense rather than weak, asymmetrical rather than balanced, isolated rather than gregarious, and passionate rather than companionable. But we shall later encounter Freud himself, jealous of his wife when passion has given way to routine, by no means socially isolated, nor a victim of unrequited regard, angrily complaining of her vivacity and sociability at a dinner party!

The balance of a relationship involves a complex piece of accounting, especially when sexual and social partnerships become the centre of activities in the form of a family or household. There are not only questions of attractiveness and attraction, but also all the economic and practical contributions being made by the partners. Hatfield, Traupmann and Walster discuss this in the language of 'equity theory'. They analysed 2,000 responses to a magazine survey conducted by *Psychology Today* in North America on the subject of love and equity.

The finding relevant to jealousy was the strong relationship between equity judgements and infidelity. People who saw their relationships as 'balanced' had fewer extramarital relationships and

27

reported that more years went by before their first act of infidelity. Partners who considered themselves superior, and hence 'unlucky' in marriage, had more and earlier extramarital sex. This was a strong effect for both men and women, with those who rated themselves as better than their partners having almost twice as many affairs as those who thought they were lucky to have made so satisfactory a match. (The only exception was younger men; both the 'lucky' and the 'unlucky' were less faithful.)

The figures are significant because normal jealousy depends on provocation. We do not need to invoke any personality theories about insecurity causing greater sensitivity to jealousy. If person A feels superior and has more affairs, person B, who is correspondingly inferior and perhaps insecure, will have more *reason* to be jealous, unless the superior partner always manages to conceal their infidelities.

When we speak of exclusivity in love we usually mean the restraint on affection, intimacy, allegiance or sexuality displayed to other people by one partner. But there is another type of exclusivity that may be relevant to jealousy: the exclusivity of the pair – the degree to which they remain in circulation or disappear into a private world. In the Middle Ages the term *chevalier récréant* was used for a knight who retired into his castle with his bride when he married, and failed to participate in the public business of knights. The honeymoon represents the institutional imposition of such isolation, tête-à-tête, and does not suit everyone. ('How nice it would be if some friend were to turn up,' says a bride in *Punch*. 'Yes!' replies the groom, 'Or even some enemy.') When one person takes the initiative it is sometimes termed 'cutting out', isolating the partner from their usual social milieu. It is sometimes a product simply of intense romantic attachment, but it can also be defensive and jealous.

Let us now turn to the final and most interesting aspect of love, the variety of its forms.

PASSION, INTIMACY AND COMMITMENT

I doubt if there has ever been a topic in academic psychology that complicated itself so rapidly as the anatomy of love. The bulk of the survey research on the subject has been published in the past ten years, with the pioneers, Swenson and Rubin, doing their work in the previous decade. I am not, of course, talking about the great historic traditions, nor the clinicians and theoreticians like Freud, Fromm or Reik, but those modern students of love we might dub the 'list analysers', who fractionated love into small atomic features before trying to reconstitute it into broad categories.

Rubin worked on a basic list of seventy features of love, Swenson accumulated 383, and Lee had about 1,500 items printed on cards for his subjects to sort. Where did this avalanche of particularities come from? In the practical sense they came from an analysis of classical and modern literature, both academic and literary, or from people describing themselves. (Swenson recruited 300 informants.) The broader explanation of the proliferation is that in our society love and matters relevant to it are richly represented in our thoughts and actions, in our goals, our dreams and fantasies. We harbour reservations and apprehensions about love, we experience its disappointments. Even when we restrict ourselves to the love of lovers and exclude parents, children and friends, the topic spreads from sexuality through personal intimacy, companionship and partnership to the practical co-management of households. We calculate its effects on our careers, our families, the possibility of parenthood. We are preoccupied with our own moods, intentions and actions, as well as with the feelings, intentions and actions of our partners or would-be partners, not just towards ourselves, but towards potential competitors. We address the topic at every level of specificity, from 'I was smitten' to 'I wonder if she read the stars this week'.

I shall outline two of the recent systems of description that have emerged from the processes of fractionation and reconstitution of love. The first was developed by the Hendricks, the second by Sternberg and his collaborators.

Six Aspects of Love

Hendrick and Hendrick set out to identify items that would best represent the six aspects of love originally proposed by Lee in 1977. I list the six categories with the most typical item in the Hendricks' scale:
1. Romantic, passionate, erotic love. ('My lover and I have the right physical "chemistry" between us.')
2. Long-term friendship; familiar love. ('My most satisfying love relationships developed from good friendships.')
3. Giving, caring, selfless, altruistic love. ('I cannot be happy unless I place my lover's happiness before my own.')
4. Pragmatic, rational love. ('A main consideration in choosing a lover is how he/she reflects on my family.')

29

5. Possessive, dependent love. ('When my lover doesn't pay attention to me, I feel sick all over.')
6. Game-playing, manipulative love. ('I have sometimes to keep two of my lovers from finding out about each other.')

The first category, romantic, passionate love, is the one that subjects seemed to equate with 'being in love'. (They gave low ranking to the items in this category if they claimed never to have been in love.) The fifth category is the one that covers jealousy. Although it is called 'love', it actually comprises physical and mental upset resulting from break-up, conflict, a lover's indifference or straying affections. ('I cannot relax if I suspect my lover is with someone else.')

The Hendricks examined the reactions of American undergraduates in two separate studies. The first analysis found only one significant association between possessive, dependent, jealous reactions and other categories of love. It was not associated, as one might have expected, with erotic, passionate love, nor with selfish love, but with giving, caring, selfless, altruistic love. In a repeat of the study there were weak associations between the dependent, possessive reaction and three styles of love: the passionate, the pragmatic and the giving; again, the link with the latter was by far the strongest.

None of these associations was very pronounced; indeed the whole object of this exercise was to separate the six types of 'love' reaction so they appeared independent, but what links remained fly directly in the face of the view that jealousy is a product of the 'wrong sort of loving'.

The Three Poles of Sternberg's Love

Tennov identifies two types of love – the passionate, obsessive, ecstatic kind I mentioned earlier – and a style of love that Walster and Walster call 'companionate love', which emphasizes affection rather than passion. It does not involve intense, ecstatic feelings, intrusive thinking, acute longing or a great need for exclusivity, but contentment and compatibility of interests and activities.

Sternberg retains the basic distinction between intense, passionate, 'acute' sexual love and companionable, intimate, caring love. But he adds a third category called 'commitment', a decision or intention to remain with a partner. It is not uncommon of course to experience more than one type of love. We can feel simultaneously passionate, intimate and committed, or we may experience them separately. Passion by itself Sternberg equates with infatuation. Intimacy appears in close friendship or strong liking, and is by no means restricted to

30

sexual relationships. Commitment by itself Sternberg described as 'empty love', presumably the sort of response to duty and public repute that Simone de Beauvoir saw in her respectable bourgeois parents and rebelled against.

Classic romantic love, according to Sternberg, involves a combination of passion and intimacy. Commitment and intimacy produce a confiding, trusting long-term attachment. The final pair, passion and commitment without intimacy or friendship, provides the model for many a damning accusation directed at insensitive spouses who share their partners' beds but not their inner worlds.

THE VARIETIES OF JEALOUSY

As we shall shortly see, jealousy has been subjected by psychologists to a process of disintegration and analysis similar to that of love, and has its own complexities. It is likely that the varieties of jealousy mirror the diversity of love. Just as love can involve passion, intimacy and commitment, so jealousy can involve anger and hurt, alienation and loss, indignation and outrage. There is certainly no basis for believing that jealousy is associated exclusively with one sort of love, and this is confirmed by an examination of case histories and biographical material. I have selected two liaisons between well-known figures of the early twentieth century to illustrate this. The first involves Bertrand Russell and Ottoline Morrell, the second Sonya and Leo Tolstoy. All four were prodigious letter-writers and diary-keepers, providing us with detailed, day-by-day accounts of their feelings and actions.

Russell and Morrell

In 1929 Bertrand Russell wrote in *Marriage and Morals*:

A good life cannot be founded on fear, prohibition and mutual interference with freedom . . . There can be no doubt that mutual jealousy, even when there is physical faithfulness, often causes more unhappiness in a marriage than would be caused if there were more confidence in the ultimate strength of a deep and permanent affection.

It would be easy to mock Russell with the chronicle of his own conduct and to charge him with hypocrisy, but that is not my aim. Russell was intense in everything he did. In his affections he was passionate and often ruthless. In his publications and political actions he was enlightened, sceptical and above all courageous. In his private writings he was unreserved and honest. Like Wilhelm Reich, who was active in Europe at about the same time, Russell was an idealist about love, sexuality and personal freedom, and as with Reich, there was a significant rift between his public advice and his own day-to-day conduct. But there were plenty of people who behaved privately as they did but made no effort to subvert the vicious and repressive social practices they saw around them. Better an inconsistent idealist than a consistent cynic. (For an account of the public and private Reich, see I. O. Reich's biography.)

What is chiefly interesting about Russell's relations with Lady Otto-line Morrell was the *range* of his reactions to her associations with others. When Russell began his long affair with her he demanded that she cease allowing her husband, Philip, a gentle and extraordinarily tolerant man, access to her bed. Russell, for his part, divested himself of his wife Alys in a most ruthless and deliberate way, which he documented in detail in his diaries and in some of the thousands of letters he wrote. The relationship between Russell and Ottoline Morrell was complex, extended and often passionate, especially on Russell's side. Ottoline Morrell juggled charmed admirers on all sides, but did not accept Russell's demand to reject her husband.

One of Ottoline Morrell's close friends and confidants was Lytton Strachey. Bertrand Russell expressed his resentment at *this* relationship. In this case it was not competition over sexuality, since Strachey was a homosexual, but jealousy over the warm, intimate and playful relations that prevailed between the two.

Finally there was an issue of commitment. Ottoline Morrell's biographer Darroch wrote,

There was also Russell's constant worry that no matter how happy they were he knew that she was not his. Once he heard someone refer to Ottoline and Philip as 'such a devoted couple' always putting their arms around each other and calling each other 'darling'. This caused Russell to be tormented by jealousy, and there was very little Ottoline could do to ameliorate his torment.

I am not suggesting that Bertrand Russell was a monster of jealousy. He was evidently an extraordinarily articulate, intense and insistent lover, and these issues of jealousy over sexuality, intimacy and commitment occupied only a fraction of the torrent of words and feelings that passed between the two. He recognized later how unreasonable he had been in trying to split Ottoline from her husband in the early days of his passion. He never denied the reality of jealousy in his writings, but given his own experiences, he did rather understate its compulsive power.

There is one theoretical point that needs to be made about Russell's reactions. We have seen that he could be jealous about each of the three types of relationship: sexuality, intimacy and personal commitment. That is not to say that each was equally significant in *causing* the jealousy. Although Lytton Strachey no doubt appreciated the playful intimacy he shared with Ottoline Morrell, it is unlikely to have fuelled any great resentment about her intimacy with others, or indeed her commitment to her husband. In other words, there may be a difference between why one is jealous and what one is jealous about, and passionate sexual attachment has a peculiar power to stimulate jealousy over a range of issues outside its own domain. Russell's jealousy started in the sexual domain and expressed itself in the domains of intimacy and commitment.

Sonya and Leo Tolstoy

For anyone who is trying to build tight connections between styles of loving and the appearance of jealousy, Tolstoy and his wife Sonya provide a perplexing contrast. I shall be discussing jealousy in their early life in a later chapter when I deal with the problem of honesty and disclosure between couples, but at this point I want to relate some incidents from their later life as recounted in Sonya Tolstoy's diaries.

Tolstoy's jealousy was provoked by his wife's very intense (platonic) attachment to the famous pianist and composer Taneyev. What is extraordinary about this is that long before it occurred, Tolstoy had written *The Kreutzer Sonata*, a classic, stunning tale of a man's jealousy of his wife and a pianist that ended in murder. As we shall see later, Tolstoy began his married life with a short period of affection and sexual passion and then began to reject his wife. But as the decades passed his passion returned, and at the time of the Taneyev affair he was making more sexual demands on his wife than she wanted, especially since his approach to her for the most of the time was distant and disapproving, if not actively hostile. He wrote in *The Kreutzer Sonata* that love dies after sexual satiety and this is how Sonya described his relations with her:

He is happy and cheerful [when he wants sexual intimacy]. It has quite a different effect on me, I feel ashamed and sad, and I long for a poetic, spiritual, even a sentimental relationship, only to get away from this everlasting sex . . . He takes from me . . . my copying, my cares for his physical welfare, my body . . . My whole spiritual life is of no interest to him, and he has no use

33

for it – for he has never taken the trouble to examine it . . . It hurts us terribly – and yet the world worships such men.

So to sum up the situation on his side, sexual passion came and went, intimacy and caring were rare and commitment was very uncertain. He continually spoke of leaving, and when in the end he did so, his decision was so irrevocable that as he was dying in a remote railway station he refused right to the end to see his wife. Yet when she found Taneyev sympathetic and attractive he became angrily jealous. Sonya said, 'And all I ever get now is that mad jealous passion which drives all real affection out of my heart.'

Sonya had continual conflicts over the publication of her husband's writings. He wanted to renounce all royalties; she wanted them for the maintenance of their large family and household. She thought his intentions were a product of vanity; he thought her venal. His promise to donate a story to a relatively high-priced magazine resulted in an especially bitter quarrel. In the middle of the confrontation Sonya recalled a chance remark about the woman editor of this magazine having 'fascinated' Tolstoy. She jumped to the conclusion that the decision about publication and his repeated threats to leave home were connected with the woman editor, 'that scheming half-Jewess':

I lost all self-control . . . I ran out into the street and down the lane. He came running after me . . . I had only one idea in mind – to die somehow or other. I remember weeping and screaming: 'Let them take me to the police station, or take me to the lunatic asylum'.

Neither of them was properly dressed. It was a February night in Russia and the 67-year-old Tolstoy struggled to get his wife up out of the snow and back into the house. Next day the conflict was renewed and again her '. . . feeling of jealousy and irritation . . . broke out with terrible violence'; again she left the house, bent on suicide:

I seemed to like the idea of perishing of cold like Vassili Andreich in the very story that was going to be the cause of my death. I regretted nothing. I had staked all my life on one card – my love for my husband – and now the game was lost.

The situation could hardly be more asymmetrical: his love confined to episodes of sex that stirred her own passion but which she said revolted her; her desire for caring, warmth and intimacy, and her incredible dedication and admiration for his genius. Almost immediately after the two suicide attempts she wrote:

I am busy correcting the proofs, and with joy in my heart am realizing the greatness of his literary work. At times my eyes are filled with tears of happiness.

So on both sides we have violent jealous reactions of a similar kind – straightforward rivalrous sexual jealousy, in neither case well founded. The practical reactions, of course, differed – the man attacked 'with his coarse and unjust reproaches', while the woman responded with despair, retreat and attempts at suicide. It is important to emphasize that although Sonya Tolstoy spent a great deal of time agonizing over her husband's callousness and lack of sympathy, the thing that triggered her almost crazy jealous flight was the thought of a sexual liaison with the woman editor.

AVOIDANCE AND ANXIOUS AMBIVALENCE

To say that the Tolstoys were an ill-matched pair clearly understates the case. There has been a recent development in theories of love and attachment that provides two contrasting self-descriptions which, while hardly Tolstoyan in their prose, none the less capture the mismatch between them:

I find that others are reluctant to get as close as I would like. I often worry that my partner doesn't really love me or won't want to stay with me. I want to merge completely with another person, and this desire sometimes scares people away.

I am somewhat uncomfortable being close to others; I find it difficult to trust them completely, difficult to allow myself to depend on them. I am nervous when anyone gets too close, and often, love partners want me to be more intimate than I feel comfortable being.

Shaver, Hazan and Bradshaw call these the 'anxious–ambivalent' and the 'avoidant' attachment types, ideas that originated in the research of Ainsworth on the reactions of small children to separation from their mothers. They found a little under half of the people they studied fell into one category or the other, and suggested that both were more than normally prone to jealousy, the anxious–ambivalent ones a little more so than the avoidant. This is not an absolute effect by any means; jealousy was also found amongst the secure. As Shaver, Hazan and Bradshaw say, it isn't clear whether we are dealing with a pattern that was set down during childhood or whether there are temperamental predispositions that produce these reactions in childhood and adulthood. Furthermore, since both types reported short personal relationships in their recent past, there is also the important possibility that in some cases at least a history of break-ups and jealousies with partners has contributed to ambivalence and the avoidance of close relationships rather than the other way around. Disappointment and hurt in relationships in adulthood can produce quite an enduring 'backlash'. Jealousy can lead to anxiety, ambivalence and avoidance as much as the reverse.

THE INTERLOPER

It is difficult to find a term for the third party in a triangle that doesn't imply intention (and bad intention at that). 'Intruder', 'rival', 'inter-loper' all imply a caricature of persons who, in reality, are simply people attracted to or in love with one's partner. The third party can be perceived by a jealous person as passive or active. The passive intruder is someone selected by an unfaithful partner. The active intruder is someone who uses certain (perhaps illegitimate) means to establish their position.

The active intruders can be subdivided into those who simply concentrate on one's partner, and those who, in addition, turn their gaze towards the jealous person. These are the real 'intruders', the people who, so to speak, press their bodies against the person you love and turn their eyes towards you. The blade of jealousy can be given a further twist if, for some reason, the partner joins this spiteful game. Elizabeth Bowen expresses this in *The House in Paris*: 'Jealousy is no more than feeling alone against smiling enemies.'

In a very early piece of research we conducted on jealousy, Kathy Ernst and I explored this issue of intentional provocation. She had a set of sound films made, in which actors portrayed a tête-à-tête between a romantically involved heterosexual couple. Each film opened with the identical sentimental conversation between the two, but the couple were shortly joined by an intruder, a young woman, who either actively attached herself to the man or was courted by him. At this point the camera moved around behind the female partner who henceforth said nothing, but sat as a spectator as a mildly outrageous piece of double-dealing was played out before her. Some of the women students recruited to watch the films were reserved at first and had little to write or say. We assumed they had not identified with the young spectator in the film, but once the ice was broken there was a sudden release of emotion and bitter comment. The aim of the study was to compare the impact of the actively unfaithful man as opposed to the pushy female intruder, but this effect was somewhat eclipsed by an unexpectedly potent consideration: the appearance and manner of the actresses. Almost as an afterthought Kathy Ernst had the intruder played by two different young women, one pleasant and rather bland, the other thinner, quicker in her gestures, more vivacious and theatrical. As far as we could tell, a key issue was the appearance and mannerisms of the vivacious actress and not whether she was being intrusive. Whichever role she played she provoked jealousy and hostility.

Many times in subsequent interviews informants have described qualities in others that seem related to this phenomenon: 'an operator'; 'she is not sincere'; 'she is using means of attracting men that I wouldn't use'. One of the few stock questions that I began regularly to include in my interviews concerned the sort of person that most provokes jealousy. Often my informants had a certain individual in mind; sometimes it was hypothetical. These are some of the descriptive terms: seems artificial; sets out to impress; putting on an act; basically insecure; fairly artistic; changeable; bitchy; puts on a front; self-centred; wrapped up in herself; assumes attitudes; shallow, a bit of a ladykiller; can impress people very easily. The picture throughout is of illegitimate success. The individuals in the film and in these descriptions are not identified simply as healthy, handsome and sexy. They are neither dominant nor admirable.

Perhaps if the intruders were handsome and highly valued they would not be thought of as active intruders. This raises the possibility that the critical qualities are to an extent in the mind of the perceiver. From my notebooks it seems that this sort of identification was more characteristic of women judging women, and it may be linked to a tendency that I shall discuss in my final chapter for women to be blamed in most cases of infidelity. Husbands blame wives and wives blame female lovers (and female lovers find fault with wives!). This is not to deny the reality of the original effect; the theatrical woman provoked more jealousy when she was not being intrusive than the bland woman did when she was. It is rather that if women are disinclined to accuse men, they are likely to exaggerate the insincerity and manipulative character of the (female) third party.

The other focus on the qualities of intruders arose from one's own self-evaluation. One informant said, 'The person who would make me jealous would be physically well set-up, confident, an amusing conversationalist.' (Pause.) 'Damn it, they would be all the things I think I'm not.' We could modify this slightly: 'They would be all the things I want to be, or try to be, but they would be better.' So a person who values being sophisticated most fears someone more sophisticated, a person who thinks their sexiness is important fears an erotic rival.

THE JEALOUS REACTIONS

The most superficial empirical inquiry into jealousy compels one to conclude that jealousy has many faces. Take this verbatim statement by a woman whose husband had transferred his attentions to someone in his office and note the rapid succession of thoughts and reactions: 'I felt rejected, and I felt insulted. I couldn't see where my life was going. There was the financial problem. I wasn't handling the children very well, that was the worst. I missed him. We used to talk a lot. I'm jealous of them having everything. How could he find it better with her?' At other times in this interview the same woman described how she had fantasies and dreams of going into the room where her husband was and 'holding forth'. She was resentful of the intruder: 'What hurt me [was] he left us because she *got* him . . . Even when we went out, went to concerts together, I felt excluded, as if he wasn't with me when I thought the occasion important. I'd have felt left-out if they had met.' Then later in the interview, 'The more I talk about it, the more I think I'm well out of it.'

This account comes from a particularly articulate woman, who in fact acted with considerable restraint. The extracts convey only a part of the rich diversity of reactions she experienced – some immediate, some reflective, some practical, some fantastic – relating to many aspects of her life and experience. Academic writers have tried to mirror this diversity. Usually they make lists and taxonomies, as I am shortly to do. Freud listed grief, wounded self-esteem, self-criticism and, of course, hatred. Kierkegaard spoke of fear, indignation and mourning.

The lists that writers compile are not necessarily random assemblages of reported emotions. Sometimes they are organized according to their intensity or the degree to which they become a preoccupation with us, so that mild or immediate jealousy is distinguished from a jealous 'complex' in which proving infidelity becomes an obsession. Kierkegaard's three forms represent stages in the development of jealousy over time. I shall describe a range of reactions according to a dimension of immediacy. Some jealous feelings have a raw, immediate quality to them, some seem more interpretative and others again seem to involve quite substantial wrestling with the problems that intrusion and jealousy create.

Also it should be recognized that people mix their own cocktails of jealousy. Personal temperament and history, the society, the situation, the audience, real or imagined, can lead to a special subset of reactions. Furthermore each individual may experience different constellations of feelings on different occasions or in different settings. I have interviewed people who are simultaneously subject to two different types of jealousy within two different relationships. A woman may suffer jealousy of one sort with her husband and of an entirely different kind in her relations with her lover. The first may be at the level of companionability and domestic competence, the other explicitly sexual. Jealousy is not simply a fixed reaction programmed socially or biologically within an individual, but it follows a personal and situational logic.

The Jealous Flash

Zajonc argues that emotional reactions may be immediate and primary. Clearly we have to take in enough information from the outside world to trigger a reaction, but the processes of assessment largely *follow* emotional reactions. As we know, people often say nothing about the feeling of jealousy, but none the less they have quick and often bitter initial experiences.

The term 'jealous flash' is used by two important students of jealousy, Clanton and Smith. It refers to an immediate feeling that arises at the moment a precipitating event is detected. Occasionally informants refer to this moment: 'They were holding hands. I froze. I couldn't move. A horrible feeling. I turned right around. I walked home. Later I cried.' 'I was just getting back into my car [in a service station] when they drove into the area there. I thought I wouldn't be affected, but I could hardly stand up. I had to reach out to support myself.' 'I realized that the reason she met me in the street was because she had A with her [in her apartment]. It was a horrible sour feeling. Then I began thinking they must have had breakfast there.'

One of my informants drew comparisons between this immediate reaction and the feelings she experienced in other crises. Her husband had once disclosed an affair to her in bed, just after love-making. Her instantaneous reaction was an indignant, angry attack – pushing him away from her and out on to the floor. Some years later, when that alliance had broken up, she became involved in an intense sexual relationship that was proving much more ardent and exciting than anything she had previously experienced. One day she telephoned her new friend. Unexpectedly the telephone was answered by a cool, pleasant and assured female voice, 'Yes, I'll get him for you.' There was then a quick, tense dialogue between them: 'I don't think I want to see you tomorrow.' 'Good.' It was when she put down the telephone that the experience occurred – it came, as she said, 'in waves of physical reaction'. She retreated to her bedroom, shut the door and sat down to wait for the crisis to take its course. 'It went down and down and down . . . After a time I thought crying would help, but I couldn't.' She thought of getting a drink, but decided it wouldn't help. The intellectual coping, explaining things to herself, didn't start for quite a time, ten to twenty minutes, and during that time she said she felt emotion 'hurtling about inside'. When her parents had died she had been shocked, but tears came immediately. Here she felt 'stuck'. She had no justification for resentment or indignation. Her lover owed her nothing. She was reacting to the combined shock of the cool female voice and the immediate rupture of relations.

It is usually difficult to document these instantaneous reactions and we have no way of telling if there is really a distinctive experience common to many people and situations. Although informants are generally excellent reporters of their jealous experiences, it is asking a lot to expect them to isolate this early reaction, which is quickly crowded out by complex feelings and thoughts.

Although we usually think of jealousy as a 'feeling', I am not sure that it is productive to concentrate just on that primary emotional experience. Like most other writers, I tend to think of jealousy more abstractly, as a larger unit, a connection between certain significant events and the various things we feel, think and do. Something critical happens in our heads and often in our bodies, but I don't think it is captured just by asking about the contents of that initial moment.

Symptomatic Jealousy and Fear

The literature on pain suggests that the intensity of 'hurt' is not related simply to the severity of injury. Pain that is interpreted as a precursor of ill-understood bodily disasters is psychologically more hurtful than that tied to specific well-understood injuries. Pain that carries a threat is termed 'symptomatic pain'.

By analogy, one might speak of symptomatic jealousy: fear of loss of control, reputation, 'face'; fear of emotional deprivation, and so on. It is not the incident itself, but what it presages that causes much of the trouble. One is always operating under conditions of uncertainty in emotional affairs and the severity of a jealous episode is based in part on an assessment of the future. One informant said, 'I should not care if he became involved with *her*. She is a lightweight. If he's going to get serious, it won't be with someone like that.' On occasions the future potential of a new relationship has actually been talked over by the partners and the 'prognosis' is not simply based on guesswork. I shall discuss pacts in the next chapter, but the motivation for some pacts is not just to limit real breakdowns, but to keep symptomatic jealousy to a minimum, that is, to remove some of the threat from possibly harmless incidents.

The balance of this chapter will describe in turn a series of important reactions that were repeatedly mentioned in interviews: anger and hostility, resentment, devaluation of the partner, broodiness and martyrdom, a sense of alienation and finally a long-term withdrawal or self-isolation. We begin with the aggressive reactions.

ANGER AND HOSTILITY

Sometimes the hostile reaction is irrepressible. People comment on their lack of rational control over what they are doing. 'While it is happening, I don't see that it is unreasonable. Later I feel bloody embarrassed.' 'What was most distressing was my appalling behaviour. I was violently out of control.' 'I cry. I want to smash things. I look horrible. Who would want to be like me?' 'I can see myself doing it. I feel guilty. I find it destructive. It's irrational.'

In other cases the hostility is under control and is only released when it seems legitimate. You may recall that some of the students who viewed Kathy Ernst's films were at first quite reticent. The event that caused a sudden release of comment was a girl saying in a frank Australian way, 'What a bastard'. This remark about the male actor who was flirting blatantly in front of the girl he had been flattering a moment ago legitimized the expression of hostility, which rapidly escalated within the group. As Bailey has pointed out, emotions are not just steam rising from internal kettles, they are strategic in their functions. We are acting on the social world when we express emotions, and anger is very sensitive to our moral position.

The hostility may be delayed. There is a classic case in the literature of a farmer who made no outward objection when the man from a neighbouring property 'moved in' and made love to his wife while he was present in the house. In the end the lovers loaded what the farmer regarded as his possessions in his car, and drove off. Ultimately the farmer remarried. After a time he got wind of a minor affectionate misdemeanour on the part of his new wife and killed her. Even under less dramatic circumstances anger may be delayed long after the discovery of a breach of fidelity, and often emerges when some other issue raises the emotional temperature. This 'incubation' of hostility can produce difficulties from a legal point of view, because the law tends to look for immediate provocation before it classifies a reaction as due to unusual emotional stress.

RESENTMENT

We now move fairly clearly into the domain of secondary reactions: feelings that arise from an assessment of the situation that gave rise to the initial jealous reaction. The implication of treating these reactions somewhat as a sequence is that one may first feel some sort of raw shock, which is followed by a process in which resentment, injured pride, and so on, are reviewed. I am by no means sure that this is always a fair account of the situation, because the feelings of resentment may develop before any jealous incident occurs. Feelings of resentment often centre around important questions of interpersonal equity that are the background for the complex emotional reactions we experience.

Any sort of investment can provide a basis for resentment. Sometimes it centres on an investment of effort and attention in the home and family, or it resurrects lost romantic opportunities, real or imaginary, or it is provoked by a breach of an implicit contract about outside relations: 'You are acting in a way that I might, but I don't.' 'You are acting as I *cannot* act,' is a frequent complaint. John Hoyland relates what transpired when, in a burst of liberal candour, he informed his wife of his infidelities: 'She was bitterly resentful. "Why don't you do the same?" I asked. She replied that she had neither the opportunity, nor the confidence, nor the inclination to do so.' (Later, to his chagrin, she acquired all three.)

One reason why sexual jealousy is so intransigent is because it converges with reactions that are not sexual at all, nor even primarily emotional, except in their effects. Jealousy can become so confounded with other aggravations that in any particular case it is hard to see how they could be disentangled. For purposes of illustration let us suppose two novice entrepreneurs each has a few thousand dollars. They agree to pool their resources and start a modest enterprise. This prospers and comes to occupy the centre stage for both of them in terms of their daily activity and their self-identities. Then one breaks the news to the other about an attractive offer to invest elsewhere, knowing that their little partnership will now collapse. It need not be a business – it could be a sporting partnership, a pop group, a political alliance – but the effects will be identical: anger, disappointment, a sense of betrayal, depression, hurt pride.

In *Group Psychology and the Analysis of the Ego*, Freud suggested that all social groups are held together by what are essentially emotional (sexual) forces, but I am not prepared to accept that. I think the goals are quite practical and the reactions have ordinary, commonsense explanations.

My anecdote is, of course, a rather obvious allegory for the setting-up of households or families, in which all sorts of effort and commitment are involved. When the rupture of a domestic partnership is accompanied by unfaithfulness, the reactions are going to be fuelled by all the upset of sexual jealousy combined with that unhappy packet of miseries that the business partner experienced. We appreciate in a theoretical sense that the pain and resentment come from different sources, but we could hardly expect to separate them in practice.

AMBIVALENCE AND THE DEVALUATION OF PARTNERS

Anger and prolonged bitterness can arise, of course, from many sources. Hostile feelings are present in some relationships from the outset. Berscheid and Fei give an account of the fear of dependency that many people experience as they find themselves drawn into emotional involvement: fear that we will become dependent and that others will become dependent on us. The process of attachment often masks reservations we may have about a partner. An old cartoon shows a woman talking to her male companion across the table: 'When I fell in love with you, suddenly your eyes didn't seem so close together. Now they seem close together again.' I encountered this sort of phenomenon in a man who reacted to his girl-friend's infidelity with complete rejection and dislike. At first I supposed that the change of feeling was a device to compensate for his feelings of humiliation and rejection. I tried to find out whether there were any particular resentments that built up during their partnership. But ultimately I concluded that about the only thing that had drawn him to her in the first instance was the fact that she showed an interest in him, and that was now gone.

BROODINESS AND MARTYRDOM

Perhaps the most common reaction amongst jealous people is chilliness, prickliness and sulking. People describe it in themselves as well as in their partners: 'I show coolness towards my wife.' 'I won't talk all night.' 'I simply sat and stewed.' 'I was like ice.' 'I withdrew, like switching the light off.' A woman said, 'He went stony on the outside; he wouldn't talk.'

Often the broodiness is accompanied by displays of virtue and martyrdom. A woman reported that while she was having an affair, her husband painted the house inside and out, 'not with a roller, but with a brush'. From the way she described it, it might well have been a brush two centimetres wide! I call this behaviour 'bucket rattling', conspicuous displays intended to point up a disparity in moral worth. Who hasn't heard the exaggerated crash of dishes being washed, the buzz of a vacuum cleaner running across an already passably clean floor, the elaborate complaints of overwork, or watched the bulging briefcase being carted in and out. The gestures often involve duties towards children or relatives. The message they carry is, 'I am pre-occupied with you and your comfort and welfare. I give a lot to this relationship and you contracted to accept it.' There are various degrees of explicitness. Sometimes of course there will be a confron-tation during which these 'credits' will be spent (and perhaps saved to be spent again). But usually that is too blatant, and the recent performance serves instead to keep alive and fresh the virtues of the past. Occasionally the martyrdom drives the delinquent partner into a state of breezy truculence, yet the performance may persist, either because to stop it would be to admit its artificiality, or because it is a source of private comfort. It still enhances the contrast between the acceptability of one's own conduct and the unacceptability of the partner, but it constitutes internal work done on one's righteousness, rather than display for the opponent's discomfiture.

I mention these strategies of management at the risk of holding them up to ridicule, but they are not ridiculous. It is no news to anyone that passion may conflict with duty, or that fidelity may stunt people's lives. The trick, I suppose, is to recognize when attempts to call people to account are a lost cause and to turn away from resent-ment when it has only an inner audience. Evidently that is often much easier said than done.

The Threshold of Accounting

Why don't people simply get things off their chests? Unequal power is one reason, but also to initiate an accounting may require a signifi-cant redefinition of personal relations. Julian Pitt-Rivers discusses the distinction between the moral ties within friendship and the tie of duties and rights within kinship. He sees the ties of friendship as needing reciprocity only in an indefinite way, but if this reciprocity is not forthcoming and one party then calls the other to account, the relationship of 'friend' is placed in jeopardy:

Once a tally of favours is kept the amity has gone out of it and we are left with a tacit contract; the relationship is no longer simply moral but implicitly jural, involving duties and rights. The injured party can declare what is due to him and can take steps towards its recovery, exercising the sanctions which relate to reputation. But these cannot be used while the moral nature of the relationship is still accepted, for the disillusioned friend who complains that his favours have not been reciprocated destroys his own reputation by implying that he expected they should be.

As Pitt-Rivers points out, the admission of a quid pro quo represents an important watershed in a relationship because once the topic of justice is broached, it is difficult to rebuild the 'innocence' of amiable (as opposed to legal) relationships.

If a marriage is treated primarily as a contract, then accounting is quite in the spirit of such an arrangement. But when, either in reality or in a mythical sense, a partnership is set up as essentially based on love or friendship, a psychological hurdle is erected between amity and legal arrangement. When partners do not marry, the basis of their relationship emphasizes amity even more distinctly, and resentment over unfairness is correspondingly more difficult to express. This is especially a problem for homosexual couples, as Vicki Morris so perceptively points out.

It is the crossing of the line from implicit mutual good-will to articulated claims and recriminations that holds back the expression of jealousy in many relationships. There is a high price to be paid for an expression of resentment. Although Pitt-Rivers was not referring to sexual partnership and jealousy, his point still applies: once an admission that rights and duties are at issue is made, 'it cannot be retrieved and the [amity] relationship collapses, for it has been revealed that the sentiment is not mutual'.

The philosophy of romantic permissiveness that flowered in the 1960s, with the boom in open marriages and other innovative personal arrangements, no doubt contributed extra weight to the idea of partnerships without accountability.

It is sometimes quite comical to witness the process of redefinition. I was once a visitor in a household where a single man lived with a young married woman whose husband had consented to the arrangement in advance. By coincidence (I assume) it was on the weekend of my visit that the husband discovered that he could not tolerate the situation he had earlier agreed to. I was not surprised at the swift, tense reassessment of relations that followed his arrival but I was amazed at the hurt, innocent surprise of my host at the overturn of his plans. No doubt there was plenty of discussion between the married pair when they got out of the house, but the husband made his entry and exit quickly, not wishing to explain in public how he had made the switch from freedom back to contract.

ALIENATION: THE JEALOUSY OF EXCLUSION

Surprisingly often, people have reported to me that the dominant component in their jealousy is not hostility or even sulking, but a feeling of being left-out, excluded and isolated. The mood is that of sorrow more than resentment or hate. Several of my informants described how, as adolescents, they looked on the developing sexual attachments of their peers as outsiders, excluded from a rather magical romantic world. I experience this occasionally with people to whom I am attracted, but to whom I have never expressed my feelings. I once was standing in a queue in a cafeteria, holding up a line of people while I stared in a completely absorbed way at a female acquaintance who was talking to a tall young man I did not know. I realize on reflection that for a minute or two I had invested their world with a certain magic significance and felt a vague jealous alienation. At this point the differences between envy and jealousy at a psychological level disappear. We are not trying to retain the partner and ward off the intruder. The intruder and the partner are now a couple, and the relationship between them stimulates a sense of desire and longing.

The feeling of alienation may be sad or bitter. One of the most telling descriptions of bitter alienation is found in the writing of Robbe-Grillet. His novel *Jealousy* is remarkable for its evocations of inner worlds through the minute description of physical objects. Robbe-Grillet develops a sense of alienation and apartness simply by describing arrangements of chairs:

They are arranged as usual: the first two next to each other under the window, the third slightly to one side, on the other side of a low table . . . This arrangement obliges anyone sitting there to turn his head around sharply towards the left if he wants to see [her].

The situation combines exclusion with the conflict of being held as a morbid spectator and agony at what is seen or imagined. Everywhere Robbe-Grillet evokes that image of excluded watching, through the

46

half-open door, through the slats of a blind, through the flaws in the glass of a window.

The bitterness in this alienation comes not just from exclusion but from a mutual awareness of a reordering of the relations among the three people. The feeling of intrusion is transferred from the rival to the jealous partner: 'Franck [the intruder] stares at the tiny bubbles clinging to the sides of his glass, which he is holding in front of his eyes at a very close range.' The lovers cannot talk because their conversation can be only trivial or intimate. In the case of a woman excluded from her lover's new affair, to which I shall shortly refer, there is no suggestion that the new pair are anything but completely absorbed in one another, but in Robbe-Grillet the jealous man is always present in the minds of the couple. The bitterness is further heightened by feelings evoked by the detail of the woman's grooming. Her hair and lipstick, her toilette – all emphasized and explored in detail – have been carefully prepared for an illicit relationship from which the jealous husband is excluded. This raises the interesting issue of what the maximum jealous provocation might be. Certainly it would involve deliberate acts by the unfaithful partner – in other words, that turning towards the jealous partner from a position of intimacy with the intruder which I mentioned earlier.

It is impossible to say at present whether personal dispositions heighten jealous alienation. Several informants who experienced such jealousy described a history of personal insecurity about their own attractiveness. The following case is typical: the woman was in her late thirties, neither beautiful nor plain, well dressed and very carefully groomed. She was clearly prepared to devote herself to being stimulating, intelligent and autonomous. As an adolescent she had only a very mediocre opinion of her own worth and attractiveness. At the time I interviewed her she had just gone through one of the most stimulating emotional experiences of her life – a prolonged sexual relationship of a quality she had never supposed was possible. It was not completely over, but it was falling apart. Her lover, whom she regarded as superior to herself (a 'catch'), was having another affair, and the predominant feeling was depressed alienation.

This was not just love lost, not simply what Kierkegaard called the 'mourning of love at the death of love', but a feeling of deprivation and exclusion from a special, rather magical world. This was the world she imagined being created with her partner's new love, not that she experienced herself. Reviewing her own experience, she recognized rationally that it had perhaps been superior to the new, but that did not banish the feeling of being excluded.

Another person (coincidentally also female, although I have no reason to suppose that this reaction is any more common amongst women than men) described the same feeling. She reacted to the exclusion with a wish to draw closer to the couple and to form an attachment to the other girl, who was a friend of hers. She wanted to 'snuggle up to them', as she expressed it.

Two other informants described their efforts to achieve this. One succeeded to a certain extent, establishing a *ménage à trois*. The other recognized that it was a vain attempt: 'They do not need me.' A male informant tried to achieve the same thing by making himself indispensable to a couple. He was constantly around their house, minding the children, keeping the wife company and countering his jealousy of the husband by trying to draw close to him.

There is some very interesting writing on the topic of exclusion. Weitman focuses particularly on public intolerance of displays of affection, resentment of 'gratuitous acts of social exclusion': 'One unmistakable meaning of intimacies to those who witness them but are not privileged to partake in them is that they are excluded from the bond of affection being cultivated in their presence.' Weitman sees the public reaction as hostile and critical, as though the exclusion were calculated, but in the cases I have described, although the bond may be exclusive, it is not provocatively so. The new pair were not flaunting their attachment; they were simply absorbed, and the reaction was not resentment so much as a resurgence of aloneness.

The Prison-house of Private Consciousness

I may be overgeneralizing but I suspect that aloneness is much more common than people admit. I do not attribute this to the growth of anomy, or the recognition of existential isolation. I think it has a more banal explanation, namely that we grow in a prison-house of our own private consciousness and only slowly learn to recognize that we are not the only ones in such prisons. It is easy to believe informally that the consciousnesses of others somehow fuse. The additional fact that we are all inclined to cultivate the appearance of confident belonging does not help us discover our common misunderstanding. Having said this, I must also admit that once we are launched on a programme of mutual comparison, some of us are bound to fare better than others. This is not a comment about justice, but about social reality in evaluative societies. Although confidence, attractiveness and talent don't guarantee invulnerability, one would none the less be rash to turn up one's nose if they were being handed out. The point is that some individuals may be unavoidably at greater risk than others of experiencing depressed alienation based on shaky self-esteem.

To take up a theme that I introduced earlier, the psychological literature on this subject is not always strong on sensitivity. Presumably it is not meant to be read by the jealous. The link it forges between experiencing jealousy and having deep-seated feelings of inadequacy is no doubt intended in some way to direct our efforts to remedying a blight by removing a weakness. But it often comes through as something of a put-down. Let us suppose you have acne, no chin and an unprepossessing physique. Your main chance has come by, you seize him or her, live a moment in the sun, and then suffer loss and jealousy. 'Jealousy', you are then reliably informed, 'is a symptom of emotional insecurity.' So now, in case you hadn't noticed, you are an emotional failure on a double score. The poor get poorer. It is little wonder that we flock to see continental romantic films. There we can look through the bars at an imaginary world in which people can play out their conflicts and crises in a public atmosphere of amused tolerance.

THE BACKLASH: WITHDRAWAL

Two or three informants described the aftermath of a jealous crisis: for a period of months they made no attempt to establish affectionate relationships. 'I felt lonely and alone. It lasted for months. It plagued me at work.' 'I went for eight months without a girl-friend.' 'I had no relations with anybody for a year after that.'

These effects are clear-cut in the sense that the informant is aware of a complete withdrawal for a specified period, but not all such effects are so clearly identifiable. One informant simply commented that he feared a relationship with girls: 'None of them lasts very long.' 'Now I cut people instantly when I'm threatened.' Another, when asked if he wanted to get married said, 'I'm not emotionally suited to it. I'm very nervous, cautious, I'm frightened of saying stupid [jealous] things.'

Experiences of jealousy within oneself or in others may lead to a general reserve in initiating relationships with people that can last a lifetime. It is in this sense that jealousy, though perhaps not a very obtrusive event from an overt behavioural point of view, may be exercising the most powerful covert influence upon our social relationships.

Finally let us ask the question, are men more jealous than women? There is no clear evidence of a difference. When I read my case notes there is much more variation from person to person than between groups like male and female, and this is what the survey research clearly confirms (Bringle and Buunk).

There is a stereotype that men are more jealous of explicitly sexual intrusions while women are said to be more concerned about withdrawal of support. The idea is part of the sexual double-standard: men are sexy, women are not; men can play about provided they bring home the pay. I never saw this reflected in my interviews. Plenty of women react strongly, even catastrophically, to the sexual aspect of their partner's infidelity, and in a later chapter I shall report a recent study I conducted that backs up this informal impression. Women are just as upset as men when they contemplate their partners in erotic escapades.

What about the form that jealousy takes? Does that vary between the sexes? Jeff Bryson, a pioneer of questionnaire research in this area, found that men claim slightly more often than women to be activists when they are jealous. They more often say they would force a discussion, assault their rivals or attack their partners. The figures on jealous bashings and homicide show them to be true to their word; their partners typically attract more direct aggression than rivals, since they are accessible females while rivals are remote and male. Men also claim to be 'benign' activists slightly more often, saying that they would more energetically court their straying partners or chase after fresh ones. (In fact what they often do is simply talk about alternatives, whether new, old or fabricated.) These sex differences in reported actions tend to be small, as I said, but they appear consistently in the survey research of Bryson and his co-workers.

The only action (other than crying) that the women reported more often than the men was seeking the support of a close friend, usually another woman. This conforms to the finding that heterosexual women regularly split their close emotional attachments between male sexual partners and intimate female friends. The major reactions that women more commonly report are not external but internal. They mention a little more often than the men feeling helpless, depressed, ill, insecure, fearful. When they report antagonism, it is often internal anger. But again we should not exaggerate the difference. Pines and Aronson found that the most commonly reported reaction of both men and women was in fact mulling over and agoniz-

50

ing about the predicament. (It was called 'using the occasion for thinking and processing'!)

The emphasis on male activism presents something of a paradox because on the whole women in Western society seem more sensitive to and inclined to talk about their emotional lives. Zick Rubin and others have shown that it is often the women who take action to terminate romantic relationships. Ailsa Burns and others paint a picture of husbands playing the ostrich when emotional troubles are brewing (including those they are causing), and they frequently act stunned, disoriented and hurt when a rupture is forced on them. Maybe infidelity is the one occasion when they notice and feel it proper to take action.

The key to all this is probably power rather than any intrinsic emotional differences. This is the theme that the sociologist Gregory White has always applied to jealous reactions. There are actually two important concepts of power in personal relationships. The one that White emphasizes is that of the balance of good fortune – which of the partners thinks he or she has made a 'good catch' and which feels less lucky. That shows little sex bias; sometimes men feel lucky, sometimes women, often both. But of course the really potent power differences, and the ones that explain best the differences in reactions to jealousy that Bryson found, spring from the situation that most men and women find themselves in within society. The greater occupational opportunities generally available to men give them greater flexibility and this, combined with their physical strength, might be expected to bias them towards confrontation. Women generally share greater dependency with their children, so their relative lack of economic and occupational resources is more inhibiting. In a way it is surprising that they are not even more inclined to absorb conflicts internally and to hold back from translating their angry thoughts into action. It is a situation that is changing rapidly among the middle classes in Western society, but the power asymmetry is still very real.

Let me now turn away from provocations and jealous reactions to the management, or attempts at management, of relationships. In the chapter that follows we will look at pacts between couples and arrangements within communities that are designed to minimize or eradicate jealousy.

CHAPTER 3

Pacts and Arrangements

———————— Q ————————

Most of us have heard of individuals making pacts to be sexually and emotionally free, or of arrangements in larger communities where people have multiple spouses or lovers, and we loosely assume that somehow these people have escaped jealousy. We then wonder why we and most of our personal acquaintances find it so difficult to manage 'open relationships' or to cope with infidelity. What can be wrong with us? In this chapter I shall dissect some of these pacts and arrangements more critically to determine just how 'freely' the participants lived, and to see whether in fact they *did* contrive to abolish jealousy. Without anticipating my conclusions too much, what I found surprised me. Jealousy appears to be a much tougher weed to eradicate than even I had thought.

I shall begin by describing two failures, one reported in my interviews, the other from the novel *Les Liaisons Dangereuses*. We can then look at some pacts and arrangements that at least partially succeeded.

The first arrangement was made by a woman who was trying to keep control of a precarious personal situation. She had been having an affair with a man while living with her husband, of whom she was very fond. This had been going on for nearly a decade when she became aware that her husband was beginning to form an attachment to a young girl. She decided to take the initiative in the hope that by controlling the relationship she could weather it. So she discussed it with her husband, suggesting 'Why don't you?' 'I kept it under control,' she went on. 'I made the call. I arranged the liaison. When the time came I was in the park. I had a crisis. I was delusional, sweating, anxious.' This little affair had complex motivations. Guilt had something to do with it, but the wish to be even-handed, to give her husband his chance, was probably the minor theme. The intention was primarily to be able to tell herself: 'He didn't prefer her: I pushed him; I arranged it.' In the event it didn't work. Jealousy took over, and it was then made especially traumatic by her detailed knowledge of the proceedings.

One of the most famous fictional accounts of a sexual pact is to be found in *Les Liaisons Dangereuses* written in 1782 by a French army officer, Choderlos de Laclos (translated as *Dangerous Acquaintances* by Aldington), which purports to be the letters exchanged by two members of the Parisian aristocracy. As Armstrong says in her review of the novel of adultery, until recently authors found it very difficult to permit illicit lovers to prosper. They always seem to end up committing suicide or are otherwise ill-fated. Laclos is no exception: the Vicomte de Valmont is killed in a duel, while the Marquise de Merteuil is first humiliated in public and then disfigured by smallpox. However, the most interesting aspect of their relationship is the way they fall out. Their pact was to pursue their affairs and tell everything in their letters. At first it appears that the collapse of their pact arises simply from an inability to tolerate the amorous success of the other, but in fact it transpires that their agreement had always been to avoid passionate engagement, and it is when the Marquise detects real attachment on the part of Valmont for one of his victims that their relationship begins to degenerate into serious conflict:

What I thought, what I still think, is that you are none the less in love with your Madame de Tourvel; not indeed with a very pure or very tender love, but with the kind of love you can feel; the kind of love, for example, which makes you think a woman possesses the charms or qualities she does not possess, which puts her in a class apart and ranks all others in a second order . . .

This will be a theme throughout the chapter: what forms pacts take, what challenges there can be to them, and particularly the power of this ultimate emotional allegiance to get under the guard of even the most confident and sophisticated treaty-maker.

DE BEAUVOIR AND SARTRE

Simone de Beauvoir and Jean-Paul Sartre established a pact of sexual freedom 'within limits'. De Beauvoir describes how it was proposed by Sartre:

He explained the matter to me in his favourite terminology. 'What we have', he said, 'is an *essential* love; but it is a good idea for us to experience *contingent* love affairs.' We were two of a kind, and our relationship would endure as long as we did: but it could not make up entirely for the fleeting riches to be had from encounters with different people.

Their 'password' was the line from a poem by Ernest Dowson: 'I have been faithful to thee, Cynara, in my fashion'. Neither the pact nor the password shielded de Beauvoir, in particular, from jealousy, although it probably in the end allowed them to sustain their very complex relationship. Sartre clearly took the initiative. It was he who suggested a 'two-year lease' of shared intimacy, followed by two or three years of living apart, perhaps overseas, then a reunion, perhaps in Greece.

Sartre and de Beauvoir were the philosophers of rationality, freedom and choice, and their pact may have the appearance of a true philosophical invention, the application of pure reason to the planning of their lives. It was not, of course, anything of the sort. In this account and in that dealing with the Russian authoress Lou Andreas-Salomé, I want to deal with the counterpoint between philosophical conviction and the personal and practical motives that lie behind such pacts. We will also see how plans sometimes collide with the reality of jealousy and disappointment. The aim is not to discredit pacts, but to show that they do not spring from pure thought and that rationality has to accept the existence of irrationality; reason must accept emotion.

The pact between Sartre and de Beauvoir certainly did not propose a series of simultaneous or successive affairs. They were not interested in what has been called 'the consciousness of the Club Méditerranée', nor the heavy, fatal passion of Tristan and Isolde. Rather they seemed to be aiming at a secure partnership from which one might emerge from time to time for emotional adventures. In this, too, they resembled Lou Andreas-Salomé. The parallel is not exact, for Lou Andreas-Salomé proposed a basic partnership without sex, which Sartre and de Beauvoir certainly did not advocate.

What made Sartre choose two years for the term of the 'lease'? Was it some wise estimate of the duration of a honeymoon? The reason was more concrete. He was about to enter eighteen months of military service and planned on receiving visits from de Beauvoir during that time (as he did). He had hoped to then take a lectureship in Japan. When this fell through (someone else got it) he abandoned the two-year lease, abandoned the idea of 'vast solitary escapades', and together they decided to substitute a relationship that would keep them together until their thirties. Both were teachers and they faced separation, de Beauvoir going south to Marseilles, Sartre north to Le Havre. At this point Sartre actually raised the possibility of marriage to avoid such a separation: '. . . it was stupid to martyr oneself for a principle', de Beauvoir reported him as saying.

I recount this not to discredit Sartre's motives, but to show how a pact can emerge from the interplay of several forces. In this instance it involved de Beauvoir's rebellion against what she saw as the hollowness and hypocrisy of the bourgeois marriage she first witnessed in her own family. Second, there was the emphasis they placed on freedom and choice, and third, the openly acknowledged partiality of Sartre for women. 'He had no intention, at twenty-three, of renouncing their tempting variety,' said de Beauvoir. To these general issues were added the practicalities of work and ambition.

Changing Views of Freedom

The concept of freedom played a central role in their philosophy and in their personal relations. It changed with time, however, and especially so for de Beauvoir. They moved away from the early existentialist emphasis on an individual's independent choice to the idea of *engagement*, whereby choice was made in a community and had to respect the free choice of others. We can see the change in the way de Beauvoir resolved the problem of jealousy in her first novel, *L'Invitée* (*She Came to Stay*). It is semi-autobiographical and deals with the problem of jealousy and its resolution. The two principal characters, Pierre and Françoise, represent Sartre and de Beauvoir, and Xavière is a fictional version of a young friend of theirs, Olga Kosakiewicz. The novel contains some extraordinary passages of introspection; Françoise experiences jealousy and a sort of desolation as the relationship deepens between Pierre and the manipulative and unstable Xavière:

Xavière must have arrived by now, thought Françoise with a slight tightening of her heart. She would be wearing either her blue dress or her beautiful red-and-white striped blouse, with the smooth folds of her hair framing her face, and she would be smiling. What was that unknown smile? How was Pierre looking at her? Françoise stopped short on the edge of the pavement: she had a painful impression of being in exile. In the ordinary way, the centre of Paris was wherever she happened to be. Today, everything had changed. The centre of Paris was the café where Pierre and Xavière were sitting, and Françoise was wandering around in some vague suburb.

She begins to re-examine the bond between herself and Pierre:

What was there beneath the phrases and gestures? We are but one. With the help of this convenient confusion she had always been relieved from worrying about Pierre . . . Now, she was aware he lived his own life, and the result of her blind trust was that she suddenly found herself facing a stranger.

When she decides to talk to Pierre about the turmoil she is in, he cuts her short to attend to Xavière:

Françoise felt the blood ebbing from her cheeks; had he suddenly struck her, the shock could not have been more violent . . . it had come to this: a pout from Xavière was more important than all her own distress.

Later she has to play the role of complaisant third party over coffee:

. . . she made no attempt to speak a friendly word. She had already lived this scene more than twenty times. She was sickened in advance by the cheerful tone, the bright smiles she felt rising to her lips, and by the irritated disgust she felt welling within her . . . For quite a while no one breathed a word.

The passion of the novel rises to a climax as Françoise recognizes that it is her jealousy that has driven her into a sexual affair with Xavière's other younger lover. When Xavière discovers this, Françoise feels compromised and trapped and kills her.

Such an ending may seem simply a dramatic narrative twist. On the back cover of the Flamingo edition of the novel it is described as 'an act of revenge by the novelist against the woman who so nearly disrupted her life with Jean-Paul Sartre'. But as Anne Whitmarsh, Mary Evans and no doubt many others have pointed out, the real significance of the lethal ending lies in the way it is expressed:

Her act was her very own. 'It is I who will it.' It was her own will which was being accomplished, now nothing at all separated her from herself. She had at last made a choice. She had chosen herself.

This is a celebration of freedom to choose in the spirit of 'one against all' and it is a version of freedom that de Beauvoir had rejected even before the novel was published in 1943. After a buffeting from their critics and a growing sensitivity to the possibilities of exploitation and victimization, de Beauvoir and Sartre shifted from individualistic freedom to freedom between equals. Other people are not simply 'wallpaper', not simply stage props for the playing out of a person's choices. Exercising freedom should not damage the freedom of others.

In a sense their original pact of limited fidelity was a concession to this more considerate view, because instead of asserting defiantly, 'I shall pursue my sexual liberty, even at your expense,' it offers security, or at least a verbal statement of ultimate allegiance between the couple.

In 1945 Sartre went alone to New York as a correspondent. He was introduced to 'Dolores V.' and after two days' acquaintance they became lovers. When de Beauvoir in her turn crossed the Atlantic it was agreed that Dolores would join Sartre in France. Dolores and Sartre then decided to prolong their interlude together and they asked de Beauvoir if she could stay longer in America. At this point de Beauvoir launched her relationship with the Chicago writer Nelson Algren. Neither Dolores V. nor Algren wanted the relationships to be terminated, and de Beauvoir, reflecting on this, makes the point that a pact of this sort is not just an agreement between two people to limit their own sexual freedom to a degree, but an encroachment on the freedom of people with whom they have affairs. These people are still in a sense the 'wallpaper'. In spite of what Sartre had told Dolores, she could not believe that he would want to break off the affair. When de Beauvoir finally arrived back in Paris, Dolores was still there and in the words of Madsen, 'Sartre practised shuttle diplomacy'. De Beauvoir later wrote:

It was normal for M. [Dolores V.] to think that things would change. That is, that she could win Sartre permanently for herself. Her mistake was to take Sartre's profound convictions for mere verbal precautions. He had misled her in so far as he had not been able to make her understand his convictions and she, on the other hand, had not told him when she began that she might reject its limits . . . Of course he had warned her that there could be no question of making his life with her. But by saying he loved her, he gave the lie to that warning, for – especially in the eyes of women – love triumphs over every obstacle. M. [Dolores V.] was not entirely in the wrong. Love's promises express the passion of the moment only; restrictions and reservations are no more binding; in every case, the truth of the present sweeps all pledges imperiously before it.

Algren expressed the same view more brutally. According to Evans, he wrote that

he felt betrayed by de Beauvoir, who, in his view, had entered into the relationship with him knowing from the start that it had no future . . . In a biting review of *Force of Circumstance* [a volume of de Beauvoir's autobiography] Algren writes of the pact that Sartre and de Beauvoir concluded: 'Procurers are more honest than philosophers.'

We will address the question of the honesty of philosophers in a moment. Here I simply want to say that de Beauvoir's approach to the dilemma is typically rationalist. She speaks with sympathy but seems to propose that all the crises of love, jealousy and disappointment can somehow be swamped by ultimately triumphant reason. Yet she knows quite well that once exclusive fidelity had been breached the most one could hope for is that, with care, the level of joy may be kept above the level of pain.

Honesty and Disclosure

The pact between these two French intellectuals rested on three legs: fidelity, variety and honesty, or, more accurately, disclosure. In *The Prime of Life* de Beauvoir wrote, 'We made another pact between us: not only would we never lie to one another, but neither of us would conceal anything from the other.'

Both of them discussed this policy in their novels. De Beauvoir refers to confessions being poured out 'to the limit of boredom'. Falling short of this is the policy of simply not volunteering information, or delaying the telling until the moment is right. The partner can of course be probing, diplomatic or steadfastly incurious. Or the partners can lie. At one time or another every one of these courses was pursued by Sartre and de Beauvoir. Again quoting from Evans,

In the case of the more serious relationships which he had with women other than de Beauvoir, Sartre seems to have maintained at least a partial honesty: in the case of others he quite candidly admitted that he lied.

And about de Beauvoir,

Sartre's deceit about his affairs might, then, be balanced by a kind of dishonesty on de Beauvoir's part: though she was deeply hurt and upset by Sartre's infidelities, she would allow herself to be deceived rather than face a rupture of a relationship which . . . was of fundamental importance to her.

Mary Evans is in fact more sympathetic to this predicament than this quotation would indicate. 'A kind of dishonesty' is one way of putting it. 'A kind of discretion' seems fairer to me. People can make up their own minds about whether they are going to be sexually faithful or not, and if they are not, they can decide how candid they are going to be about it. Candour can sometimes be like scalding water, and I would never demand that someone reach up and pull it down on themselves.

RETROSPECTIVE 'HONESTY'

People can be as jealous of the past as of the present, and the question arises whether one should be honest, or rather revealing, about the past. The obvious answer is 'It depends'. It would be absurd to suggest that a current lover has an absolute 'right-to-know'. It is also questionable whether we do someone a favour by pushing information on to them. There are sometimes pragmatic reasons for doing this of course: 'Better to hear from me than someone else.'

Tolstoy provides one of the more breathtaking examples of 'total disclosure'. Immediately after proposing marriage to Sonya, who was eighteen, and a week before their wedding, Tolstoy presented her with the volumes of his diary to read. In these she found a full account not only of his extravagant and destructive gambling, but also of his prior sexual life. Edwards writes,

That evening Sonya went to her room directly after dinner and began to read the diary. At first she was timid, then fascinated, then shocked, and finally appalled. She knew he had gambled away fortunes, but she had been almost completely ignorant of his erotic life. And now, less than a week before their wedding, she discovered that the man she loved had been to bed with every sort of woman – gypsies and whores, women who were her mother's friends, even his own serfs – and had recorded each encounter.

What was Tolstoy's motive, and what was the effect? First it must be said that everything Tolstoy did in this relationship seemed precipitate. He seemed out to defy his fortune. He was passionately attracted to this young woman, one of three daughters of a doctor. He had picked up something of her attitude towards him from a story she had written that he insisted on reading. It was obvious that the story concerned Tolstoy, the three sisters and one of Sonya's admirers. The message it conveyed was, first, that Sonya was attracted to Tolstoy, but, second, that she really did not find him physically very attractive. At the age of eleven when she first began to appreciate his presence in their house, she had idolized him – the brave soldier, aristocrat, etc. But the Tolstoy in her story was described as middle-aged, unstable, lacking in convictions and finally 'repulsive'. Tolstoy could deny none of these things about himself. He agonized about Sonya's ambivalence, but tried to satisfy himself that love would conquer her reservations.

Tolstoy also knew that his years of scandalous conduct, which he now despised but which were not so far behind him, could wreck her idealized view of him and subvert her growing attachment. Hence giving her his diaries – an act of 'total honesty' – was a defiant and desperate gesture. If he had been calm enough to be calculating, he might have been more optimistic about the outcome, for there were three strong forces binding Sonya to him: her love; the power of his position as a count and his reputation as a great literary figure; and the fact that her acceptance of his proposal had just destroyed her older sister's passionate hopes of becoming Tolstoy's wife.

What was the effect of the disclosure? In the short-term, disgust and turmoil rather than jealousy. But later when they were installed in their house in the forest, jealousy arose on both sides. Sonya's main preoccupation was with Axinia, the peasant woman who had born Tolstoy an illegitimate son, now four years old. After a short period of apparently ecstatic personal relations between Tolstoy and Sonya, matters deteriorated. Sonya was bored during the day when Tolstoy was absent. The possibility of encountering Axinia, and the consciousness that the peasants on the estate knew of the liaison, tainted her relations with them and increased her isolation. She began to suffer sexual rebuffs and rejection from her husband when they slept together. The idea came into her head (and into her squabbles with Tolstoy) that perhaps she could not trust his assurances that he now had nothing to do with Axinia.

One November morning in the entrance-hall of the house, Sonya came upon a strong-looking woman scrubbing the floor on hands and knees, and beside her a slim, fair-skinned young boy. Again, quoting Edwards,

Slowly the peasant woman sat back on her sturdy haunches and, as she drew her son close to her, glanced towards the mistress of the house. No words were exchanged . . . after a few moments she rose majestically to her feet, and grasping her child strongly by his shoulders, forced him to stand on his own . . . This was a horrifying moment for Sonya. Not only did she suspect the woman's identity, but for the first time in her life she had looked at a peasant – a former serf – and seen her as an equal, having the same sense of pride and dignity she had.

Within moments Sonya was out of the house, running, and ended up clinging to her dog under a pile of old fabric in a shed while the household searched for her. She was hysterical for weeks. She had in her mind a passage in the diaries about Tolstoy and Axinia: 'Never so much in love'. Later she wrote, 'So that's how he loved her! If only I could burn his diary and his whole past! . . . If I could kill him and then make another man exactly like him, I should do it joyfully.'

The impact of the diaries extended beyond this immediate crisis. It is not just that they confronted Sonya with past conduct she saw as 'filthy' and threatened the present, but they also produced in her a feeling of alienation, of having been excluded from the significant events of his earlier life. She wrote,

He doesn't understand that his past is a whole world of a thousand different emotions – good and bad – which will never belong to me, just as his youth, spent heavens knows on what and whom, will never be my property.

If someone were perverse enough to arrange a jealous predicament, this combination of brutal disclosure, isolation in place and time from her family and from his life, ambivalent but passionate love, rejection, and finally unannounced confrontation could hardly be improved upon. To it Tolstoy added another twist: that they should regularly read one another's diaries, and the diary he now wrote in was one of those that he had given her before the wedding. It is hard to comprehend that these were the actions of a man who wrote some of the most perceptive and penetrating studies of jealousy in fiction, in *Anna Karenina* and the *Kreutzer Sonata*.

I should add that the creation of such fiction, as in the case of Sartre and de Beauvoir, itself constituted a significant form of emotional disclosure. It is scarcely avoidable when authors draw so directly on personal sources for their fiction. Sonya, who acted as a scribe or copyist on endless versions of her husband's novels, had the experience of watching the development of the personality of Natasha in *1805* (later *War and Peace*), realizing that in life this was her younger sister Tanya, and that Tolstoy had developed a deep affection for her. Tanya lived with them for long periods and Sonya observed their intimacy and the sort of light-hearted enchantment that her sister could exercise over Tolstoy. Yet apart from one brief episode, this knowledge never had the corrosive effect that the diaries produced.

To pursue this matter of honesty and disclosure much further would require a major treatment of moral dilemmas, which would stretch the boundaries of the topic of jealousy. Perhaps I can recommend Bok's excellent book, *Lying*. If anyone thinks at the end of it that absolute frankness and truth is always the path to take, I can only say I admire their single-mindedness.

LOU ANDREAS-SALOMÉ: ONE-SIDED PACTS

The complex and often equivocal relationship between philosophy and action that we encountered with de Beauvoir and Sartre emerges even more dramatically in the life of a Russian novelist, essayist and critic, Lou Andreas-Salomé. She was born into an affluent St Petersburg military family that had come originally from western Europe. By the age of seventeen she had already developed impressive psychological independence. She was a religious disbeliever, and a

61

political idealist. She saw no reason to be less intellectually ambitious than her three elder brothers, and she absolutely opposed her mother's view that a woman should submerge herself completely in her husband's welfare. H. F. Peters, from whose biography of Lou Andreas-Salomé I have derived most of my information, writes that while still a young woman she had heard stories of 'fictitious marriages' advocated by certain of the Russian intelligentsia – marriages in which a couple lived together co-operatively, a sort of two-person intellectual and moral mutual-improvement-society from which sexuality was excluded. (It is intriguing to see the difference between H. F. Peter's account of 'fictitious marriages' and that given by Judith Armstrong. She points out that fictitious marriages were designed to provide women with passports, documents that they needed to travel around, even within Russia, and which could be obtained only through a father or husband. Even so, some of the Russian nihilists of the time do seem to have diminished their sexual possessiveness, and their passion, almost to vanishing point.)

Lou Salomé's education expanded dramatically when, at seventeen or eighteen, she came under the intellectual and emotional influence of Gillot, a fashionable minister of the Dutch Reformed Church in St Petersburg. The experience she had with this man, who was twenty-seven years her senior, set the pattern for almost every relationship throughout the next twenty years of her life. They were plainly fascinated by one another, their intellectual interaction was furious and passionate, but their affectionate and sexual intentions were quite different. Gillot had developed a plan to divorce his wife and to marry this attractive, vivacious and intelligent eighteen-year-old. Lou was not disgusted by this; she clearly found him attractive. None the less she rejected the proposal outright, brought the tutorship to an end and immediately began to campaign to leave Russia for Switzerland to attend university.

Over the next decade Lou Salomé entered into a succession of intellectual and emotional alliances with distinguished men on terms ultimately dictated by herself. She effectively created the 'fictitious marriage' relationship, but with a difference: in no case did the men really understand or freely consent to the exclusion of physical relations, or if they said they consented, they either did not really mean it, or were incapable of sustaining it. This is not to say that the liaisons were without profit for them. Although Lou is not regarded as one of the great original minds of the late nineteenth century, she had a formidable intellect and she was more clear-headed than many of the luminaries with whom she associated, Friedrich Nietzsche in particular. In every case these men had to acknowledge through the fog of anger and depression in which she left them that she had contributed much to their thought and creativity.

The sequence of events is not hard to follow. Each man was attracted by her combination of candour, intelligence, warmth and vivacity, not to mention her considerable physical charm. She came very close to them in order to participate in their intellectual and artistic worlds, typically spending long hours alone in their company, issuing and accepting invitations to live with them, and then finding it necessary either to fight them off or to desert them to maintain her independence. The overall result was a mixture of exaltation and disaster.

Lou went to Rome to visit a distinguished German feminist in exile there, Malwida von Meysenbug, and she met two of Malwida's protégés, the philosophers Nietzsche and Paul Rée. Rée was the first of the pair with whom she established close relations. On long walks at night they talked and argued, and in the process Rée fell in love with her. When he was told that physical relations were not on her agenda, he sensibly planned to leave, but Lou held him back. She proposed a non-sexual joint living arrangement, an apartment with herself, Rée and some third party, perhaps Malwida, perhaps Lou's mother, perhaps a second man. This didn't happen because the third person was never recruited. Lou simply lived with Rée on a 'fraternal' basis, and then took time out to establish an intense and similarly asymmetrical relation with Rée's friend Nietzsche. After that affair collapsed in turmoil she returned to Rée. Andreas, a 41-year-old Professor of Persian Language, then proposed to her, and after dramatizing this with a suicide attempt, persuaded her to marry him. She accepted on two conditions: first, that it should be a marriage without sex, and second that she be permitted to keep her relationship with Rée. This marriage endured for more than forty years, and the first condition was consistently held to, although not without considerable conflict. However, when Rée heard that Lou was to marry, he moved out and disappeared. He trained as a doctor, lived a sad, isolated existence working for the poor, and in the end drowned himself in the river close to a place where he and Lou had had one of their happier encounters.

Lou's relationship with Nietzsche came close to ending equally tragically. She went to stay with him for several weeks and informed him he had been 'selected' to be the third member of the *ménage à trois* with Rée. Nietzsche's sister Elizabeth was in a state of bitter and frantic jealousy over this proposal and over the long days and nights the two spent together. Nietzsche, too, fell in love and although there were evidently some tender moments, Lou rejected all his serious advances. It is hard to tell if she knew what effect she was having. According to Peters, 'All her life she found it hard to distinguish between her own imaginary world and the world in which other people lived.' Yet she wrote, 'All love is tragic. Requited love dies of satiation, unrequited of starvation. But death by starvation is slower and more painful.'

Nietzsche and Rée became more and more jealous of one another, Rée because Lou prolonged her stay with Nietzsche week after week, and Nietzsche because he had been told of the plan to come and live with Lou, but it never eventuated. Lou's feelings for Nietzsche had changed from fascination to doubt and from doubt to pity. They all met together in Leipzig, but Lou never committed herself, and in the end Nietzsche was simply left standing on a railway platform on an early winter's day watching Lou and Rée's train depart.

He stayed on in Leipzig for two despondent weeks, then went south to Italy, staying in cold and bleak Genoa. He heard that Lou and Rée were living together in Berlin. He wrote but got only evasive answers. In Leipzig he had felt sad and humiliated. In Italy he came close to suicide. He was alienated from his family, who believed he might be living with Lou. He had lost his friend Rée, whom be began to blame for Lou's indifference to him. His friendship with Lou was 'dying a painful death', he said. He began to hate her but could not get her out of his mind. His letters swing from reproach to self-blame and pleas for forgiveness: 'I want you . . . to consider that I am after all nothing but a semi-lunatic, tortured by headaches, who has been completely unhinged by solitude.'

Then suddenly within a month or two he began to write his *magnum opus, Thus Spake Zarathustra,* the book of the Superman that was so influential in Nazi Germany. He completed it within a year. Peters shows that one passage after another of this book echoes the affair with Lou, including the remark,

He who is consumed by the flame of jealousy turns at last, like the scorpion, the poisoned sting against himself.

Nietzsche for a time became more calm and reflective about Lou, but his sister kept up an active campaign of hatred, and in time Nietzsche was reinfected by her malice. But instead of directing it just against Lou, he turned on her innocent companion and his old friend, Rée:

I have not known the gravest facts of this bad affair until the last three weeks . . . Rée now suddenly stands exposed. It is terrible to be forced to revise one's opinion so completely about someone with whom one has felt linked for years in love and confidence.

Nietzsche's sister described Lou as a 'low, sensuous, cruel, and dirty creature' (Freeman and Strean). Nietzsche now went one better, describing her as, 'This thin, dirty, evil-smelling little monkey with her false breasts'. This was the woman to whom he had once written, 'I owe to you the most beautiful dream of my life.'

All the parties to this particular disaster survived it, although the combination of his sister's fury and his own grief and disillusionment almost brought Nietzsche to the end of his resources. Lou, to a certain extent shielded by Rée (who kept many of Nietzsche's letters from reaching her), maintained her composure and her will. Peters remarks,

It was *her* life, the rest was unimportant. To become more and more herself, to grow according to the law and rhythm of her own nature – *that*, she believed, was her supreme task.

We cannot pursue Lou Andreas-Salomé throughout her whole career. While she lived out the long period of her unconsummated marriage to Andreas she wrote, travelled and began a long liaison with the German poet Rainer Maria Rilke, then with her doctor Friedrich Pineles, and later with Tausk, one of the psychoanalytic circle in Vienna.

Shortly before she met Freud she wrote a book entitled *Eroticism*, in which she talks about the double aspect of the life she had led as though it arose from some philosophical policy: a stable, quiet and peaceful household love combined with constantly renewed passions (which she called 'divine madness'). Yet one gets the impression that she never really saw far into relationships, that she pursued life with a detached obstinacy, and turned her face to something else whenever things began to disintegrate. Whether it was the exhilaration of new possibilities or a philosophical doctrine that motivated her, it was certainly better suited to entering relationships than leaving them. Possibly there was no kind of disengaging from a man like Nietzsche, and perhaps the very intensity of the passion she provoked in all her companions and lovers made the exits perilous. But Peters quotes one of her lovers: 'There was something terrifying about her embrace, elemental, archaic . . . When she was in love she was completely ruthless.'

The rather gentle and fey philosophy of the 'fictitious marriage' gave her scope for her mobility and productivity. She nurtured the creativity of others, especially the poet Rilke. But it also provided the armour for the most ruthless progression through the emotional lives of those who became attached to her. In many respects she must be considered a heroine of liberated feminism. But only those who are implacably hostile to men, and to their emotional and sexual hopes in particular, would regard as benign the way she applied her philosophy.

GROUP ARRANGEMENTS

Let us move now from Europe to North America and from pacts between two people to arrangements made in larger groups. I shall begin with a contemporary Utopian group, the Keristas, who have developed a well-articulated philosophy enshrined in their 'social contract' and a set of working procedures to deal with local problems.

In 1981, when they were studied by Pines and Aronson, they had been in existence as a group in California for about ten years. Kerista Village then comprised nine women, six men and a couple of children. I referred to them as 'Utopian' not in any derogatory sense, but to indicate that they set up the group deliberately and optimistically to pursue their personal and global ideals. We are concerned only with their personal relationships. These were governed by two major constraints: first, they were not to engage in sexual affairs with people outside the group (so they were faithful to one another) and second, within the group they did not 'play favourites'.

Their sexual activity was regularized by a roster system governing sleeping and they placed stringent limitations on public expressions of exclusive intimacy. (The concept of a roster or time-table is something we shall encounter again. It arises, of course, from the fact that one of the most potent signals people can give one another and the outside world about their preferences is the amount of time they choose to spend in one another's company.)

Their 'social contract', a document of sixteen clauses, is published in Pines and Aronson's report. It dealt with certain practical matters such as group size, housekeeping and finance. It specified 'group parenting' for the children. It also placed restrictions on various sexual practices including not only sadomasochism, paedophilia, etc., but also group sex and voyeurism. These last two restrictions effectively limited sexual intimacy to couples interacting in private, and another clause banned any overt display of affection between adults in public. (That, too, is something we shall encounter again both in

66

other American sub-cultures and in certain kin-based societies.) The 'package' that the Keristas thus put together – the ban on outside affairs; the set time-table; the restriction of sexual relations to complete privacy; and the ban on public demonstrations of affection within the group – ought in theory to completely insulate all the members from the usual provocations to sexual jealousy. I should add that if there was any 'leakage', presumably in the form of impressions forming in the minds of one member or another, this was contained by a ban on 'gossip'.

The Keristas went even further than this, however, by cultivating a sort of 'anti-jealousy', a deliberate celebration of one another's relationships in so far as they were detected or inferred. Finally if jealousy did arise in spite of these precautions, there was a safety-net to deal with it. In a process of group confession the details of the reaction were explored and the group's intention to maintain mutual attachments was reaffirmed.

The group had a theoretical view about jealousy, an ideology derived from mainstream environmentalist psychology, couched in the language of 'socialization', 'learned norms', 'conditioning' and so on. We could take two different views of this ideology. The sceptic might ask, 'If jealousy is in fact just an unfortunate learned habit, why take such elaborate precautions to avoid provoking it?' The other more pragmatic view is that this ideology provided members with the confidence that if they worked at it they could exorcize any imps of jealousy that popped through the cracks.

A couple of items remain to be mentioned. At the beginning of the 'social contract' they asked for lifetime involvement with the community, its ideals and the 'family clusters'. These were simply statements of intention much like the 'death-do-us-part' clause in the traditional wedding vows. There was also an 'exile' or 'transportation' provision, not stated in the contract but evidently understood by everyone, so that if two people *did* form a preferential attachment, they were expected to pack up and leave.

THE MORMONS:
THE PRINCIPLE OF PLURAL MARRIAGE

In the early to mid nineteenth century two large-scale American communities were established that are famous for their unorthodox sexual and family arrangements, the Oneida community and the Mormons. Let us begin with the latter. The Mormons practised polygamy from the proclamation of 'The Principle of Plural Marriage' by

Brigham Young in 1852 until it was officially abandoned thirty-eight years later. A descendant of that Mormon leader, Kimball Young, has written an excellent account of the successes and failures of these marriages in the book with the rather off-putting title *Isn't One Wife Enough?*

What makes the Mormon community significant is that it was not established by well-to-do, well-educated Utopians, but by people of all ages, of varied economic backgrounds, many of them recent immigrants whose social and political views were on the whole far to the right of the centre. Their heterogeneity and the absence of a strong theme of humanism and permissiveness means that the experiment lacks the 'preciousness' of many of the communes set up in or around university communities in America and elsewhere.

The principle of plural marriage was an article of Mormon faith and was preached very vigorously both inside and outside church. Marriage had a double significance; it established earthly alliances and made preparation for alliances in the afterlife. (People whose spouses had died before entering the church could be married posthumously to ensure celestial connections and men could be 'sealed' to unmarried women who had died.)

I shall now quickly outline the social philosophy of the nineteenth-century Mormon community, following Kimball Young, and then review what he saw as the successes and failures of the family arrangements.

General Policy

The society was heavily and explicitly patriarchal. The husband was the chief wage-earner (or was supposed to be) and lord and master in his house or houses – daily discipline, moral teaching and all major decision-making were his responsibilities. The Mormon project of exploiting the frontier involved a drive to increase population. It is described by Young as a 'child-centred culture', with a high priority placed on fecundity and child education. Wives were childbearers and housekeepers. Courtship was '. . . brief and to the point'. Sex was 'not a means of personal pleasure'. A husband's love, although often real, was not a policy issue. There was flat opposition to birth control, and disapproval of sex during pregnancy and nursing, on the grounds that such intercourse was non-procreational.

There were no fixed rules about how a polygamous family was to be set up. Sometimes weddings involved a man and more than one wife; more often wives were recruited at intervals, either as additions

68

or replacements. There were no firm rules about the status or power position of wives relative to one another, nor about housing or inheritance, although there was a general admonition of 'equal treatment for all'.

Mormonism and polygamy in particular were under continual political, moral and legal attack, so that as time passed, families had to change their habits. Men originally appeared with multiple wives in public, then when police harassment worsened, they might attend church with the first ('legal') wife while others followed at a distance, and finally marriages 'went underground' or families emigrated.

The ultimate effect of these attacks was that, as Young puts it, 'their system did not last long enough to develop any standards'. In other words lessons that were being painfully learnt never became the basis for general policy. People improvised, sometimes with compassion, sometimes not. Many simply did what suited them as individuals and tried to paper over the cracks with preaching.

Most of the arrangements I will now review in terms of their success or failure are institutional – housing, children, public behaviour, etc. – but I must emphasize that the personal characteristics of the people seemed to play a big role in the outcome. Sometimes a woman with two co-wives would find life with one a pleasure and with the other a constant source of rancour and bitterness, even though the formal arrangements did not differ. One of the most successful marriages was attributed to the qualities of the man and his judicious selection of his three wives:

. . . they admired father. He was a bright man and a kind man . . . He chose well. All three of his wives had the same ideas. They wanted education and culture, and they wanted a peaceful home.

Take the problem of an older husband adding a young wife to his ménage. The example of one man would seem to mark it as a dangerous practice: he proposed marriage to an 18-year-old domestic they employed. The first wife's reaction was 'pure gall'. Again quoting Young,

I think I have never seen more unadulterated hatred than she [the first wife] shows when speaking of this woman . . . she refused to visit her husband on his death-bed though her children told her that he had been calling for her all day and begged her to go to him . . . 'I haven't spoken to Annie [the newcomer] for thirty years and don't expect to speak for thirty more if I live that long.'

And yet in a parallel situation:

he married when he was fifty years old . . . a shy girl of twenty years. She was taken to the home of the first wife. A daughter of the latter said of her: 'she was so young and quiet and timid that she was treated like one of the children. She had her own room, but during the day she joined in the housework exactly as one of the daughters.'

It is obvious that in some cases the difference arises from how people use their emotional power. One husband brought two new wives into the household together. The original wife could tolerate one but not the other:

Nora was a good girl, and she couldn't even look at him if she thought I wouldn't like it. But Rebecca, this one just gloried when she could get out alone with him. There's all the difference in the world between those two women.

This 'first wife' did not have the personal resources to assert herself and evidently the husband had his own reasons for not helping her. She said that over the first year she nearly lost her mind. By contrast another more assertive first wife simply moved her competitor out. At first the new co-wife slept in an adjacent room, but while she was away on a visit with the husband, the first wife picked up all her rival's clothes and belongings and dispatched them to a small house a few blocks away that belonged to an old woman who had died. Moreover, when the husband slept there, the first wife would demonstrate both her household virtues and her emotional attitude by rising early, doing all the housework, and then walking down the road to hurl stones at the roof of the house to stir the couple within.

Because there was strong moral pressure against the expression of jealousy, much of it was concealed. One wife simply paced up and down all night while her husband slept with his new wife; another retreated to the granary to cry. A third went out, climbed on the roof in winter and froze to death.

Of course some women bluntly rejected the addition of further wives. Young reports how one man, apprehensive about speaking of his intentions, finally told his wife that he had a 'divine revelation' that he should enter polygamy. Next morning his wife announced that she too had a divine revelation: 'To shoot any woman who became his plural wife'.

One might hope that sooner or later women would realize their common predicament, and this did in fact happen. Young describes alliances between women, even when they were of very different ages. They could achieve things together that neither could manage alone: 'He always said he had two to fight.' But the addition of still further wives often meant that tension returned.

Accommodation

It seems from all the reports that segregated accommodation was a great aid to co-existence. However, there were some resilient souls who managed under pretty rough conditions. There is a story of three women sleeping in beds one above another. The first wife, who slept at the top, would consent to her husband descending to 'visit' the wives below only when she thought it was time for another child, and then the husband was not permitted to spend more than the minimum time necessary away from the first wife's bed.

There was a regular pattern for men to build or buy houses for each of their wives and families as they became more prosperous. This practice has its echoes in a great number of polygamous societies, as Murdoch has shown. Of course the issue of accommodation is confounded with that of status and affluence, since only the more successful or well-endowed families could afford multiple residences. Material affluence was certainly no less important to marital harmony in polygamous families than in more conventional ones. Many failed marriages were directly attributable to the inability of the man to provide for multiple wives and the growing tribes of 'little images of God', as the children were called.

Women did not necessarily stand by in silence when they saw that a husband was about to extend his family beyond his resources. I liked the story of a man who brought a prospective new wife home to dinner. The children of his first wife were making a racket, and he demanded she take them out so that he could carry on the courtship in peace. To this the first wife responded, 'Children, howl all you want to.' In another case it was the 16-year-old daughter who intervened, ordering her father out to the barn because he was not supporting the family properly, simply turning up on his 'rounds' from time to time to impregnate his wife. However, other remarks indicate that something more than material survival was at stake: 'One first wife . . . was all right about the second marriage until she could hear her husband's boots drop on the floor in the second wife's room.' This is an eloquent example of how those small signals that carry us from the assumed to the explicit can be so unexpectedly devastating.

When there was trouble much of it revolved around status – status in the household, status between households and status in the eyes of the community. Within the household women competed over their attractiveness, their attentiveness, their industry, and even their fecundity. In one family everyone watched as year by year one wife gradually gained on her 'sister' by getting pregnant just a little sooner after each confinement. Although establishing separate households solved certain problems of jealousy and power, one man reported that housing his wives separately set off an unpleasant rivalry that was not previously a problem.

Status played a big role in the public sphere. The Mormons strongly discouraged shows of affection in public, but there were plenty of other grounds for distinctions. Some men insisted their wives take turns sitting beside them in their carriages or cars, in other cases the favourite or first wife always had that privilege. One husband drove up to the house of one wife and put everyone down so that the less-favoured wife had to return home on foot. In another case the less-favoured wife walked everywhere. Some arranged matters by turns, so the 'wife of the week' was the one who danced with the man or sat with him in his pew in church.

This policy of having a rota also applied in the home. A surprising number (75 per cent) of families applied it to sleeping. According to Young, 25 per cent alternated daily, 25 per cent on a 2–3 day roster, and 25 per cent on a weekly one. This was modified by pregnancy and nursing, illness, seasonal absences, etc. But not keeping an appointment with a wife without good reason could cause great bitterness and humiliation.

There was then the issue of affection with the household. The daughter of a Mormon said to Kimball Young, 'I don't think those polygamists knew what romantic love means.' Many outsiders saw polygamy as simply organized lechery, but as I said, the official attitude was that all this was duty and pleasure had little to do with it. To this religious and social puritanism was added the lesson, learned quickly by many, that displays of affection in the presence of other wives were perilous. Any sign of affection had to be perfunctory or clandestine. Romantic partiality had to be a well-kept secret because it could cause more trouble than anything. As I pointed out earlier, this discretion was sometimes as actively enforced by the wives as by the husbands, because many wives were acutely sensitive to the pain they could cause their 'sisters'.

Finally let me refer to another whole area of difficulty – the attitudes of unmarried men. Young reports that the balance of males to females in Mormon society at this time was about equal, so every wife added to a plural family was a wife 'taken out of circulation'. It is interesting to see patterns emerging here that appear in various kin-based societies. Some wives were recruited from new arrivals, but most were local. It was quite common for sisters to marry the same man – Young reports a figure of 20 per cent and says that these 'Adelphic' marriages were on the whole successful ones:

Of the thirty families . . . in which sisters or half-sisters were spouses of the same man, three-fifths of them may be rated as successful or moderately successful; seven families were definitely not successful; of the others there is too little data . . .

Sometimes there were swaps between the offspring of male friends, which sounds like something straight out of Lévi-Strauss. Sometimes widows or widows and their daughters married into plural families. This included what is termed the 'levirate', a man marrying his dead brother's widow. The marrying of widows was in general problematic, because of the conflict in what we might call the 'celestial continuation'. The women would normally expect to unite with their dead husbands in the afterlife. (Nobody discusses the possibility of jealousy in heaven. It may well be the sole prerogative of the Almighty.)

Young indicates that there was male hostility to plural marriages to young women, but he provides no details. There are two possible reasons for this lack of information: to protest publicly would be to defy a very autocratic religious establishment; and the men who established the most extensive plural households were the Elders, the senior and influential people in the church and community. This also explains why there were so many young women who actively sought polygamous unions (some took the initiative and proposed). They were not just seeking glory in eternity, but security and prosperity in 'time'. The frontier society was a very competitive and stratified one, and had no place for women trying to operate on their own. So in spite of the jealousies and power struggles in many plural families, entering them was often a way of 'marrying up'.

Girls and their families had to be particularly careful about male newcomers to the town. Young speaks of the 'winter Mormons', men who came into town, married, and then in spring deserted. For a dependent woman, a man with an established family might be a considerably better bet. We have to realize also that the Elders were often very heavily occupied in the public domain. In some cases they were almost like uncles or strange visitors to their various families, so that the greater part of the women's time was spent in a sort of female commune.

My very truncated version of relations in plural families has necessarily emphasized the conflict, but there were plenty of very well-advertised polygamous Mormon families that were clearly busy, successful, happy households and probably compared very favourably with some of the monogamous unions of the time. Murdoch said that the Mormon experiment with plural wives collapsed from internal stresses as much as from the very virulent external opposition, but the internal stresses were only in part due specifically to sexual jealousy. They arose also from economic pressures, conflicts of power and too little respect for the problems of status.

ONEIDA: MOVING AROUND OR OUT

The members of the religious community of Oneida were known as the 'Perfectionists'. Unlike the Mormons, whose sexual and marriage practices evolved haphazardly, the Oneida community was carefully planned by its founder, John Humphrey Noyes. Noyes had an acute awareness of the power of sexual attachment and jealousy. The community, located in rural New York, persisted in its classic form from 1848 to 1878. Within it there were two systems of sexual relations, one designed to provide sexual outlets without procreation, the other exclusively for childbearing, involving specially selected couples. The first system is of more interest to us, because it involved all the adults in a web of temporary liaisons in which casual affection was encouraged. Within this system conception was kept to a minimum by the practice of 'withholding'. The men learned, relatively successfully it seems, to suppress ejaculation. The second feature of the arrangement was the exclusion of any intense, exclusive love relationships, according to their major chronicler, Carden.

The battle against emotional attachment was waged in five ways. First, all liaisons were negotiated through an intermediary, usually a woman, and records were kept so that participants were kept moving from partner to partner. Second, they followed a principle called 'ascending fellowship', which ensured that there was always a substantial age difference between couples, and intercourse between supposedly more 'susceptible' younger pairs was minimized. Third, although sex was celebrated and affection encouraged, the couples were prevented from staying together too long at night – they ended up having only an hour or two together. Carden comments – 'such separation also helped prevent the long private conversations that might lead to "exclusive love" '. The fourth method of control was the exile of people who failed to keep their relationships 'cool'. People were banished to a separate community or departed altogether. (It is notable that of the forty people who chose to leave, half did so with partners.) Finally, like the Keristas, the Oneida community had public discussion sessions. The tone was critical rather than therapeutic, however, and there was constant denunciation of the 'marriage spirit', 'false love', 'special love' or 'exclusive love'. There was even posthumous criticism of a man whose diary and letters were found to include evidence of 'special love'.

Noyes had started a small spouse-exchange community involving sex and rather high-minded affection before he established Oneida, but his motive for creating the carefully controlled pairing system in the main community was to avoid the unhappiness he had experienced from an earlier sexual rejection. He wrote, 'Exclusiveness, jealousy, quarrelling have no place at the marriage supper of the Lamb.' So transient, continually shifting sexual liaisons provided community members with a generous volume of sexuality and with short-term affection. It liberated women from constant childbearing or childrearing. It ensured that older people, women in particular, were not neglected in love-making in favour of their younger colleagues. And except amongst the occasional back-sliders who failed to resist intimate attachment, it evidently kept exclusivity and jealousy at a low level by the radical control of exclusive attachment. Oneida was an extraordinary social experiment both in duration and radicalism, and it anticipated by a century the procedures adopted by groups like the Kerista community to minimize conflict and jealousy.

THE SWINGERS

We shall now move forward a century to the 1960s, and contrast the Mormon community that, officially at least, abhorred hedonistic sexuality, with groups that were formed in North America specifically to get more of it: the 'swingers'. James and Lynn Smith point out that the term 'swinger' is applied to couples who organized themselves into groups for recreational sex, but in fact covers a great variety of sub-cultures. They investigated well-educated inner-city swingers from San Francisco, whose behaviour and backgrounds differed greatly from the Midwest group that I am about to review.

The swingers are popularly regarded as examples of people who have emancipated themselves from jealousy and who show their emotional freedom by their easy tolerance of extra-marital intimacy. Indeed they often talked of themselves as the 'cosmopolitans', or the 'beautiful people', and set themselves apart from the 'straights'. But according to Gilbert Bartell, an anthropologist, the swingers were often very straight indeed outside a certain area of physical sex.

Bartell used interview material from 280 men and women from the Chicago suburbs. They were predominantly middle-class, predominantly white, all married or claimed to be married. They were politically conservative (60 per cent voted for the Southern Democrat, Wallace, and most of the remainder were Republicans). They were regularly anti-blacks, 'anti-hippie' and anti-drugs. Ninety per cent of the women were housewives. Salesmen were the biggest single occupational group among the men (40–50 per cent) and although they listed a great range of interests – dancing, travel, theatre, etc. – their actual recreational activities (apart from swinging) rarely extended beyond watching television. I mention these things to place the people socially. Apart from being white Americans, these people had almost nothing in common with the Kerista community, and were in fact more similar in certain respects to the Mormons in social background. The contrast between the three groups may be seen in terms of their political stance and class background. They also differed in their commitment to lasting relationships, and their attitude to hedonistic sex. Gilmartin uses a distinction between *body-centred* and *person-centred* sexuality. The swingers (in so far as they were swingers) concentrated on body-centred sex, the Mormons rejected it and the Keristas demanded both. The Keristas were Utopian, the Mormons pioneering, and the swingers recreational.

In discussing the Kerista group I placed emphasis on what they *didn't* do as well as what they *did*, and the same must apply to the swingers. The Chicago swingers followed about five patterns of sexual activity, which Bartell neatly summarizes as follows:

1. Partner exchange (or 'closed' swinging), where two couples simply swapped partners for the evening.
2. 'Open' swinging where the same sort of foursome made love together in various combinations and different ways (although it virtually never involved male homosexual activity).
3. 'Closed' parties where at some point couples paired off and disappeared for sex in various parts of the house.

4. 'Open' parties with group-sex accompanied by some watching and even a little photography.
5. 'Threesomes', usually a couple with a second female, but sometimes a couple plus a male.

What didn't they do? Although some couples met together over a period the major rule throughout was that there should be no evidence of commitment or attachment outside the actual sexual situation. Bartell comments, 'It is taboo to call another man's wife or girl-friend afterwards or to make dates on the side.' It is hard to believe it didn't happen, but the point is that if it occurred, the whole meaning and significance of the event altered; it ceased to be swinging and became adultery or at least infidelity (a third of the participating couples falsely claimed to be married). As Bartell says, 'They are absolutely terrified, even though they think of themselves as liberated sexually, by the thought of involvement.'

They placed great emphasis on the consolidating effects that swinging had on their married lives. Bartell says that most moved into swinging from boredom with their marriages. The majority were well past the 'seven-year itch', if there is such a thing; most had been married twice that long. They were on average in their early thirties. The key fact is that swinging was not an arena for courtship and new life directions; there was no place for emotional intimacy. Indeed some who tried swinging and rejected it did so because it was 'too mechanistic . . . there is a loss of identity and absence of commitment . . .'

What did the physical encounters involve? In some of the arrangements, such as the closed foursomes and closed parties, people never witnessed sexual encounters between their partners and others. The swingers here created on a casual and shifting basis what Kerista Village arranged more permanently: no demonstrations of public affection and no visible sex. The open trios, foursomes and open parties involved more drama, especially it seems, for men. When drunk, straight sexual rivalry sometimes broke out on both sides. This was made less frequent by 'exile', that is, people who made trouble once were simply not invited again. Gilmartin reports that some partners kept feelings bottled up until they got home and that their jealousy then expressed itself as passionate lovemaking. Presumably if it expressed itself otherwise, the couple would be 'ex-swingers' and unlikely to be among the interviewees.

More common than straight aggressive jealousy was a feeling of exclusion. Bartell gives a graphic account of the reactions to an open party. A number of people (especially those who were older or who regarded themselves as less attractive) simply gave up immediately and retired.

For those who remain, other negative aspects include sexual jealousy. The male may find after a number of parties in which his opportunity for satisfaction is limited and he sees the women around him engaging in homosexual activities and continuing to satisfy each other over and over again for the duration of the evening, he may feel, and this is verbalized, that the 'women have the best time', that the swinging scene is 'unfair to men'. *We find that less than 25 per cent of the men 'turn on' regularly at large scale open parties* . . . The male experiences disaster. Sixty-five per cent of the female respondents admit to enjoying their homosexual relationships with other females and liking it to the point where they would rather 'turn on' to the female than to males.

There are three paradoxes here. First, one might expect the source of men's jealousy to be the same-sex participants rather than, as in this case, other women. Second, it doesn't sound as if the men were jealous of individual women as competitors, but felt envious, inadequate and 'left out' by women in general. Third, ever since Kinsey the view has been that men are stimulated by sexual relations between women, whereas here we have the reverse effect. The size of the group appears to make a difference. As we saw earlier, the most popular 'triplet' by far is one man and two women. The first interpretation of this is simply that men call the tune. But there is clear evidence that these relations are more stable, and the stability seems to arise from the combination of voyeurism by the male and mutual satisfaction on the part of the women.

Gilmartin found many of the same features among his suburban Californians. He refers to the whole scene as 'psychological monogamy through the management of context', which I think is very apt. The management included the selection of participants: 'Most swinging groups will not permit single men to participate, nor do they allow married men to attend parties without their wives.' Not every group forbade the expression of tender feelings but they seem universally vigilant about any hint of attachment or exclusivity and banned contacts outside the regulated encounters. As we saw in the Chicago study, there were various levels of exposure in both the physical and emotional sense – many swingers simply retired from sight to make love, and presumably people adjusted their daring to what they felt they could handle.

Just as the Mormons exerted religious pressure on people not to confess jealousy, no doubt the 'cool' image of the swingers kept what agony existed underground. As Bartell indicates, it tends to surface under the effect of alcohol, a phenomenon also observed among the Marquesans by Linton:

Jealousy between plural husbands or even between married men over some woman outside their households was considered very bad manners. Such men never quarrelled over women when sober, but when drunk there were numerous fights, some quite serious, when knives were used.

What all the pacts and arrangements reviewed in this chapter indicate is that no matter what jealousy's origins may be, people who decide to break exclusivity in one way or another and who have gained some experience at it seem more elaborately protective of themselves, their partners and friends than we might have been inclined to think. By the exercise of care and sometimes by considerable effort, they can manage surprisingly well. But there never seems to have been a full-scale 'withering away' of jealousy to the point where people could form multiple, fully demonstrative, emotionally charged sexual attachments without risking adverse reactions. The picture almost everywhere is of the elaborate evasion of jealousy and rarely, if ever, of its abolition.

CHAPTER 4

Jealous Instincts?

——————— Q ———————

In this chapter I want to develop a distinction between two varieties of jealousy: *reactive* jealousy, which we see whenever someone throws a tantrum or becomes gloomy and morose over an incident of straying affections, and *preventive* jealousy, which includes those societal and personal manoeuvres that we use to isolate our partners from temptations or opportunities to stray. I then want to explore the possibility that one or both of these varieties of jealousy owes something to instinct, to biological, genetic predispositions to be jealous. Some readers may be surprised that a modern writer would even mention instincts. Don't we live in an age of infinite human perfectibility? Given the right environment, anybody could, in theory, be anything, or not be anything. But I have developed a belief that at least in the area of the emotions there are some reactions or tendencies to react that could be called instinctive, inborn, innate.

Instinct has had several births and deaths. Sigmund Freud saw two major instincts as the engines of our psychology, and later we will examine the mechanics of his 'sexual instinct', which was supposed to generate normal and delusional jealousy. Over seventy years ago an Anglo-American psychologist, McDougall, defined a small clutch of broad human instincts: curiosity, gregariousness, the reproductive instinct, and so on. These fledglings thrived, then grew alarmingly to a flock of almost a thousand, only to be dispatched almost overnight by the guns of indignant academic hardheads. After an interval during which the concept of instinct was virtually outlawed, 'microinstincts' were born in Holland and Germany out of scrupulous and patient observation of lower animals: beetles, spiders, fish, seagulls, wolves. This is the tradition of 'instinct' I am going to call on in considering the role of biology in the two main categories of jealousy.

We begin with the most radical conception, that there might be a universal 'jealous imperative', a basic drive found in all animals, including humans, that gives rise to cock fights, cat fights, the combat of red stags on the mountainside, even, perhaps, the pet dog menacing the new baby. Consider the fur seal patrolling his enormous harem of females, or, if he can't keep them together, charging desperately about trying to chaperone each consort as she cools off in the sea on a hot afternoon; or the tropical fish repelling rivals from his patch of reef and trying to cope with 'streakers' who occasionally flash in to fertilize the female's eggs.

But is it legitimate to make inferences about ourselves from deer, dogs, cockerels and coral fish? What about our closer genetic relatives, apes and monkeys? Hamadryas baboons, like seals, assemble harems, watch them carefully and will bite the back of any faithless female whose attention wanders to the younger males. Gorillas live in one-male harems and are intolerant of intruders. Male orang-utans fight only when a sexually receptive female is at hand and have been reported to attack humans who are in contact with their females. Gibbons live in monogamous pairs in the high tree-tops and repel interlopers.

Doesn't this begin to look like a general jealous instinct, a 'jealous imperative'? Unfortunately the idea encounters trouble at the most critical point: Our *closest* genetic relatives, the animals with whom we share all but 2 per cent of our chromosome pattern, are the chimpanzees. Rather than being jealous and rivalrous, male chimpanzees commonly display a remarkable indifference to sexual competitors. They have been observed again and again going about their bodily affairs or idly watching while other males mount and copulate with females with whom they have just mated. The baby chimpanzees or young juveniles interfere with mating much more vigorously, pushing at males who are mounting their mothers. However, this is not sexual rivalry, but rather a way of postponing their mother's next pregnancy and so continuing to monopolize her care and attention. (I am not claiming that baby chimpanzees are wise to the reproductive significance of copulation; the reaction itself is probably inborn.) Female chimpanzees sometimes attack new females trying to enter their ranges (the females are exogamous, that is, they leave their own groups to mate), but according to the primatologist Ghiglieri, this may have more to do with food resources than sexual competition.

The bored sang-froid of the adult chimpanzees deals a fatal blow to any idea of a *universal* genetic mechanism of jealousy. There is no all-embracing biological 'jealous imperative'. But that does not in itself rule out some instinctive or organic basis for jealousy in humans. It rather means that we have to evaluate the idea on its own terms.

Perhaps it would be helpful to explain why I think there probably *are* biological roots to human sexual jealousy (and to the jealousy we discussed earlier in children). I can offer no final proof, only a developing conviction. It rests ᴖn the fact that adult jealousy seems to obtrude itself in all societiᴇ where emotionally charged sexual attachments form, and also on the unexpected difficulties experienced by individuals and groups in our own society who have attempted to evade it. Before I began reading intensively on the topic and talking to allegedly 'jealousy-free' people I was much more prepared to see it as an entirely cultured product, but my confidence in that has given way to a hybrid view that combines biology, culture and personal history.

Saying that jealousy has some biological or genetic basis does not imply that it is either stereotyped or inevitable. We can draw a useful parallel with grief, which I am even more convinced has biological roots, but which is not such a political and moral 'hot topic' as jealousy. To say that the tendency to grieve is inborn seems unobjectionable. It doesn't imply that everyone must grieve or that they must grieve in the same fashion. An appropriate prior attachment is necessary, along with a recognition of loss. In other words, one needs an appropriate personal history to set up the process, just as one does with jealousy. Further, we can, with effort, hide our grief or hide jealousy. On the other hand, social practices can elaborate and amplify both the emotion and its expression. We can also develop rituals (like wakes) to deflect and swamp our grief, and we can occasionally block jealousy with well-timed humour or reassurance.

The Survival of Instinct

Let me persist a little longer on this theoretical point. If we can establish a model for jealousy that combines the forces of biology and social influence, we will have an idea that can be applied to many emotional states – love, embarrassment, panic, depression, etc. – where we suspect there may be an underlying organic 'instinctive' mechanism or predisposition.

Is this fusing or interlacing of instinct and social experience something that we encounter only in humans? Humans are dominated by culture and develop institutions that are not found in animal societies, but the principle of socially modified instincts is by no means rare in animals.

I will restrict myself in my explanation of this to two examples related to rivalry or jealousy in lower animals. Take first the notorious stickleback. I say notorious because almost anyone who has read any psychology will have been subjected to tales of the behaviour of this nondescript pond fish. Male sticklebacks attack rivals. Their attack is triggered by the sight of the red belly of the intruder, and it seems to be so automatic that a stickleback raised out of contact with others of its species will attack a crude wooden decoy painted the appropriate red. One could photograph the standard signal that triggers the reaction, which doesn't seem far from a sort of complex reflex. This sort of behaviour provides an example of a 'micro-instinct' of the sort I mentioned earlier. However, note that the stickleback reacts in this way only when the red belly enters its territory. So could we get a photograph of stickleback territory to indicate what the fish's brain is responding to? But there isn't 'a territory' in the sense of an innate map in the fish's brain. Its territory is just whatever piece of pond or tank the fish has settled down in. What is home territory for one fish is foreign territory for its rival. In other words, it chooses and then learns its territory and this local geographical learning is somehow automatically incorporated into the innate mechanism that releases the attack on the rival.

Take as a second example the jealous behaviour of the hamadryas baboon. These monkeys organize themselves into large groups of females and young under the control of a dominant male. The male behaves aggressively both to intruders and to any female who reacts to the presence of competitor males at the periphery of the group. The attack on the females is quite recognizable; the male tries to bite the back of their neck and in fact the females have a tuft of thick hair on their necks at this very spot.

So, in line with the 'micro-instinct' idea, is there a trigger that inevitably produces jealousy in the baboon like a key fitting a lock? If we took a photograph, what would we see? Some female monkey walking across some piece of ground. The events that trigger the characteristic jealous biting of the female's neck are local signals that have to be 'read' by the dominant male's brain and they depend upon his own developing social history. The male will have entered into a sexual relation with certain females in oestrus. The visual appearance of those females who are his consorts is not branded genetically on his brain. Nor are the walking movements that carry one of the females towards a young mature male near the periphery of the group innately recognizable to him. Yet he is clearly biologically programmed for a jealous reaction: *that* isn't something he learned or thought out for himself. But the programme includes a sophisticated, rather *abstract* recognition of a misdemeanour by one of his harem based on his learning of consort and dominance relations that are themselves partly instinctive.

It is these precedents, aspects of behaviour in lower animals that clearly arise at one level from genetic endowment yet in other ways require experience and complex interpretation, that make me reluctant simply to abandon the instinct idea on the grounds that meaning and experience are involved.

Male and Female Differences Again

The biological idea that I am trying to retain can be both useful and dangerous. It is useful because without it jealousy appears an ephemeral thing, something that a few contemptuous words or a little social conditioning can banish. The danger lies in extending the biological idea too far into areas that properly belong to culture and social arrangement. We have already encountered this in the surprisingly widespread view that male jealousy is somehow naturally or genetically different from female. Let us start with a quote from Scot Morris, describing a discussion involving the primate anthropologist Irven de Vore in 1977. One of the topics concerned

a genetic approach to the question of why men and women seem to react differently when their mates commit adultery. That idea developed into the concept of parental investment . . . Because of the greater investment a human female makes in having a child, she would be more sensitive to desertion than adultery. The human male on the other hand would be most disturbed by cuckoldry, because raising another man's child would delay the reproduction of his own genes.

Here we have a quite plausible biological explanation for a phenomenon that very well may not exist (that is, a gender difference in the trigger for jealousy) and which, if it does exist, may well have a completely social explanation. I recently inquired into this with a group of university students in Sydney; the outcome was not very favourable to the sex versus desertion idea.

The students had no prior idea of the purpose of the study, which was divided into two stages. In the first the students were given ten short scenarios that they had to rate on a scale from 'extreme jealousy' to 'not jealous at all'. They then rated the same items along the dimension to which Morris refers: emphasis on sexual intrusion at one end and emphasis on loss of affection and support at the other. In this second exercise, distinguishing sexual intrusion from something analogous to desertion, the male and female students were in absolute agreement. Not surprisingly they rated spending the night with a person of the opposite sex, dancing close and acting guilty at a party as very 'sexually intrusive'. Brushing a person's cheek, straightening hair and cleaning off lipstick were somewhat the same. Writing a long personal letter, shopping for a personal gift and spending money and time with the person were classified as indicating loss of affection and support.

How did this relate to their jealousy ratings? The most jealousy-provoking scenarios were the sexually intrusive ones – spending a night together, dancing close. The significant fact from the point of view of the biological hypothesis is that the male and female responses to these items were virtually identical. Indeed, the most striking overall outcome was the extraordinary similarity of the jealousy ratings of men and women on all items. The biological hypothesis of sex differences could draw comfort from only one item: 'You discover that your partner has been spending time and money with someone of the opposite sex'. The item was put at the top of the list in emphasizing loss of affection and support by both men and women, but there were more than three times as many women as men giving it the extreme jealousy rating ('Likely to make me extremely jealous'). I should point out that although it did receive high ratings from women, it was still much less jealousy-provoking for women than the explicitly sexual items. Spending a night with a lover was twice as jealousy-provoking as spending money and time.

At this point I looked at the identity of the women who gave higher ratings to the item. Across the whole study the subjects were young, the majority being eighteen and nineteen. Unmarried students greatly outnumbered married, and only about half were in 'steady' relationships. The higher jealousy ratings on this 'economic' item tended to come from older women and included *all but one of the fifteen married women and all the women with children*.In other words, it isn't a general characteristic of women in contrast to men, but is dependent on the family situation in which people find themselves. (It is also worth remembering that it is much more likely for a man to be spending money on another woman than a woman on a man, so the item was not a very plausible scenario for the male respondents in the first place.)

I am not suggesting that this study closes the issue, but it does indicate two things: first, we cannot simply accept a stereotype on the 'sexual' man and the relatively asexual 'domestic' woman that this sort of biology draws on – both men and women are most sensitive to explicitly sexual intrusions; second, we have to recognize that any differences there may be in jealousy over a threatened transfer of affection could as well be associated with economic dependence and lack of options as with genetically determined differences between men and women.

PREVENTIVE JEALOUSY VERSUS REACTIVE JEALOUSY

The other area to which biological ideas have been applied is that of preventive jealousy: those practices that limit the freedom of partners and serve to restrict sexual access to them. Biological causes have been suggested because the motivation for many of these often cruel and exploitative customs seems to be to guarantee the parenthood of offspring.

First let us take an example of *reactive* jealousy to dramatize the difference. Reactive jealousy is that which shows up after infidelity, not something you do to prevent it. The quotation is from Chimbos, an American investigator interviewing a man who shot his wife:

You see, we were always arguing about her extramarital affairs. That day was something more than that. I came home from work and as soon as I entered the house I picked up my little daughter and held her in my arms. Then my wife turned around and said to me: 'You are so damned stupid you didn't even know she is someone else's child and not yours.' I was shocked! I became so mad, I took the rifle and shot her.

Was this lethal reaction biological? In line with what I have said about the socialization of instinct, it is obvious that it isn't *all* biological. To begin with the man wasn't genetically programmed to understand English. He was not born with the equivalent of a computer disc or a set of punched cards in his head with this woman saying these words to him, any more than he was born with the knowledge that guns kill people. So it obviously isn't *all* genetic. Yet neither am I prepared to say that this is simply a learned role he was acting out, like a person saying 'I will' at a wedding. Somehow the particular social and emotional history of this man, woman and child in this cultural predicament seems to key into a potent motivational system that drives the explosive reaction. In another family and another culture the provocation will differ in detail, yet preserve some essential quality. Jealousy triggers are not templates, they are social computations.

Preventive jealousy includes things like the coercive control that the law, until recently even in 'advanced' Western countries, gave men over women, the stress placed on the virginity of women, the idea that men can drink alone in hotels but that women should be accompanied, and so on. Preventive jealousy lacks the immediacy of reactive jealousy, and although it seems to serve biological purposes, it is much more difficult to see how it could be tied to organic programmes in our brains. This is because it so often involves whole social institutions rather than individuals. I can perhaps clarify this with a couple of diagrams. In the first we have a simple, direct link between need and action. We need food, we collect and eat it; we need exclusive sexual partners, we seek them and repel rivals. From the simple pair, need and action, we find it easy to extend backwards to genes and forwards to survival:

genes → needs
     ↓
   actions → survival

And finally we close the evolutionary loop: survival controls genes.

The second model is needed to deal with much preventive jealousy, because our needs do not necessarily give rise to *direct* actions on our own behalf, but flow through institutions: rituals, laws, religion, moral teaching, even the structure of the building people occupy, the jobs they do, and so on. So if there is to be a link between genes and actions and ultimately the survival of genes (which is what biological systems are about), the path must be more like this:

genes → needs
     ↓ ↑
   institutions
     ↓
   actions → survival

We will see that economic, family and political systems, laws and even medical practices are involved in preventive jealousy; explaining how genes and biology could affect these isn't so easy, as we shall see.

Paternal Confidence

I want to draw on a very challenging article by Daly, Wilson and Weghorst entitled 'Male sexual jealousy', which is largely about preventive jealousy. It ties together a wide range of practices and arrangements in many societies: adultery laws and penalties in Europe; sequestering and incarceration of women in countries extending from the Mediterranean to the limits of Asia – veiling, chaperoning, virginity tests, female 'circumcision' and other forms of genital surgery. Much of the material is depressing and the detail swings from the unjust to the macabre and horrifying. The authors describe

various practices that are commonly subsumed under the misleading label of 'female circumcision'. These range from partial through complete clitoridectomy to surgical removal of most of the external genitalia and the suturing shut of the labia major (infibulation). Hosken (1979) documents the continued existence of these practices in twenty-three countries extending across Northern and Central Africa, as well as Arabia, Indonesia and Malaysia. She estimates that more than sixty-five million women and girls presently alive in Africa have been 'circumcised'.

What Daly, Wilson and Weghorst are emphasizing is that these practices that limit access to females by 'inappropriate' males have one thing in common: they all serve to increase 'paternal confidence'.

There is an obvious and inescapable asymmetry in the position of mothers and fathers with respect to offspring. A mother is not ordinarily in any doubt that she is the parent of the child she bears. The male has no such *automatic* source of confidence, and this, according to Daly, Wilson and Weghorst, is a primary source of what I have called preventive jealousy. Concern on the part of men about the biological parentage of their children is not universal. There have been societies in which people simply don't believe that there is any direct link between copulation and childbirth, or at least no link that connects the father's characteristics with that of the child. There are many societies in which children are accepted no matter who their genetic father might be, and of course fostering and adoption are very widespread. But there are many more societies where paternal confidence is very important, indeed one might almost call it an obsessive preoccupation. It isn't the only reason why in so many societies men keep such control over women, but none the less it is of vast social importance. It has helped shape the whole texture of male–female relations in societies all over the world and throughout history and continues to do so. For example, in almost every major culture men move more freely geographically and participate more in public life. This is not because women are more naturally fearful or less competent, or even because they have to be close to the children. It applies long before they bear children and persists long after the children are independent. And if women are more fearful, it is often because they are made more fearful, and made to associate mobility and independent action with risk, irresponsibility, immorality and shame. We can think of many societies where this is extreme; I shall be describing some in Chapter 6. But although in Western societies the restraints are more moderate, the same structures are there.

The horrific details of Hosken's report on topics like repeated infibulation makes it seem more than a trifle bizarre to be pursuing fine points of theory, but let me just say that to explain this institutionalized barbarity towards women in terms of the direct operation of male jealousy in individuals is unsatisfactory to say the least. On the other hand, to think it has nothing to do with the control of genetic paternity is equally unreasonable.

Genes and the Law

This is the comment of Daly, Wilson and Weghorst on adultery laws:

Both cross-cultural and historical reviews of adultery laws reveal a remarkable consistency of concept: sexual intercourse between a married woman and a man other than her husband is an offense. It is often viewed as a property violation. The victim is the husband, who is commonly entitled to damages, violent revenge, or to divorce with refund of bride price.

The authors document a long line of cultures with a double standard in this area: ancient Egyptian, Syrian, Hebrew, Roman, Spartan, Inca, Maya, Aztec, Islamic, tribal Germanic, African, Chinese, Japanese. In Europe and the countries around the Mediterranean 'male infidelity was not criminalized until 1810, and then only in a very limited way when a French law made it a crime for a man to keep a concubine in his conjugal home against his wife's wishes'.

There is quite a bit of work to be done if we wish to explain the way that 'paternity insecurity' translates itself into cultural institutions like the law. Of course, one might simply say all of this is traceable to male power, which it is. But how are we to conceive of this process: laws being passed by a clutch of red-faced, angry and indignant male parliamentarians, their innate jealousy inflamed by the spectre of female looseness of morals, backed up by equally red-faced and furious male judges interpreting and administering these laws on behalf of male defendants and complainants? And did the genes under the waistcoats and wigs change their tune when they inspired and administered law on the behalf of wronged women? It is good theatre; it contains perhaps a grain of truth, but it lacks conviction and rigour as a description of institutional processes.

But the complementary question is, why was male power exerted over *this* issue? It is not just sexual services that are being conserved for males by these institutional arrangements, but control over progeniture, over the paternity of offspring. Biology has to answer the question 'How do genetic mechanisms come to work?' The quick answer is 'evolution through natural selection'. A full answer has to spell out exactly how cultural institutions provide a link between genes and their survival. But social and cultural theories have their own tricky question to answer: 'How do cultural mechanisms and social practices, which do not flow directly from genes, come to serve the survival of these genes, as biology suggests they do?'

Is There a 'Biology' behind Female Sexual Rivalry?

De Vore emphasized male rivalry and its possible basis in genetics. Mildred Dickemann discusses certain cases of *female* competition and considers them biologically. Dickemann has put the view that the restrictions placed on women by men (or on women by women for men) is part of a quid pro quo. She describes societies in Northern India, the Middle East, China and to a lesser degree Japan, where the old, wealthy élites kept harems. These institutions contained women of widely differing status: wives, consorts, concubines, servants and female slaves. They sometimes operated on a grandiose scale: 4,000 women for a ninth-century Islamic caliph; 1,200 for an Ottoman sultan; 1,200 for an Indian maharajah, and so on. There are two features of the harems that were not familiar to me before I read Dickemann: female infanticide was a common feature; although some women in harems were bought or captured, certain socially ambitious women competed for the privilege of becoming members of the harem. The two currencies of this competition were dowries and virtue. Families tried to outbid one another in the size of the dowries they offered and the women themselves offered their virginity and their fidelity as inducements to acceptance. Why would some women compete for membership of an institution into which others were enslaved? It was not that the competing women were the social inferiors of the servants and slaves, quite the reverse.

The key to the situation is the question of status within the harem. The élite women of the harem could expect their children to become the next generation of the élite of the society. Wives and concubines could expect their sons to acquire wealth and power, and with wealth and power, harems of their own. The killing of the female offspring was part of the system, so that in each generation there would be a high ratio of males, who would produce a high ratio of males in the next generation – a sort of 'compound interest' system for the production of descendants.

The most common biological idea about sexual competition and rivalry is that males compete for females when the females devote great time and effort to the rearing of offspring. The term used is 'parental investment'. Rivalrous males compete for women because they commit themselves so heavily as parents. In the harem situation this idea has to be turned on its head. Males were 'investing' not in personal care, but in the resources they provided both in the present and through inheritance. This, according to Dickemann, is what the women and their kin competed for, and one of the elements in the deal was the assurance that the female who was marrying up into the harem élite was not 'damaged goods':

Child betrothal and child marriage . . . are the inevitable result of many families competing over a few grooms . . . Upper status males . . . demand virginity at marriage, and the socialization of the female to value and manifest ideals of feminine modesty, purity and shame . . .

Dickemann sees the procedures of preventive jealousy – cloistering, veiling, binding of feet, and so on – as a price paid in this trade; access to inheritance and proliferation of (male) offspring in return for virginity, fidelity and large dowries.

All this has to do with 'biology' in the sense that the males and females are preoccupied with their descendants. They want many and they want to be sure of their origins. They act as though they were driven by 'selfish genes'. But whether we can attribute the elaborate social paraphernalia of the harem, the dowries, the infanticide, the sequestering of women, to biological evolution is another question altogether. Consider Dickemann's account of the routines in the Tang dynasty imperial harem, which included

copulation of concubines on a rotating basis at appropriate times in their menstrual cycles, all carefully regulated by female supervisors to prevent deception and error, showing what can be achieved with a well-organized bureaucracy. Given nine-month pregnancies and two- or three- year lactations it is not inconceivable that a hardworking Emperor might manage to service a thousand women.

The Emperor no doubt had his work cut out to cope, but think how hopeless it would be for the selfish genes to orchestrate all that without a little help from culture.

Reproduction and Labour

I don't want to leave any impression from Dickemann's work that male preventive jealousy was something found only in the exotic upper strata of Asian harem societies, although it certainly flourished there. Practices like the excision of the female genitals and infibulation are found in tribal societies throughout central Africa today. Excision even extends to the Europeanized sectors of the communities and is carried out in modern hospitals. Currently it tends to be associated with Muslim beliefs, yet the practices are many centuries older than Islam. For centuries they were seen simply as local cultural practices, condoned even by European churchmen, but not emanating from any particular religious teaching.

Hosken has suggested that infibulation (the surgical closing of most of the opening of the vagina) is a practice adopted to restrict female sexual activity in societies which cannot sequester women. Where there is enough wealth women can be kept in special quarters. In less affluent families they can be segregated at the back of the house, but when they are involved in non-domestic labour they often cannot be kept geographically isolated.

The ostensive reasons for excision of the female genitals are as varied as they are unconvincing – religion, hygiene, aesthetics. But a common explanation was simply the reduction of 'wantonness' by reducing sexual pleasure. This is obviously related to sexual jealousy and control of reproduction. Within the African societies in which these practices continue on a large scale wives are not only child-bearers and providers of sexual services, they are also a major source of agricultural and pastoral labour. Rendering them sexually 'tranquillized' by surgery from childhood is part of a programme that maintains male power in both reproductive and economic spheres. Hosken points out that work considerations sometimes took precedence: infibulation was practised on female slaves not to keep them as sexual servants but to ensure that childbirth did not interrupt the availability of their labour.

The fact that these procedures serve more than one purpose is not fatal to a biological explanation, but what are we to make of the fact that it is not the males themselves who actually carry out the surgery? They may be the beneficiaries, but they are almost always excluded from the actual excision or infibulation rituals, and may not even know when they occur. It is females who do it to females, the old to the young. In other words 'preventive jealousy' is institutionalized and in the process delegated to the victims themselves.

CONCLUSION

First let us deal with the biological contribution to reactive jealousy. It is in this area that I am most sympathetic to the idea of an abstract biological mechanism shaped, exaggerated or deflected by culture and dependent on a personal history of attachment. The technical arguments *against* some biological involvement in direct 'face-to-face' jealousy are based on a model of rigid micro-instincts that I reject. It is not that I am unhappy about species-specific micro-instincts. That is a more respectable idea than jumbo-sized instincts like 'the sex instinct' or 'the reproductive instinct'. But when we carefully analyse instinctive behaviour in lower animals we find that it involves an important ingredient of experience. The social history of a particular animal in the short to medium term determines what will be a significant event for the release of a jealous or rivalrous reaction. This learning is not completely arbitrary. The baboon doesn't get jealous of the waving of the trees or the rise of the moon. It is a tricky issue: the genetic mechanism is changed by learning, but the learning itself is genetically limited or channelled – that is, the events that can become significant for the jealousy mechanism are themselves limited by biology.

This situation is much more intellectually challenging than either simple social learning or a simple reflex-like instinct. It is a significant idea because it provides the model we need for human jealousy – a process that may on the one hand be biologically given, but that can be deeply affected by certain cultural experiences. As I remarked above, it is also the sort of mechanism we need to explain many other important human emotions like love, grief, loneliness, even aesthetic reactions and humour. They all seem to combine some biological predisposition – a different one in each case – and a heavy contribution from culture and development.

When we turn to preventive jealousy – laws, rituals, social and domestic arrangements – we are dealing with institutions and with actions that may even be delegated to people who are themselves victims of preventive jealousy, and it is here that biological theories run into their greatest difficulties. Yet it has to be said that certain practices, such as sequestering in harems, infibulation, the restriction of freedom of young girls and the jealous guarding of wives, make a sort of macabre biological sense against the background of paternal uncertainty. They seem to favour the survival of genes of the individuals who practise or support them, and the genes of their close relatives. The practices themselves, however, are part of complex cultural arrangements and nobody has provided a good account of how genes can shape and control such systems.

Daly, Wilson and Weghorst include in their review a discussion of what happens when there is a jealous attack by a man who discovers his partner with a lover. It includes the original act of reactive jealousy and the operation of public institutions, in this case the criminal courts. 'Cuckoldry mitigates responsibility for otherwise criminal violence.' In other words, courts regularly reduce penalties for spouses (usually men) who are confronted by sexual infidelity *in flagrante delicto*. Now I would not claim that courts or the law-makers (in spite of the fact that they themselves are largely male) are in the grip of a jealous instinct when they make a law and apply it in this way. But I do not rule out the possibility that somewhere in the original jealous act they are condoning there is something like the buried stump of an innate jealous mechanism, watered and fertilized by the culture in which it continues to live.

CHAPTER 5

The Anthropology of Jealousy

—————————— Q ——————————

Let me begin the discussion of the anthropology of jealousy by considering those writers who work from vignettes or examples, such as: 'The eskimos lend their wives for the night'; 'On some Pacific islands unfaithful wives dress up and jump from coconut palms'. We can divide the vignettists into two groups: those who use vignettes to prove that jealousy is universal – in every society we can find some examples of it – and those who use vignettes to prove that jealousy is *not* universal – in many societies there are practices (like a wife having more than one husband, a man marrying a widow and her daughter, or, indeed, eskimos lending their wives) that would surely provoke jealousy if it were universal, but don't.

Both groups are correct in their basic claims. It is extremely difficult, if not impossible, to find societies without jealousy. Sometimes jealousy appears only when people are drunk; often it is not evident until an anthropologist starts talking on intimate terms to people about their private feelings. On the other hand, there are plenty of practices that in one society would produce jealousy but in another do not.

If jealousy were a reflex, like blinking when something hits your eye, you could use the vignette method to establish if it were universal or not. But jealousy isn't like a reflex nor even like a cluster of reflexes, so the battle of examples is inconclusive. Both groups can support their arguments. Jealousy is very common but takes a variety of forms, and what provokes it depends to a large extent on cultural practices and meanings.

It would be wrong to be dismissive of the vignettists, because they have brought to light much interesting material about jealousy and it is their success in supporting their two contrasting views that has taught us a lot about the nature of the phenomenon. But the anthropology of jealousy can be approached in another way. We can look at a few societies in more depth, as Hupka has done – or Les Hiatt in his inquiry into the outcomes of polyandry in Sri Lanka. The object is to establish whether there are certain social arrangements, political and economic considerations, or systems of belief and attitude that help us understand where jealousy is likely to be more pronounced, who might display it, and under what circumstances. This is the project of the present chapter. I shall begin with a brief comment on 'the family', and then plunge into a quick (and rather ruthless) classification of societies.

THE FAMILY AND SOCIETIES

Defining a family can be tricky. Even in our own society we use the term in different ways. When we ask 'Are there children in the family?' the implication is that a childless couple could constitute a family. We talk of 'single parent families', so a couple is not essential, and we even ask 'Do they have a family?', where the term refers to the addition of children. None the less the common stereotype of a family in Western society is the independent married couple with children, which is known as the 'nuclear' family. This is by no means a world-wide standard model, however, and various configurations and variants occur in different cultures. In Sri Lanka there were wives with multiple husbands, sometimes brothers, sometimes not, coexisting in the same society with monogamous families, so even within one society there may be a variety of models. Furthermore within any family constellation there are several different relationships: husband–wife, parent–child, brother–sister, brother–sister and sister's child, and so on.

Immediately we accept this variety, we see that our emphasis on the adult partnership as the key family relationship shapes our pre-occupation with a certain sort of jealousy. Jealousy between partners is only one of a number of jealousies within families. In many societies it is not the most salient. Indeed, as we go from family to family within our own society, we may find all sorts of other rivalries that we didn't at first focus on.

Bearing in mind the diversity of family forms, let us move on to a classification of whole societies. For convenience I have adopted the three-part classification of Eric Wolf. First, there are capitalist industrial societies like our own. We have a strong interest in them simply because they *are* our own. Second, there are highly organized 'tribute' societies, such as existed in India, which I referred to in Chapter 4: societies in which rulers maintained themselves and their élites by extracting wealth from their subjects. We discussed them in connection with competitive hypergyny (marrying up) by certain women and the tight supervision and control of those women by various physical, economic, educational and other procedures. Wolf calls these 'tributary states' and includes traditional oriental and many middle-eastern societies. Wolf's third category is 'kin-ordered' societies. These include most of the societies we ordinarily think of as 'primitive'. They are the societies that classical anthropologists typically studied, and it is from these that most of the interesting examples quoted by the vignettists are derived: the American Indians, eskimos, Pacific Island societies, African tribal societies, and so on. Within the kin-ordered societies there exists or existed a rich variety of relationships, in families, descent groups and clans.

These three types of society are distinguished on the basis of their productive organization, but they are not eternal and unchanging. They alter themselves and intrude on one another so that modern anthropologists are now mainly occupied in watching their 'primitive' societies transformed, often with brutal rapidity and brutal results, by the impact of industrial and commercial societies.

Let me now turn to questions of kinship, where I shall borrow from Robin Fox. Although I shall be describing certain kinship systems from 'kin-ordered' societies, kinship is obviously not restricted to these societies. We all have 'kin'. It is just that in capitalist societies productive processes – economic life, accumulation of capital goods, the use of labour, etc. – are not centrally organized around kinship. Kinship systems in urban Europe, North America and other industrialized countries tend to be rather stripped-down, minimal affairs.

What has this to do with jealousy? I believe that in order to understand the likely impact of new sexual and emotional alignments between men and women, we need to know how central the personal relationship is to the whole structure of people's productive lives. In Western society we tend to think of infidelity and reactions to it as simply a matter between a couple themselves. It spreads to the children if there are any, and may affect domestic property. But it has negligible effects in the sphere of work: when a man and a woman work in a factory or office, these institutions are not usually transformed in an immediate way by disturbances in their personal affairs. If, as in a kin-ordered society, the land, the animals, other workers and the patterns of exchange are all organized around the family, there are many parties whose fate will be affected by personal rearrangements. Consequently the people themselves attach a completely different significance to shifts in affections.

In order to talk about kinship structures, we have to consider two things: the actual patterns of kinship and marriage; and the way these are related to rights and obligations, not all of which are economic. As a psychologist, kinship structures were never part of my basic education, and my primitive knowledge of the primitives will protect the reader from too much technical detail. But the more serious we become about jealousy (or any other emotion) in relation to society, the further into the details of these structures we need to go. This idea is at the heart of a systematic study of the anthropology of jealousy. I have chosen my examples from three of the major kinship arrangements: the patrilineal, the matrilineal and the nuclear family. I shall begin with the last one.

THE NUCLEAR FAMILY

The nuclear family, common in industrial societies, can appear either in its complete form (mother, father, children), in an augmented form (including grandparents, etc.) or, very frequently, in an incomplete form (one parent and children).

I won't elaborate on the way the structure gives rise to new families except to point out that it is symmetrical, each child marrying and usually moving out. Who they marry outside is not controlled by kinship but by various class, religious and racial limitations. The formal expectation is that each new family will be a stable, full-time affair, irrespective of whether it is a son or daughter who is marrying. Property is nowadays split between husband and wife and passed on to sons and daughters. Jealousy is usually thought of in terms of outside intrusions on the sexual partnership, or rivalry between the siblings. But other jealousies occur: one partner may resent the other's attachment or allegiance to the offspring, or adults may react badly to their children forming outside attachments. Because of the authority relations between parent and child, there is probably more scope for the expression of resentment about outside attachments in the case of father and daughter, and more opportunity to conceal what jealousy there is in the guise of moral control or perhaps anxiety for the daughter's physical safety. The situation is not just one-way of course; children can feel resentment at parents' attachments to new partners.

Competition for allegiance also occurs where members of earlier generations are present, bringing with them long-standing attachments and dependencies. For example, a man may progressively withdraw from general family activities and finally from his sexual partnership with his wife as a result of conflicting allegiances involving his wife's mother (Clark and van Sommers). Obviously there can also be problems between a woman and *her* in-laws that express themselves as jealousy, although according to Levinger this is a less common source of tension.

Before we look at other kinship structures, let me make a brief comment about the issue of the separation of the Western nuclear family from work relations. There are two opposing considerations. On the one hand one might think that a couple in a nuclear family could form new attachments with less trauma simply because there is rarely any direct impact on the work sphere. On the other hand the elaborate paraphernalia of the Western family is made possible only by the participation of at least one family member in outside work, and for women in particular a break in marital relations often means being cut off from that source of subsistence. I hardly need to dwell on why this might be a reason for heightened sensitivity to serious outside attachments. The other equally well-known fact is that the nuclear family and our residence patterns tend to isolate people from broad social networks or at least represent the critical link through which the networks are sustained. So even a relationship that does not threaten the survival of the household itself may produce strong jealousy, anxiety and resentment in both males and females because social life and personal identity are focused upon the little knot we call the family. Work also separates couples for long periods of the day. This allows clandestine relationships that are not possible, for example, in certain kin-ordered societies where people are working together all the time, or where people are under the eye of other family members virtually every minute of the day or night. We are invoking here the regulatory aspect of jealousy, which implies that the level and style of people's infidelity are adjusted to detectability and the estimated hurt and disruption it may cause. The structure of the family and society affects not only personal predispositions to jealousy but also the level of provocation, both in volume and visibility.

PATRILINEAL SOCIETIES

The patrilineal arrangement is perhaps the easiest alternative kinship structure for Western readers to understand. We ordinarily follow a patrilineal system where children are given their father's name and wives take their husband's. Hereditary titles go down the male line. If you think of the 'ancestral hall' and how the eldest Lord Bloggs inherits it and brings his new Lady Bloggs to live there, you not only have patrilineality but patrilocality as well: the son lives with the father, and his son brings *his* new wife in, and so on.

In fact this family arrangement combines four features: patrilineal descent (tracing descent through the father, the father's father, etc.), patrilocality (living in the paternal home), patriarchy (male power and authority), and property being passed down the male line. When we discuss the Mediterranean situation, one of the contrasts we will encounter is that between nuclear or bilateral families in Europe and patrilineal families in the Middle East and North Africa. This has marked effects on who is expected to react strongly to female infidelity: husbands in the one case, and fathers, brothers and cousins in the other.

History and literature are full of dramas associated with male infidelity in patrilineal families, especially when a male ousts (or attempts to oust) an old wife in favour of a new wife and new heirs. Jason plans to cast off his wife Medea to marry the daughter of Kreon, and Medea, the barbarian sorceress who once killed her own brother to serve Jason, now the classical portrayal of jealous vengeful hate, murders the prospective bride, her father and finally her own two children. King David, discarding his wife Mikal for his new wife, Bathsheba, arranges the death of her husband, Uriah, and those of his own two sons in favour of Bathsheba's child, Solomon.

Patrilineal societies offer the most spectacular examples of the double standard, gender segregation and institutionalized jealousy. All the great tribute-taking societies of China, India and the Middle East were (and many still are) patrilineal. Fox remarks,

we might expect in patrilineal societies to find a lot more fuss being made over marriage and the rights over wife and children than in the matrilineal. Logically, marriage is only a marginal institution in matrilineal societies. This does not mean that it may not have its importance, but compared with the central place it has in patrilineal societies it is as nothing. In a patrilineal system, a man wants sons. So he must get hold of a woman, or preferably women – the more chances the better – and hang on to her until she produces him some.

This may or may not be accompanied by a fierce preoccupation with *geniture* – the question of who is the biological father of the male child. Preoccupation with having a son doesn't always mean obsessiveness about genetic paternity, but when it does we have the most potent prescription for jealous behaviour on the part of males – not just personal jealousy, but institutional precautions and sanctions.

Exogamy, Exchange and Alliance

Some kin-based societies, such as the Mae-Enga, are organized on a patrilineal basis. Mae-Enga jealousy (or the lack of it) is dominated by questions of alliance. When I was discussing chimpanzees I made a brief reference to exogamy – female chimpanzees move out of their own group to mate. In a crude sense we could say that the females who are recruited into the group are 'exchanged', since exogamy involves two-way traffic, but there is no social significance to the movement. The male (and females) within the group feed together, associate together, groom one another, but they have no such relations with the groups from which the females come, and the arrival of the females makes no systematic impact on relations between the groups. As Robin Fox points out, it is only between human groups that such exchanges become socially significant. Exchange between human groups is the instrument of alliance.

In his book *Kinship and Marriage* Fox quotes Tyler: 'Again and again in the world's history, savage tribes must have had plainly before their minds the simple practical alternative between marrying-out and being killed out.' Fox goes on,

We might call this the 'hostage' theory of exogamy. Our palaeolithic hunting-and-gathering bands . . . exchanged women in order to live with each other. If it were made a firm rule that no man of the band must marry any woman of it – or rather that each man should marry a woman of some other band – then each band would become dependent on the other bands for marriage partners . . . 'enter into marital alliances with other groups in order to live at peace with them'.

The principle does not stop with the symmetrical exchange of women; as Lévi-Strauss observed, women may circulate (or be circulated) serially or in irregular ways through much larger groups, and exchanges may involve not just the women but other 'commodities', including bride-wealth. Again, we are not so conscious of this within nuclear families in industrial societies. Although in a sense offspring are circulating within a pool of families restricted by class, race, religion, geographical location, and so on, the alliance functions are very woolly, and issues of fidelity are much more likely to be family issues, the preoccupation of family members. This in turn makes it easy for us to ignore the tricky problem of how a biological mechanism of jealousy can be mobilized in a society where not just the husband or potential husband is seriously interested in the sexual conduct of the woman in question; where women are community property, the community can be jealous.

The Patrilineal Mae-Enga

The Mae-Enga, a patrilineal society of the highlands of western New Guinea (now Nuigini), was organized in such a way that large numbers of people had a strong interest in having marriages endure. This is not because of any romantic ideas about marriage, quite the reverse. Mae-Enga marriages involved the transfer of a woman from her clan or descent group to the control of her husband. Marriages were preceded by prolonged negotiation between the clans about the terms of exchange. For a month after the marriage there was little contact between the couple. When both had been appropriately tutored in the magic needed for their association, there were a few days of meeting for intercourse, after which, in the words of Meggitt, their ethnographer, 'The husband gives his wife a new digging stick and a net bag, then sends her to the gardens to begin the round of drudgery that continues until she dies.'

The marriage was cemented by a bride price (mainly pigs) given by the groom and his descent group to the bride's group, who made a smaller gift in return (also mainly pigs, but not the same ones). Not only was the woman transferred to the man but the children also became members of the husband's clan, except perhaps for a period when they are young and may stay with their mother should she leave her husband. The bride price was not massive in material terms, but it involved contributions from a number of donors – usually between seven and thirty people – and it was distributed to a variety of people in the woman's clan. The marriage was both a material transaction and an important act of integration between the clans, and was followed by further exchanges so long as the marriage persisted.

If divorce occurred (and it rarely did), the bride had to be returned intact to her family if a husband hoped to see a refund on the bride price. He could react to any misdemeanours on her part by cutting off fingers, cutting her nose, or worse, but if he did so, neither he nor the clan members who supported him when he married could expect the bride price to be returned. If he obstinately proceeded to divorce without convincing grounds, the same problem arose. It was not simply a matter of the pigs and other gifts that were at stake; the whole alliance system that they symbolize was under threat. (It is in this sense that we refer to patrilineal *societies* rather than simply patrilineal *families* affecting attitudes to marital behaviour.)

People on both sides were very jittery about short-term separations because of the risk that they might become permanent. So, according to Meggitt, in the absence of the safety valve of 'going home to mother', beating and mutilation or occasional banishment of a wife to a remote garden were more likely. Remarriage involved a repetition of the whole exchange process, so neither the man nor his potential backers were very enthusiastic about the replacement of one wife by another. Since all but a few marriages were monogamous, and since the man depended crucially on the woman's labour to maintain himself within the community, bachelorhood was not a reasonable alternative. All these and other considerations meant that the man's actions with respect to an unfaithful wife were dominated by kinship and clan interests.

The same conservative influences arising from alliance and exchange affected the woman's response to her husband's adultery. Her family rarely had any interest in divorce, because not only would they have had to establish fault if they hoped to retain the bride price, but divorce would unravel all the exchange relations between the clans that had continued since the marriage. They were much more likely to seek some simple compensation. So adultery by a husband did not figure significantly in the effective grounds for divorce.

Meggitt describes how an older, impotent or sterile man might occasionally connive at sexual relations between his wife and younger men to acquire children and perhaps to satisfy the woman. This had to be very carefully orchestrated. The younger men had to be ineligible to marry the woman, even were she single. (We shall see this again in the Tubetube people.) The men must also be unable to identify who was the father of any children, and above all the matter had to be carried through with the utmost tact, or it could precipitate a 'spill', that is a divorce, with compensation added to all the other complications.

I think I have said enough about patrilineality as it operated in Mae-Enga society to illustrate how the political and economic networks can shape and channel the reactions of husband and wife. From Meggitt's account the Mae-Enga seem to have been a rather belligerent people, but it is not even necessary to go beyond the division of labour between husband and wife and the structure of the exchange systems to get a feel for the forces affecting their personal relations.

MATRILINEAL SOCIETIES

The great majority of societies studied by classical anthropology were patrilineal and patrilocal. Perhaps for this reason there is a special interest in the exceptions – in matrilineal societies. These societies constituted only 15 per cent of the 250 societies examined by Murdoch in one of the early comprehensive summaries of kinship, but almost everyone discussing kinship will at one point or another mention the famous matrilineal societies of the Nayar, the Ashanti or the Trobriand islanders.

As with patrilineal societies, descent, residence, power and property provide the basis for classification: in a matrilineal society descent is traced through the mother; if it is also matrilocal, the husband goes to live with the wife's group. There do not seem to have been examples of matriarchal societies, where power and authority are invested primarily in women.

A vital issue in matrilineal societies, as elsewhere, is property: land, herds, stored crops, buildings, tools, domestic equipment. With major items like land and animals, we can ask two questions: to whom is it passed on, and who manages it? In the case of the Tubetube people women may manage the property, and this makes a big impact on their independence and hence on their ability to weather domestic crises. However, major property resources are usually passed between males. In some matrilineal societies husbands are largely peripheral, but that does not mean that property falls into the possession of women. It may be transmitted from uncle (mother's brother) to nephew (sister's son). In this sense matrilineal descent can be seen as a variant on male power rather than as an exception to it.

It is important to see that the family structures that are associated with certain personal interactions don't necessarily arise from those interactions themselves but may very well have their bases in external practical realities or beliefs about those realities. There is a widespread view, described by Fox and Marvin Harris, that kinship systems arose from the interplay between people and the environments in which they live. When resources were scarce and widely distributed, hunters and gatherers tended to move in small nuclear-family groups and came together to negotiate marriages. When economic activities require men to pass on knowledge and skills to younger men; then fathers and sons tended to live together in patrilocal groups. When men were obliged to be absent for long periods for trading, hunting or warfare, they seemed to prefer to leave things in the hands of sisters rather than wives, and matrilineal systems were common. Let me now describe two matrilineal societies: the Nayar and the Tubetube people.

The Nayar

One basic matrilineal arrangement introduced in the early chapters of Fox involves brothers and sisters remaining in residence together and bringing in their spouses from elsewhere. The sons remain with their mothers, becoming uncles when their sisters' children are born and providing the male care for the next generation of sons. The husbands visit, sire children, but live in their own matrilineal households. The resident 'uncles' likewise function as visiting sexual companions for lineages elsewhere.

The most-often quoted case of this sort is the Nayar from southern India, described by Gough. Their kinship system was rapidly replaced by monogamy after the British put an end to the warfare that was one of the mainstays of this society at the end of the nineteenth century, but the women originally had a series of male associates of three different types. Before puberty they were married to a local man as a sort of 'holding operation'. Then they may have stayed in a Brahmin household as consort to the upper-caste males and may have had children as a result. When they returned to the village to live with their mother and brothers they had a 'batch' of up to twelve temporary husbands, who visited sequentially. So casual were these arrangements that one lover would announce his presence to another hopeful simply by leaving a weapon resting beside the door.

The view has been put that the transient relations between the warrior husbands and the Nayar women were a result of the need to keep the men free from heavy emotional dependencies. To think of it as a long-term 'rest and recreation' system is probably too flippant a view, but there was an element of this to it. The reports say little about rivalry between the visiting husbands beyond the observation that they negotiated freely and easily. Yet from time to time men of high status formed more enduring relations with the Nayar women, and other men were excluded. Members of the woman's own caste could not set up exclusive relations of this kind.

There was a powerful undercurrent of control over a woman by the men of her lineage, which belies the general impression of free association. When a child was born, one or other of the multiple husbands claimed it. This was not a matter of economic responsibility or even personal control of paternity, but rather a formal way of asserting that the woman was consorting with the right men. If no husband came forward, the supposition was that the child was a product of a liaison with a lower-caste man, a highly dangerous situation. The woman was considered a source of pollution. Even though she was still alive, her funeral rites might be staged and the whole community remained under a cloud until it was decided whether she should be executed or simply enslaved. The men of the matrilineal descent group, not the husbands, handled this caste infidelity. According to Gough, the woman's brother was the key figure:

A man's hidden concern for his sister's sexuality seems to have found an approved outlet in the jealousy with which he was expected to guard her from any taint of contact with lower-caste men . . . If a woman were finally judged guilty of sexual relations with a man of low caste, the law permitted her brothers to vent their jealous fury by putting her and her lover to death.

There is a vague suggestion in the way this is expressed that the brother's jealousy arises from some sort of suppressed attachment felt towards his sister, but it is his authority over her that seems important. Brothers experienced great rivalry with one another over authority according to Gough. Older brothers could physically punish younger ones. The question of external public reputation was also involved, because there were duels and battles between lineages arising specifically from slander about the sexual reputation of women, that is, allegations about liaisons with men of lower castes.

Finally, there was a third source of jealous tension. Although the temporary husbands did not seem to show hostility towards one another, a husband's *kin* sometimes reacted badly if one of them seemed to be becoming too involved with the Nayar woman and her children. The husband's brother might practise sorcery towards the wife or her kin to induce illness. The motive was jealousy over the possible transfer of goods from the husband's lineage should the attachment to the casual husband become too strong.

The Nayar situation illustrates that the strongest tensions and jealousies are not between those that we would select as the most vulnerable – the multiple husbands – but between the wife's brother and the husband's brother. We might have expected mayhem to break out between competing husbands over sexual access or paternity. The reporting on this is not as full as one might like. I have the impression that the (male) travellers on whose tales we depend may have been rather titillated by the possibility of several good-natured men sharing a woman, in what they saw as socially acceptable female promiscuity. But, for what it is worth, the husbands were said to be urbane and tolerant, while in the relationships with brothers in both lineages jealousy arose over allegiance, resources or caste.

The Tubetube People

The Nayar society was large and complex, highly differentiated by caste, and split into families, lineages, chiefdoms and kingdoms. In the seventeenth century, warring kingdoms in this area could send as many as 60,000 soldiers into the field to fight. In contrast, the Melanesian people who live on the small island of Tubetube off the New Guinea coast are a very small-scale society. There are around 2,000 people on the group of eight islands called Bwanabwana and only about 140 on the island of Tubetube. I have selected them to discuss for three reasons. First, they too are a matrilineal society. Second, we do not have to depend on historical records as we do with the Nayar. Martha Macintyre has written a report on them based on recent field work and I have had the opportunity to talk to her about some of the details of Tubetube family relations. Third, although jealousy certainly occurs amongst the Tubetube people, the society has several interesting features that seem to make jealousy and domestic strife much less harrowing for everyone, even though marriage break-up, divorce and remarriage are almost universal.

I will briefly summarize three areas of Tubetube society: work, property, and marriage; relations between parents, other adults and children; and strategies for handling jealous conflict. Marriages follow on personal attachments, and the couple lives alternately with the wife's family and the husband's, year by year. Each relocation is accompanied by a balanced exchange of gifts and labour, so that neither partner builds up an excessive amount of credit. Both husband and wife have a garden, so each can maintain considerable economic independence. Their work differs, but not dramatically so. When men travel they have to cook and look after themselves, and women take over men's jobs in their absence, including the management of land.

Because of the close bonds between a woman, her brothers and other men of her lineage, a single, divorced or widowed woman can depend on these people for assistance. Although such matters are not directly relevant to the occurrence of jealousy, they make a considerable difference to the humiliation and anxiety that might otherwise accompany an impending split-up and which in our society so greatly amplifies jealousy.

In line with the general approach we have been adopting, I have emphasized the structural features of this society – the matrilineal kinship, the balanced division of labour, the property-management skills the women exercise, the continual flux of gift-giving and labour service, the close proximity of villages to one another, the mobility (one might almost say the *portability*) of children, who are readily adopted or simply given to one person or another. But there are also important intangible factors, the most significant being the feeling of belonging to a lineage, of having unqualified acceptance into an extended group to which one can return. Macintyre says, 'The word for a lineage, *susu*, means "breastmilk" and conveys the ideal of social unity that is sustained as one generation bears and nurtures the next.'

The most likely time for a split-up to occur is during the second year of marriage, while the couple is living with the husband's household. The role of the wife as an outsider in this setting, where she is treated to a degree merely as a helper and is separated from her kin, probably has much to do with it. It is not that women in this situation are maltreated or bossed about, but they have less self-respect and, as strangers, are at a disadvantage. Few first marriages survive beyond these initial years. There is no formal divorce, but rather a change in residence. The most usual precipitating event is infidelity; when the aggrieved partners find out, they often take themselves off to sleep elsewhere. Moving away is the approved way of handling the situation. Quarrelling is strongly disapproved of, and people who lose their tempers, scream and hit may well prejudice their long-term chances of remarriage. A public display of anger is much more humiliating than the infidelity that gave rise to it; bystanders will avert their faces and move away, signalling their disapproval.

Seeking allies to brew up trouble is quite out of order, and there are mechanisms in the community to bring things to a proper settlement. Macintyre writes:

The reasons for divorce are, in most instances, similar to those prevailing in our own society, with incompatibility and adultery as the main causes of breakdown. Emotional responses to the discovery of a spouse's infidelity are apparently similar. People express anger and dismay at their betrayal. The aggrieved partner is often jealous and very unhappy. But he or she has only a brief period of time for the legitimate expression of such emotions before the senior members of each lineage involved insist on separation. Sometimes the matter is sorted out at a public meeting, more often the relevant groups simply discuss the most appropriate solution and insist that the couple behave in ways that do not create general unrest. By the time a marital quarrel involves other people apart from the couple it is usually assumed a divorce is necessary.

The children in a matrilineal society such as this automatically go with their mothers – but the geographical and emotional situation is such that children move backwards and forwards very easily. Fathers usually have very relaxed and regular contact with their children both during marriage and afterwards. Their upbringing is, in any event, shared between the father and the mother's brother, who has responsibility for educating them.

When an act of infidelity occurs and people begin to recognize that a new attachment is forming, the change may be attributed to 'love magic'. Men believe other men use it and women think other women use it. The Tubetube people are affectionate and romantic lovers, but they are not 'paraders'. They do not make conspicuous displays of their attachments. When an attachment is forming the first evidence of it may be that the man starts treating the children of the woman's family with more than customary affection. Irregular affairs are never conducted in public, and never in houses. People disappear into the bush. Such love-making is not disapproved of, but it is regarded as different from the standard premarital and marital relations. When men go on trading and fishing trips, it is expected that their wives may have affairs, although these are certainly not advertised. A woman may have a casual relationship for a day or two. It is note-worthy that the partners in these relations are often people they could not technically have as marriage partners – people in certain special kin relationships or of different generations.

To sum up, there are many features of Tubetube society that defuse the jealous situation. There is also a certain amount of direct sup-pression. Throughout their lives the Tubetube people, like the K'ung bushmen, are socialized to behave with restraint, but it is not a repressed society, quite the contrary. We can contrast it in this respect with the highland New Guineans, the Duna, described to me by Nick Modjeska. The Duna do not have a well-developed language of emotions and men in particular avoid displays of feelings, including both affection and distress. There is nothing of the egalitarianism in work and power relations between the Duna men and women that one finds amongst the people of Tubetube. When I inquired whether they displayed jealousy, Nick Modjeska replied that, as far as he knew, there wasn't even a word for it. But, he said, consider this incident of interaction between a husband and one of his wives: the wife had expressed a wish to join another family group. Her husband dismissed the 'request for transfer' with impatience, the reason presumably being that he would lose her domestic and sexual services. Finally, when her request became very insistent, the husband said in a matter-of-fact, peremptory way that rather than listen to her continual requests, he would simply take her and give her to the other man. They then set off through the forest. On the way the man suddenly requested intercourse. The wife consented and lay down on the ground, whereupon the husband took his axe and killed her. In a society in which men's standing depends upon avoidance of the discussion of emotion, it is naturally difficult to establish what the motives for this act might have been, but the whole situation could not be more different from Tubetube society.

CHAPTER 6

Societies of Honour and Shame

———————— Q ————————

In the societies we have been discussing the jealousy experienced and displayed has by no means been restricted to the members of the sexual partnership. We have seen examples of other family members reacting to what seems to them excessive commitment, or intervening when liaisons breach caste rules. I am now going to discuss a group of societies in which the community at large as well as close kin (husbands, fathers, brothers) exerts strong pressure on people (usually women) who transgress or are believed to have transgressed rules of proper sexual conduct. In these societies we will encounter situations where these 'outsiders' may in fact act with more anger and vehemence than the people that we think of as directly involved, so that sexual partners may be torn between the jealous demands of the outside world and their own desires and affection. We shall also encounter the very opposite, when outsiders occasionally counsel restraint on the passions of the jealous.

MEDITERRANEAN STEREOTYPES

Before I begin a discussion of these 'societies of honour and shame' and the institutionalized jealousy they involve, I want to counter any impression of a uniform bloc of patriarchal societies jealously guarding subjugated women. The Mediterranean region contains a great variety of sub-cultures, indeed most of us have not one but several images of even a single Mediterranean country such as Italy. Let me illustrate this with four of my Italian stereotypes. The first, which is probably closest to the material in this chapter, is that of the men of a small town drinking in the café, the women on their doorsteps dressed in black, the boys idolized by their mothers, the young daughters dressed in bright clothes but subject to jealous control over their sexuality. The second, which for me probably derives from *La Dolce Vita*, is of the dynastic upper classes, powerful, amoral, the women sophisticated, cosmopolitan and independent, fashionably dressed. The third is of the rural poor (pictured, for example, in *The Tree of Wooden Clogs*) – tenant families being dispossessed and driven out by displeased rural landlords. The fourth comes from the industrial north – Milan, noisy, political, organized and disorganized. All of these stereotypes share to one degree or another the influence of the church, the shaky hand of the state, male domination, female strength and female subjugation. I will return to the problem of heterogeneity and historical change later, but I thought it wise simply to activate the awareness that all of us already have about these societies as a counter weight to the narrower vision of tyrannical patriarchy portrayed by the literature of honour and shame.

THE 'STANDARD THEORY' OF HONOUR

To cut off an unfaithful woman's nose or breast, to kill a woman because she has been raped while at the same time admiring the prowess of a male adulterer, to discredit a woman simply because she has been the subject of idle or malicious gossip, to outwit neighbours by deceit and to destroy their reputation by slander – none of these actions seems to us honourable, yet all at one time or another have been accepted as indispensable to honour in the countries surrounding the Mediterranean.

The description of these societies and the explanation of why the behaviour developed or survives is contained in a series of books and articles that emerged during the 1960s. For example, Campbell's *Honour, Family and Patronage* describes the rather extraordinary Sarakatsani communities of nomadic shepherds in highland Greece not far from the border with Albania. Material was published about Spain by Pitt-Rivers, about Greek Cypriots by Peristiany and about the Kabyle of Algeria by Bourdieu. The Sicilians, Corsicans, Sardinians, Turks, Bedouins of North Africa and the Near East, the Montenegrans of southern Yugoslavia all provided accounts that I shall refer to for simplicity's sake as the 'standard theory on honour and shame'. Without exception the societies were centred on villages, small towns or the countryside rather than large cities. All tended to be fragmented into small groups – families, lineages or alliances that competed or conflicted. Conflict needed to be played out in face-to-face relations, that is, people reacted and interacted in a personal way and were for one reason or another less influenced by the laws of the state and the church.

Our interest in these accounts is that they offer dramatic stories of institutionalized jealous behaviour, which is displayed by individuals but stems from social demands and social vigilance. The demands are often quite explicit and are designed in the first instance to protect sexual exclusivity and to punish and avenge sexual misdemeanours, real or alleged. I say 'in the first instance' because the explanations for why these societies proclaim and to a certain extent carry out these acts of institutionalized jealousy are not just sexual or procreational. Men certainly expect to control sex and reproduction, but in so doing they are demonstrating their general power and at the same time are guarding themselves against breakdowns in family and group allegiance. While they keep women in they are keeping other men out.

In talking about a 'standard theory' I will often be using the past tense, not because these practices have vanished since the 1960s, but because in many places they have changed, and also because our view of them has changed. What makes them so significant and interesting to us is the fact that they often involve societies pressing for actions by husbands, fathers, brothers, cousins that may conflict with their personal desires. In our society we tend to think of jealousy as something that follows or is caused by love and attachment. When certain groups within societies expect or demand death, mutilation or banishment, this may well conflict with love and attachment and people may try to evade the pressures. However, the social influence is not always in the direction of inflaming jealousy. As we shall see towards the end of this chapter, violent resolution of a conflict over infidelity doesn't always suit either the wronged partner or their kin. It depends who the rival is. A demonstration of jealous violence may upset an alliance or involve a group in a serious backlash. So there may sometimes be spouses who have to keep their feelings under control, or if they are not inclined to do that, kin who, rather than inciting violence, try to contain it. It is therefore important to establish not simply what informants say are the social attitudes and practices, but also what actually emerges from this conflict in each particular village, camp, family group, etc.

This does not imply that the standard theory is wrong or the theories about its origins irrelevant; it is simply that since the classic writers of the 1960s mapped out the broad picture, more detailed accounts have begun to show that these societies, like our own, are complex and changeable. I shall therefore state in broad outline the classic account of honour and shame. I shall then discuss the deviations from the standard theory and finally the reasons that have been given for the existence of these societies around the Mediterranean.

We tend to think of honour as an individual quality, associated with honesty, incorruptibility and perhaps high achievement and good works. If we speak of an honourable woman as distinct from an honourable man, the emphasis shifts perhaps towards moral issues, but we do not need two separate definitions. We also use the term 'honour' for rich and poor alike, although honour and honours in the upper orders might stress achievement and public service, and honour amongst the poor might stress integrity in hard times.

The Mediterranean concepts of honour and shame differ on every count. First, they do not simply concern an individual in society. A loss of honour by one person may result in a whole section of a community losing its livelihood or falling under the shadow of virtual excommunication until it has rid itself of the offender. Abou-Zeid recounts how a substantial group of Bedouins in western Egypt had to completely uproot themselves from their traditional home as a result of an incident involving a single person.

Second, honour does not necessarily involve honesty and integrity. The Bedouins regarded honesty as a key issue but Campbell's Greek shepherds fostered cunning and deceit in competition with their neighbours. Meanness, ruthlessness and aggressive destruction of the reputation of others did not by any means lose a man his honour. What *did* affect honour, according to Campbell, was a reluctance to acknowledge a piece of deceit as the hostile, defiant action it was meant to be. Close kinsmen might safely depend on truth and co-operation, but economic competition with other groups generated slander, hostility and vengeance, all couched in the language of honour.

Third, within these societies honour and shame did not have the same significance for men and women. Male honour tended to be active and competitive. Should it be compromised, it could be reconstructed. Female honour and shame were, by contrast, passive and defensive and once lost could not be reclaimed. (This fragility of female reputation prevailed well beyond Mediterranean Europe; Mary Wollstonecraft described the fragility of a woman's moral reputation in eighteenth-century England.) Women were widely regarded not just as weak and vulnerable, but as active sources of potential dishonour. It was not necessary for a woman to take any particular action to have this effect. According to Campbell, the attitude in northern Greece was that 'even unconsciously she may lure a man to disaster without a glance or gesture'. Even if she tempts no one and does nothing, it is still possible for her honour to be damaged or destroyed if enough people say she has lost honour and shame. This was especially the case amongst the Sarakatsani, because of the continual battle to bring down a competitor's repute, either in private, where it might go undisputed, or in public, where it led to challenge and retribution.

Campbell's book contains a photograph of a group of women in northern Greece in the 1950s, their faces averted from the camera, dressed from head to wrists and ankles in black.

After she reaches the age of sixteen or seventeen a maiden must discipline her movements. No movement even in domestic labour must be hurried. She ought to walk with a slow and deliberate step. In the dance she must not lift her feet more than an inch or two from the ground. A girl who is seen running risks ridicule and a reputation for shamelessness. If, by evil chance, she were to fall backwards 'with her legs in the air' . . . she would virtually lose her honour.

She had to carry herself upright, eyes downwards and show no public emotion except grief. The theme was repeated in one form or another throughout the Mediterranean region. According to Bourdieu, the Algerian Arabs referred to their women as 'cows of Satan', to a son-in-law as 'the veil cast over shame', and 'shame is a young girl'.

To control women was a challenge to the honour of men. In other words, premarital relations, adultery or even rape were not simply failures on the part of women, but failures by men. Pitt-Rivers comments on the Andalusians:

the woman's adultery represents not only an infringement of his rights but the demonstration of his failure in his duty. He has betrayed the values of the family, bringing dishonour to all the social groups who are involved reciprocally in his honour: his family and his community.

Which Men are Responsible?

Note that the 'he' referred to in the above quotation was the *husband*. In Spain until the woman was married the possibility of dishonour threatened her father and brothers, who were expected to act jealously. At marriage responsibility shifted to the husband. If the wife was accused of infidelity it destroyed the honour of her family including her children, and her husband might earn the title '*cabrón*', or cuckold (literally, 'he-goat'). It is he who metaphorically bears the devil's horns, not the adulterer. The adulterer was not socially dis-

115

honoured. He was a criminal in the eyes of the law and a sinner in the eyes of the church, but the husband was the object of ridicule and disapproval, both because he allowed the infringement to occur, and (perhaps more fiercely) because he did nothing about it when it did.

Pitt-Rivers points out that this attitude is found throughout southern Europe, but in earlier times it was even more widespread. This is a passage from a criminology text quoted by Elwin:

There have even been times when, if a man has failed in such circumstances [finding his wife with a lover] to kill both his wife and her lover, this has been so strongly disapproved that he has been punished with loss of life. Such an instance is quoted by Galo Sanchez from the old fourteenth-century Castilian law. In a collection of judgments, one is described in which a knight was condemned to the gallows because, when he surprised his wife *in flagrante*, he was content with castrating the lover. He did not punish the wife at all. He ought to have killed both. This omission brought him to the gallows.

Segalen describes the communal criticism of the cuckolded husband in rural France in the nineteenth century: 'The cuckold, or his effigy, was paraded around the village, bringing everyone up to date with his sexual misadventures.' Even neighbours might become victims of social criticism:

It was thought, in effect, that the neighbour's responsibility was implicated in the scandal, since he had been witness to what had been going on during the year without intervening.

It is clear from Segalen's account that what attracted social disapproval was the failure of the husband to exercise control. Public mockery was directed at men whose wives dominated their households ('Hens who sing like cocks') as well as to the husbands of unfaithful women. The theme of a whole village subjecting cuckolds and henpecked husbands to exactly the same symbolic humiliation occurs in Quaife's book on seventeenth-century Somerset. Mounted backwards on a horse (in France it was a donkey) the 'culprit' was beaten with a giant ladle (skimmington) as a symbol of his wife's domination.

Jealous Husbands or Jealous Brothers and Cousins?

While in Mediterranean Europe the husband is expected to punish his wife and exact revenge on the intruder, the situation in North Africa is different. According to Abou-Zeid, amongst the Egyptian Bedouins the responsibility remains with the woman's family and especially with one of her parallel cousins – the father's brother's son.

The husband may divorce her and reclaim bride-wealth (the sum paid to her family at marriage) and in spite of the fact that her conduct is held to destroy the honour of their children, the husband's honour and that of his lineage is not directly compromised.

Why the difference? Schneider points to a broad difference between the European Mediterranean societies, where nuclear families involve the husband in responsibilities for sexual honour, and the patrilineal societies of North Africa and the Near East where brothers and cousins keep their responsibilities as guardians first of virginity and then of marital fidelity. This difference in the whole kinship situation is augmented by more personal matters. A brother in a country like Turkey may attack his sister and/or her illicit lover, not simply because he is expected to do so, but because of the special social and emotional relationship each has to the other. Older brothers, in particular, may exercise strong authority over younger brothers and over sisters, and at the same time brothers depend on their sisters for an entrée into the networks of females – the sister knows about other girls and the brother knows about other boys. This sibling relationship is often the only channel through which information can flow in gender-segregated societies. So brother and sister are often emotionally close and socially dependent. At the same time they are involved in a relationship of authority that is particularly intense because the young man is 'on the make' as a patriarch.

In cases where the revenge for a sexual intrusion can be expected to start a cycle of retribution, it may be a matter of considerable judgement who should take the punitive action. The vengeance may resemble less an act of jealous passion (which it often is with brothers) than a calculated move in a political system. The person chosen to act may well be a young man without family ties of his own, so that an escalation of violence does not leave a widow or orphans. In the southern Italian town where Davis worked, homicides associated with sexual honour were rare; they were preceded by attempts to arrange marriages or cash settlements, and were the result of considerable consultation and premeditation. There is an implication that motives other than 'moral outrage' may be involved when a homicide is finally decided on. It is not hard to believe that a background of prior malice or political conflict may tip the scales in favour of a lethal resolution of an affair of sexual honour.

Bourdieu points out that in Algiers there was a special place for the 'scoundrel' in a family; on the one hand he could meet insults of inferior persons without losing the family its honour, and on the other could be disowned by the family if the matter were settled amicably after all.

Emotional Relations between Wives, Husbands and Brothers

We have seen that there are two patterns: husbands take over responsibilities for guarding sexual honour in Spain and other European countries while in North Africa and parts of the Middle East it is brothers and cousins who keep their responsibilities as guardians of virginity and marital fidelity. Is this just a mechanical difference or does it affect the quality of emotional relations between a woman and her brother as compared to those between a woman and her husband?

Meeker explores this issue by comparing Turks and Arabs. In this matter the Turks act as Europeans do, and can be contrasted with the Arabs to the south, who follow the general Middle-Eastern pattern: the patrilineal family retains responsibility even after marriage. Meeker begins by saying that in both societies, Turkish and Arabic, the relation between a sister and a brother is said to be one of 'love' and that between a wife and husband one of 'control'. He quotes a classic account of Palestinian Arabs written in 1931 by Granquist, who refers to

. . . an extraordinary romanticization of the brother–sister tie. The women say: a husband may always be had; a son can also be born; but a beloved brother, from where shall he come back when he is once dead . . . The love between sister and brother finds expression in many ways and is most beautiful and attractive. According to the conception of the *fellahin* it is more beautiful than the love between wife and husband, because [it is] not founded *on passion*!

Although such love between brother and sister is said to prevail amongst both Turks and Arabs, there is a difference in how it develops. Even before puberty young Turkish girls begin to look outwards from their own families to the new relationship with a romantic husband into whose control they will pass. When this happens, says Meeker, the love between the girl and her brother declines at the expense of her love for the husband and then for the children. The transfer of the Turkish girl's attachments from her own family to her new husband affects the quality as well as the intensity of her love for her brother. As the husband takes over the responsibility for her sexual honour, this issue ceases to contaminate her affection for her brother. Prior to marriage the sister–brother relationship is intense and ambivalent; it needs to be continually expressed and affirmed, according to Meeker. But after marriage it becomes purer and less conditional, and at the same time weaker. The change in power and in emotional quality is accompanied by a decline in jealous behaviour by the brother. The Arab girl keeps her family name and is kept within the scope of family honour. She is likely to be betrothed very early, and right from birth is generally regarded as less of an asset to her family. The payment of bride-price by the Turks reverses this, and in Turkey marriages take place later and are arranged more quickly. If the Turkish marriage should fail, the situation is difficult, since the wife cannot be sent back to her family. Meeker observes,

Sending a woman back only serves to insult the woman's natal kin by 'improperly' forcing upon them a fallen woman. In the Arab case, the disgrace of the woman is already in the laps of her natal kin.

There is even a difference between the two societies in their attitude to abduction. Amongst the Arabs it is regarded as an extremely serious and abhorrent act: 'only an enemy abducts a woman'. But amongst the Turks, Meeker says, 'abduction is not rare, and it is a matter of high, fascinating adventure'.

As we follow through the patterns in these two types of society and see affection, control and retribution resting now with a husband, now with a wife's brother or cousin, it is obvious how jealousy is tied to social meaning and social structure. Although the jealousy is more heavily institutionalized, with family conferences and political considerations often very prominent, the feelings and reactions are no less passionate and direct. Indeed the social expectations are the very things that allow the emotions to build up and to be expressed so publicly and sometimes so violently. It would be an error to think of jealousy by partners as emotional and that of relatives and interested parties as merely acted out. Although Mediterranean societies have a reputation for jealousy, tyranny and oppression of women, it would be absurd to think of love and sympathy as somehow freakish or intrusive. What Meeker underlines is that love and authority are both fundamental forces in Mediterranean family life. Within English or American society jealousy typically arises from a personal reaction to a breach in exclusivity, but of course the public knowledge of the breach can aggravate the reaction. In Mediterranean societies what is defined as a breach is different, the range and identity of those who monitor exclusivity is different, and the significance of public repute is much more patent.

I shall now turn aside from the standard account of these 'societies of honour and shame' to briefly consider some of the evasions and compromises that occur in practice. They can arise from problems of power, particularly class power, but also because of collisions between honour on the one hand and sympathy and love on the other.

Because a particular breach of sexual honour may not necessarily be followed by the sanctions prescribed by opinion or religious law, this does not mean that the sanctions are ineffective. I have mentioned earlier the idea of regulation, how there is a balance between provocation and reaction. In 1968 Antoun wrote about an Arab village of 2,000 people in the Jordan valley. According to a footnote, he was told of only three incidents involving illicit sexual relations occurring over a period of fifty years. Presumably this means that only three cases 'went public' to the extent of involving the community in resolving the issue of sexual honour. We shall see that in one of these cases, where the outcome involved a killing, there were strenuous efforts to resolve it in other ways.

The regulation of sexual behaviour is usually set at a point far removed from explicit sex. The limiting case is given by the boast of a Bedouin man: 'My wife has never left the house except to be carried to her grave.' A young man said to Antoun, 'If she as much as turned her head . . . to glance at others, if she did not cover her head properly in a head wrap, or if a man greeted her by saying, "Good morning, how are you?" we would take good care of her and him too.'

Major misdemeanours like pre-marital affairs or adultery can be dealt with privately or publicly. A case may simply be denied or negotiated privately, but if it has entered the public arena, and the fault is acknowledged, the issue is then whether there should be a formal settlement or punishment.

The following example of a private resolution comes from Gilsenan:

if certain acts are performed, certain others should follow, and the line between honor and dishonor is absolute and clear, a kind of all or nothing proposition. But people actually live by secrecy and *kizb* [deceit, sometimes lying, sometimes fooling] in complex situations, by tacit collaboration and flexibility, and by blurred definitions.

Gilsenan relates the story of a man who returned to Lebanon from a spell abroad and learnt informally that his wife had had an affair with a family member. The man was 'highly regarded and a very forceful, assertive personality of almost the classic type . . . To acknowledge infidelity would be desecration of his total social self unless he killed the wife and challenged the alleged offender. The latter is a member of a large family of brothers.' The resolution of this dilemma, which could only turn out badly if confronted head-on, was an elaborate charade in which the family co-operated. The husband ostentatiously met with and cultivated the seducer. When a drunken relative made reference to the situation on a public occasion, he was treated to hostile silence and disapproval. We could call this hypocrisy, although common sense seems a better term where the system of honour and shame is over-developed and threatens reasonable existence. Whether or not the man felt jealous of his wife is obscured by the conflicting demands of sexual honour and the tactical moves that brought him into close and ostensibly cordial relations with his wife's lover.

The second example, for Antoun, ended tragically. There was at first an opportunity for the families to deal with the matter privately, although that would not have been easy because the police were involved. They had arrested three young men with an unmarried girl in a taxi on their way to a tourist resort in Jordan. The three men gave the police a full account of what they said was a repetition of an earlier exploit of the same kind, involving drinking and serial sexual relations with the girl. The confession was passed on to the girl's father, into whose custody the girl had been given, and to her influential uncle. Although by now the case was in a sense 'public', it could have been negotiated privately if compensation had been paid and if one of the men had been prepared to marry the girl. But time passed and the story spread about. When the marriage possibility fell through, the young men's relatives soon began to feel the necessity to protect themselves against public attack. In response the girl's uncle mobilized his considerable influence, and the possibilities of a negotiated outcome were gone.

The denouement occurred outside the house of the young men's guardians on a major Islamic feast day. The girl's father took his daughter there and stabbed her to death. The village men then set off to close the shops of the young men's kin and would have burned down their houses except for the intervention of the police. They then all returned and publicly acclaimed the girl's father. In one sense what is extraordinary about the story was not so much the killing and its aftermath, but the preliminary efforts to resolve the issue by cover-up and marriage, since the original offence to honour in that community was so great that, according to Antoun, the only way people could explain the girl's behaviour was to say that she was mad. Another significant facet of the case was that the girl was engaged to another man, 'who in that very week had completed the marriage payment and begun preparations for the wedding'. *His* role in the affair was not mentioned except in so far as his existence affected the girl's alternative marriage prospects.

In emphasizing the early efforts to avoid an ultimate showdown, I do not wish to lose sight of the actual ending of the tale. In reading it I found myself becoming almost mesmerized by the struggle between the demands of honour and attempts at accommodation, and I had to remind myself that in the end a terrified and humiliated girl was taken out and assassinated by her father in public, the young men who had told the tale of their sexual exploits to the world had the protection of the police, and the men of the girl's family were acclaimed as moral heroes, which in that society they were.

Class Differences

As well as honour and shame applying differently to men and women, they also differ according to the affluence of the people claiming honour, and in this context honour may become confused with prestige. In village and rural communities in Europe the greatest vigilance over sexual honour occurs in the middle stratum of society. This has been attributed to the competitive situation of the middle classes, combined with their resistance to the intrusion of church and state into community affairs. Before discussing the paradoxes of honour among the upper classes, let me say something about the poorer groups. The situation is encapsulated in a remark made about a Greek shepherd reported by Campbell and quoted in several sources: '. . . you could copulate with this man's daughter and he would stand by and hold your coat.' The remark is particularly offensive for two reasons: first, according to Campbell, it was untrue (or at least untested), and second, it was made by a fellow countryman who was looking on while the man's small son was pelted with dung, a humiliation that no one did anything to stop because the bully was the son of an influential man upon whom they were all economically dependent.

The general conclusion is that the very poor, or at least those of the lowest status, cannot afford honour, and can be subject to sexual and other abuse and humiliation without recourse, and significantly, without protest from 'honourable' bystanders, who furthermore insult them. Cutileiro reports a similar situation in a town in southern

Portugal where 95 per cent of the men could not properly provide for their families. Quite a range of powerful people in the town – large landowners, estate managers, professionals, wealthy shopkeepers – sexually exploited their female employees or the wives of their male employees, and many of these affairs began before the women were married.

Cutileiro makes a distinction between daughters of a tinker's family who became prostitutes, and women who maintained a moral standard that admitted certain extramarital relations according to the needs of their families. A woman was accused by her rich (and jealous) patron of having another lover beside himself and indignantly denied it: 'What do you think I am? Only my husband and you lay their trousers on me.'

Prior to 1960 large landowners not only exploited the women, but also controlled the private lives of their employees. For example a labourer was instructed by his employer not to take back his unfaithful wife (who had absconded for two weeks with a travelling salesman) because of the poor moral precedent it set! Unfortunately what is lacking in these cases is documentation of what the labourers thought of their wives' and daughters' participation in these 'contracts', but I do not believe that 'holding his coat' would have been a very common attitude.

Davis reported a similar though less extreme situation in a village in southern Italy.

A common pattern . . . is for the seducer to be the employer of the whole family; in the country entire families of womenfolk have been seduced in this way. The men already dishonoured by taking their women to the country cannot insist on their honour to exact a more grievous penalty.

The community's attitude to the woman's conduct was simply, 'She does it to feed her family.' Davis neatly sums up the preferred strategy of the seducer: 'When equals are involved in cases of seduction, homicide does follow: and a prudent amorist pursues the women of his social inferiors.'

Pitt-Rivers discusses the situation among the Spanish upper classes and tries to resolve the paradox of why in many European countries those with most honour seemed most careless of it. It appears that their honour did not have to be struggled for; because it came automatically with rank, title and birthright, it was therefore not precarious. Sexual obedience and proper conduct by women became matters of conscience and religious duty, but transgressions did not dishonour as they did in the middle ranks of society.

The European élites also shared in an international culture that emphasized civility and sophistication. As Elias shows, they set themselves up in opposition to the supposed crudity and violence of the (rural) lower orders. Pitt-Rivers attaches considerable importance to the economic contribution that upper-class women could make to a family's social and financial standing. In Spain titles could pass through the female line in the absence of direct male heirs, and this significantly weakened the patriarchal bias. He also points out that women married young and on average survived their older husbands, giving rise to a group of responsible, affluent and active women in the prime of life, who could hardly be compared to the economically helpless rural women dominated by shame. According to Pitt-Rivers, the most fiercely jealous behaviour in Spain was to be found in the well-to-do middle classes, where a woman had the fewest responsibilities.

She enjoys relatively less liberty of action, since she has servants who perform the tasks that take the plebeian houseife out to the fountain or the market. She is seen in public much less, spends her day in her house, or in visiting her or her husband's female relatives, or in church . . . The middle-class woman is noticeably more restrained than the plebeian, her husband more authoritative and more jealous.

This link between usefulness and liberty is echoed in villages and farming communities in central Italy. In both places women commonly join their husband's extended family, that is a family with a spread of relatives living together, but according to Silverman the demand for the labour of women and their children leads to significant differences. In the countryside there is a call for a large pool of labour, including female labour, and a new bride and young children have ready-made tasks to do. In the village or town, by contrast, the woman has to train herself in some way, and a dowry has to be provided. When she is married large numbers of children are hardly an asset. The town engagement is typically longer and the girl is older when it begins. Pregnancy at marriage, although common, is not as happily accommodated as it is in country families, where, according to Silverman, there may occasionally be trial marriages. Not only are girls in the town exposed to a more provocative social situation during the long courtship and engagement period, but there is also more gossip and scandal (including unpleasant anonymous letters), difficult break-ups and, at the same time, much more emphasis on public reputation. In other words the whole economic setting deeply affects personal tension and jealousy.

The theme of much of this chapter has been that aspects of personal relations in families affecting jealousy can be traced back to the material circumstances of the lives of men and women. I don't want to exaggerate the simplicity of this approach. After all, as we have seen, work brings economic independence and a relative release from sexual monitoring in some societies in Europe, while in Africa it can lead to one of the fiercest sexual assaults – infibulation.

The materialist view – that the emotional relations between people are determined to a degree by the organization of their productive activities – has led to some absurd oversimplifications, which are summed up by the quip that romantic love emerged with the invention of the steam engine, and jealousy began when capitalism taught people to conserve their property. However, the problem remains of why societies of honour and shame, with their patterns of institutionalized jealousy, have survived into modern times around the shores of the Mediterranean. It is unreasonable to suppose that modern economic conditions gave rise to them directly, since they were present and indeed much more widespread in previous centuries. Yet there is some reason to believe that certain general economic and political forces have supported their survival in particular communications and within certain classes.

The classical treatment of this subject is that of Schneider and Schneider, who describe the situation in Sicily, which I will briefly review. It is difficult to find any region of the Mediterranean that has not been successively occupied by one predatory imperial power or another, but Sicily seems to have had more than its share. The Roman orator Cicero made some of his legal (and literary) reputation from his description of how Roman governors plundered and exploited the island. Much of the Sicilians' hostility to state power has arisen from the fact that it usually meant foreign exploitation of its agricultural resources. In Corsica, according to Chiva, foreign intrusion was military rather than economic but it had the same effect – local communities, resentful of the external power, did their best to keep control of social practices and gave family solidarity and strength a high priority.

The second relevant factor, poverty, arose partly from exploitation by foreign large landowners and partly from too many people trying to survive on land that was once forest, but which is now relatively arid and overused. The result is that people below the level of the prosperous élites and their henchmen built alliances and emphasized family lineages, which were as fiercely loyal to their own members as they were hostile to their competitors. It is between these groups that competition over honour, jealousy over reputation, violence, and vengeance prevailed.

The Sarakatsani, the Greek shepherds that Campbell describes, provide a dramatic example of this. Under conditions of great economic insecurity they waged incessant petty warfare against competing lineages, the reputations of whose women they continually sought to destroy. Meeker describes the same pressure on the Bedouins – nomads always in danger of losing their herds to their neighbours, preoccupied with group loyalty, military prowess, manliness and honour, and fanatically jealous of their women.

Sexual jealousy here is no doubt the product of a combination of forces : personal feelings, concern about paternity, and allegiance. Denich, talking about the Montenegrans of southern Yugoslavia, describes the murder and facial mutilation of unfaithful women by husbands and lovers and the leniency of the courts:

Although there is an undoubtedly psychological component – 'jealousy' – to this repressive control over women's sexuality, it plays a small part in explaining such severe sanctions. The explanation must be sought in structural terms: why should women's sexuality be such an extreme focus for the exertion of the male control? Why should the reactions against women's sexual freedom be so severe? There are two components to the control of women's sexuality – one practical, the other symbolic. On the practical side the tenuous bond between a woman and her husband's household would be further undermined by liaisons with other men. However, the more significant dimension of the severity of measures for sexual control over women stems from the symbolic importance of sex in the competitive social environment . . . The ability of a household's men to control its women is one of the many indicators of its strength . . .

JEALOUSY OR SOCIAL THEORY?

The task of finding explanations for particular cultural practices of the sort I have been describing is formidable. Obviously we can't merely say, as psychologists once did, people *learn* to behave that way; since people learn to behave in a great variety of ways, that explanation takes us nowhere. In trying to get to grips with the shape of societies, of families, of belief systems, we are torn in two opposing directions: towards the general and towards the particular. When we encounter practices of a similar sort throughout the villages and countryside across a whole region, we are driven towards 'big' theor-

126

ies. The theory of honour and shame deriving from the competition between families and lineages living pastoral and particularly nomadic lives is one attempt at such a broad explanation. But immediately we are drawn into qualifications and doubts. We must separate European from North African societies, nuclear families from patrilineal, lineages from alliances, nomads from other pastoralists, one system of belief from another. This is the situation in a Turkish village, this amongst the Bedouins, this in towns in Portugal or in Sicily, and so on. Before we know it we are submerged in a mass of local detail and local explanation. We have then to ask, 'Is it a coincidence, after all, that in so many of these separate and apparently different societies across the region this pattern of gender segregation and jealousy prevails?'

It is tempting at this point to say, 'I just came here with an interest in jealousy, not to tackle these massive problems of social theory and anthropology.' I agree that there are many interesting things to say about jealousy even if the basic problems of social causes are not solved, but the social causes are far from irrelevant. To use a metaphor: the study of the emotions is a small dinghy being towed behind a large vessel, which is the study of society. The little boat can hardly be expected to direct or drive the big one, but neither can we cut the rope. What I have been trying to do is to stand up in the dinghy to peer at the ship to get an idea where we might be heading and why.

A study of the social causes of jealousy also has practical, political and historical significance. If institutionalized jealousy is weakening in certain of the Mediterranean societies we have been examining, this is the result of the operation of major social forces: the penetration of the laws of the state, urbanization, immigration and emigration, changing patterns of participation in the work force, tourism, youth culture and the women's movement. I do not believe that these forces will ever transform societies and individuals within societies so that there will be no more jealousy. Rather they may reduce the volume of male 'preventive' jealousy and shrink the numbers of people who are recruited into the guardianship of honour and the cultivation of shame.

CHAPTER 7

Freud and Jealousy

———————— Q ————————

It is common knowledge that at the heart of Freudian theory is a bitter jealous conflict: the Oedipus complex (or, as we shall see, the Oedipus complexes), the sexual triangle of mother, father and the young child in the early stages of sexual awakening. One might suppose that this drama, involving rivalry, hatred, ambivalence and guilt, might stir up interest in the subject of sexual jealousy, but in my experience Freud's views seem actually to inhibit empirical curiosity about the topic. 'That's all Freud, I suppose', is a typical comment. Sometimes it implies that Freud settled the question of jealousy by tracing it directly to that early rivalrous infantile confrontation, but often it conveys another message: 'Don't let's start on that!'

At the risk of boring the psychoanalytic *aficionados* and affronting the disbelievers, I am going to outline what Freudian 'standard theory' says about normal jealousy and the Oedipus complexes, before progressing to less familiar territory, Freud's ideas about abnormal jealousy. This will take us through some exotic themes: narcissism, hate, moral guilt, fear of rejection, fear of love, fear of incest and fear, above all, of homosexuality.

Almost everything about Freudian theory is controversial. It is sometimes more like a field of battle than a field of study, so I think it would be wise from the outset if I were to come clean about my attitudes. Are you in the hands of a believer or a debunker? A 'cautious sceptic' is the way I'd like to describe my attitude to Freud, although on several issues I move from scepticism to frank disbelief.

One basis for my reservations is that Freud believed in very strong laws of mental life and I don't. When in everyday life we hear a personal biography, it often seems a rather idiosyncratic thing; events and decisions, although determined in one sense, could well have taken off in different directions at a hundred points. But Freud adhered to the position that once you had traced a sequence of events in a patient or a small group of patients, or thought you had, you possessed a template that could confidently be applied to other members of the class. He was over-inclined to see the universal in the particular. He believed we are not bowling a ball across a randomly irregular surface, we are letting it enter a maze of channels, made deeper or shallower perhaps by personal history but having a very regular configuration. If you were to read, for example, Otto Fenichel's paper written in 1931 on the forms of neurosis and the history that is supposed to lie behind them, there seems at first to be no end to the variety of early experiences that caused psychological problems. Yet ultimately they are always organized around childhood sexual attachment and early sexual experience in the family triangle. Furthermore these fundamental mental structures will be created from within if the external conditions of life do not provide them. Take this remark by Ernest Jones about the Oedipus complex:

Every little boy finds himself in the same situation, for he has had two parents of opposite sexes and he cannot escape an attitude of jealousy for the exclusive possession of his mother's love. *This is just as true whether the father is still present or already dead* . . . An emotional attitude towards the father is then developed which contains all the elements present later in the adult situation.

At first I interpreted this to mean that the jealousy will persist in maturity even though the father is no longer alive. In fact it means that the Oedipus complex will shape adult reactions even if there was no father to be jealous of in the first place; indeed there will be an Oedipus complex in children even if they are not brought up in a family at all. According to Fenichel, if individuals spend their childhood

constantly moving from place to place and being exposed every year to fresh influences and brought into contact with new people . . . their Oedipus complex is fantasy.

Many people with whom I have discussed sexual jealousy have suggested that the best way to escape it is just this sort of free life in childhood, never forming possessive, exclusive or dependent relationships. But traditional Freudian theorists would certainly have disagreed, because they believed that the Oedipus complex upon which jealousy rests will assert itself no matter how much variety the child experiences, and no matter how little opportunity the child has to love just one person. They believed that the mental apparatus was constructed to create parents even where none existed. Furthermore, according to Fenichel, a free life in childhood would later produce much worse problems of adjustment than life in the nuclear family.

It will yield adults who are narcissistic, contradictory and asocial. Is this true?

A carefully orchestrated upbringing of the sort that Fenichel condemns did in fact occur in the Oneida community to which I referred in Chapter 3. At Oneida nearly sixty children lived in a special house separated from their parents and cared for by three men and fifteen women. They ate together and slept either with other children or in rooms with one or other of the adult child-minders. According to Carden, the explicit aim throughout was to 'discourage the growth of special attachments'. Carden seems to have no doubt that the children turned out extremely well; the only issue he thinks worth pursuing is whether their success was due to the deliberate selection of their biological mothers and fathers (they were the product of a eugenics programme) or to the way they were reared. We have no data on their jealousy as adults, but there is no evidence whatever of the sorts of mental abnormality that Fenichel predicted.

In any case, I am not reporting these opinions because I believe them or want you to believe them, but simply to emphasize this point: according to Freudian theory we create ourselves and our symptoms in conscious and unconscious thought, yet these creative thought processes are not infinitely flexible. They are dominated by structures in the brain that can only be assumed to be inborn. So when we come to describe Freud's view on delusional jealousy, we should not conclude that by coincidence everyone has accidentally hit on the same strategy that takes them, for instance, from repressed homosexuality to paranoid jealous delusions. Rather they are said to be in the grip of mechanisms so imperious that, given a certain starting point, the steps in the process will drive them almost inevitably along that path.

Freud was, in my view, an intellectual long-odds gambler. He desired and he achieved a great scientific reputation. He knew that what creates such a reputation is the uncovering of laws that are both powerful and surprising – probing into some familiar jumble of material and extracting a startling new order. Freud's tactic of generalizing from one or two cases to the whole class of cases provided the power. A certain startling paradoxical logic in his interpretations provided the surprise. Anyone who reads Freud's books and papers will recognize a pattern of analysis repeating itself over and over; let us call it the logic of contraries. We all know the formula. This person is a pacifist? She is really unbearably aggressive. This person is a great Don Juan? He hates women and fears impotence. It is a formula that has galvanized generations of readers as no other

130

psychological theory ever could, and it has become part of our polemical weaponry: these people hate pornography? It really fascinates them. These people want homosexuals prosecuted? They are themselves closet homosexuals. This is an efficient career-woman? She is really a frustrated mother.

One interpretation is that Freud made one mighty discovery about the 'channels of the mind': when currents strike an obstacle, they turn back on themselves. The less sympathetic view is that this was not a discovery but an invention – a riveting and ingenious invention, but an invention. Perhaps this is *not* a special feature of how the human mind works in sickness and in health, but rather how Freud's mind worked when he set out to establish a reputation for himself as the great detective of the psyche.

Some critics have said that Freud's theories cannot be tested, that they are not about specific, concrete facts. I disagree. I think his theories can be evaluated in two ways: first, are his broad allegations about jealousy supported by carefully collected case material? second, is there within the case material sufficient convincing circumstantial evidence to make his extended lines of argument believable? We shall be looking at both these questions.

WHAT FREUD SAID ABOUT JEALOUSY

Freud classified jealousy into three types: normal, neurotic and pathological. Freud referred to them as *layers*. Layer 1, normal jealousy, is present in everyone. If it is not manifest, then it is repressed. In certain people layer 2 is also present. This is neurotic or oversensitive jealousy, that is, excessively strong jealousy, or jealousy without good reason. It is supposed to be based on guilt and projection. Layer 3 is frankly delusional, pathological jealousy, which may be added to the other two.

Freud illustrated the layering of one type of jealousy on another with a case history. I will first outline it in a factual way, without interpretation, then add Freud's analysis:
(a) A young man reports a homosexual trauma (not specified) in his youth.
(b) He was very attached to his mother and jealous about her.
(c) He evidently helped his mother financially in some way when he chose his wife.
(d) He was more than normally suspicious and jealous about his wife's prior sexual experience when he married her.
(e) None the less his early marriage was free of further jealousy.

131

(f) He then had a prolonged sexual affair with another woman.
(g) When he broke it off, he began to be irrationally jealous about his wife's behaviour.
(h) Finally this irrational jealousy became frankly delusional and bizarre when he believed that his 'rival' was his wife's father.

How is this interpreted? According to Freud the homosexual experience (a) at the beginning of the sequence will form the background to the delusional jealousy (h) at the end, so we will set it aside for the moment. In the next four steps, the young man's strong attachment and jealousy about his mother is shifted to his wife, at least when he first transfers his feelings to her. This is layer 1, normal jealousy, based on the Oedipus complex, although exaggerated in this case by a desire that his wife be like the virgin mother he would have liked to have possessed (presumably without his father).

The patient then has an affair, which produces guilt. To suppress this sense of guilt, his unconscious fills his head with beliefs about his *wife's* supposed infidelity, protecting him from musings about his own. This is layer 2, projective jealousy. Note, as I said before, that this is not the patient's own unique conscious invention. According to the theory, unfaithful people are *bound* to have guilt and are strongly disposed to handle it by projection on to their partners. Indeed, so inevitable is it that any irrational jealousy short of delusional jealousy is labelled 'projected'. It is no great impediment to the theory if the person has no affair, because it is quite likely that they will have *thought* about having an affair. And what if one has an affair or thinks about infidelity but feels no guilt? Then the guilt is repressed and operates unconsciously. In fact, the more repressed and inaccessible it is, the more likely it is to be projected as extreme jealousy. (It is hardly necessary to say that it is over this sort of manoeuvre that the believers and the sceptics part company.)

Finally in the severely delusional state, layer 3, the young man believes that his father-in-law is his sexual rival. This is explained by reference to three tenets: first, that everyone is bisexual, so the young man is both heterosexual (loving his mother) and homosexual (loving his father). Second, his homosexuality is repressed by the trauma mentioned at the beginning of the short biography and this repressed homosexuality re-expresses itself as attraction to his father-in-law. Finally this unacceptable love is converted by one of those psychoanalytic 'U-turns' into a belief that his wife rather than himself loves her father, and that his father-in-law is not his love object but his hated rival.

The theory stated baldly (but I think faithfully) is not strong on immediate plausibility. There are two aspects of it on which I would like to expand, however. First, what exactly is the significance of the Oedipus complex supposed to be? If we did not experience the Oedipus complex, would we feel no adult jealousy? As I said earlier, this is an unanswerable question because even if we were to deprive children of parents or deny them knowledge of sexual relations, classical Freudian theory says they would create the Oedipal triangle in fantasy. But surely adult jealousy can't be said to be *caused* by the complex. After all if the child inevitably treats the parent as a rival, and feels grief and hostility at the rival's success, then whatever jealous mechanism was being mobilized there would still be available in later life. Presumably we don't need to practise on our parents to feel jealous later. What we are supposed to get from the Oedipal experience is not jealousy itself but the *intensity* and *form* of our jealousy.

Fenichel puts it very plainly in a paper written in 1931. All children have an Oedipus complex at between four and six years, 'which seems to vanish'. In fact it has simply become unconscious and later, in adulthood, it can be more or less easily reawakened. This reawakening will be easiest and jealousy most intense in people who did not resolve it well in childhood, but it may be resurrected even in normal people under particular emotional stress.

The second point is the particular emphasis that the complex is supposed to be given by surrounding events. As I hinted earlier, there are supposed to be *two* complexes because boys and girls are both said to be constitutionally bisexual. They desire both mother and father and in each case the opposite parent becomes the rival. In the boy's heterosexual triangle he desires his mother and feels grief at his loss of her to his father. Towards his father he feels guilt, fears retribution and develops hatred. Finally he suffers a loss of self-esteem (known as the 'narcissistic wound'). The scenario is duplicated in the case of his (homosexual) love for his father, but here it is his *mother* who is the rival. And of course for the girl one simply changes about all the roles to produce two corresponding patterns.

From this it can be seen that all the key aspects of adult jealousy – desire, grief at loss, wounded pride, hatred, fear and guilt – are first experienced, according to the theory, at this early age. In my view we should not be too blinded by the neatness of the fit, since it isn't too far-fetched to believe that in developing the theory Freud in fact began with adult jealousy and reflected it back into his account of the childhood drama. The only ingredients that are unique to childhood

133

are the guilt and fear that arise because the rival happens to be a powerful figure who is loved and whose claims are legitimate while the child's are not. From this guilt and fear comes anger.

PREDICTING THE DIRECTION OF HOSTILITY

Given that all this is supposed to happen to all children, what predictive power does it have? The theory says that particular irregularities, traumas or fantasies may determine the *shape* of later jealousy. For example, one of the hitherto unresolved mysteries of adult jealousy is why it is that some people show hostility to their partners, while others are preoccupied with hatred of the intruder. The Freudian explanation is that anger towards the partner is less mature than anger towards the rival. If a boy emerges prematurely from the Oedipus complex still fearful of his father and still trying to placate him, he will turn against the woman. If he fears his father less, he will express his anger against the male rival. So in order to understand adult jealousy, we do not necessarily have to involve ourselves with the form of the adult relationship or the circumstances of the infidelity, we do not concern ourselves primarily with issues of power in society that might affect where we direct our hostility; we are advised instead to go back to events in the first five or six years of life.

What evidence is there for this explanation of the direction of hostility and resentment? I have been through the twenty-three volumes of Freud's collected works, reading every index entry under 'jealousy', and I found no single case report to support this view about the direction of jealous hostility, much less a systematic set of cases. So it seems to have been a theoretical prediction rather than a factual observation.

Note, however, that in the vast majority of both normal and pathological cases of jealousy documented in the general literature it is in fact the *partner* who is the prime object of anger, abuse and violence. What should we conclude from this – that only a negligible number of people make it through to a mature resolution of their Oedipal problem? Alternatively we could conclude, as I am inclined to do, that the issue has little if anything to do with the childhood Oedipal situation, but rather arises in some way from accessibility, adult power and sexual politics.

I have briefly described 'projective jealousy', the idea that abnormal (but not delusional) jealousy arises from projecting on to the partner guilt about one's own actions or wishes, conscious or unconscious. I do not have any basis for refuting the idea and just as little reason for believing it. We could test it empirically if the theory required that there must be first, actual infidelity, and second, patent evidence of guilt. But since, as I said, the infidelity and the guilt could be completely imaginary and completely repressed, the theory is safe from refutation in any place other than on the psychoanalytic couch. And I can't say I would expect it to be refuted there.

Freud's view on layer 3, delusional jealousy, is part of his general theory of paranoia, which includes not only morbid jealousy but delusions of persecution, megalomania and erotomania. There was one background condition that Freud felt was essential to all these conditions, namely latent homosexuality.

The theory is expounded in Freud's analysis of the Schreber case, or rather his analysis of the Schreber *Memoirs*. Schreber was a German who suffered the most diverse and severe mental symptoms, as we shall see. Ironically, morbid jealousy was one of the few pathologies that Dr Schreber did *not* display, but this does not mean that it is irrelevant, because our concern is with Freud's argument and he regarded the various disorders as variants on the same pathological process.

Schreber came from Dresden. Born into an eminent family, the son of a highly eccentric father, he was appointed to the highest ranks of the judiciary and was an unsuccessful candidate for the Reichstag. He had two breakdowns that he described in his *Memoirs* and a third towards the end of his life. He kept notes whenever he could during his illness. He published his memoirs when he was fifty-nine. They stand as a unique and extraordinarily honest account of the state of his mind. By legal argument he eventually succeeded in having himself released from an asylum, and although he maintained his elaborate delusional system throughout the remainder of his life, he was in other respects a sensitive, sophisticated and rational man. I shall not go into detail about his illness. His *Memoirs* fill 360 pages, to which 155 pages of court testimony were added. While in the asylum periods of mute withdrawal alternated with times when he was violent, noisy and suicidal. He suffered delusions and hallucinations and much of his bellowing and noisy behaviour was produced to drown out the voices in his head.

During his first hospitalization relations with the doctor (Flechsig, a famous neuroanatomist turned psychiatrist) were good, but Schreber subsequently claimed that Flechsig was converting him into a woman, so that he could be made a prostitute for the doctor and/or hospital staff. At the next and final stage of his disorder he did not treat the conversion as an evil plot but saw it rather as a benign supernatural process. He was being changed by God into a woman and would in time give birth to a new population of human beings. These beliefs were tied up with delusions about influences on his nerves by God, physical disintegration and feminizing changes to his body.

Freud picked up one recurrent theme, Schreber's comments about 'voluptuous female feelings', and tied these to the delusions that the psychiatrist was trying to make him a prostitute. Freud concluded that Schreber had unacceptable homosexual desires and defended himself against them by projecting them on to the doctor: 'I don't love him; he loves me'. The agency was then moved from the doctor to God and the intentions from evil to good. The doctor and God were in Freud's view representations of Schreber's father, and Freud suggested that it was his original homosexual feelings for his father and brother that began the whole delusional process.

The translators of Schreber's *Memoirs*, Macalpine and Hunter, point out that in cases like Schreber's there are actually two separate problems. The first is the issue of what meaning Schreber's delusions had. The second is why he had delusions in the first place. It was Freud's belief that you looked for the solution of one of these problems in the other. You have the delusions just because of the meaning they have. Once you have interpreted the content you understand where the delusional state came from. So let us review Freud's proposals about the various delusional systems, including delusions of infidelity.

A Language Game for Delusions

In his paper of 1911 Freud set out his ideas about paranoid delusions in the form of a language game. It invariably began with the assertion of a homosexual desire. For a man the proposition was I LOVE HIM, and for a woman, I LOVE HER. These desires are unacceptable, since according to Freud the HIM is the father and the HER is the mother, and both are forbidden. Therefore the propositions have to be negated in one way or another, and the way they are blocked or negated determines the type of paranoid delusion one acquires.

There are three outcomes, associated with changing the action (LOVE), the agent (I) or the object (HIM or HER).

Taking the male case, if we solve the problem by changing the action, we first try going from LOVE to HATE, but since that is still threatening, we reverse its direction:

I *love* him
I *don't* love him   (negation)
I *hate* him   (reaction formation)
No, *he* hates *me*   (projection)

This yields persecutory ideas, the classic form of paranoia. If, instead, we change the subject, the agent, we must find someone else to do the loving, so we project it unchanged on to our heterosexual partner. Hence morbid jealousy is supposed to follow this logic:

I love him
I don't love him   (negation)
She loves him   (projection)

Finally if we change the object (HIM), we get erotomania, a false belief that someone loves us when they do not:

I love him
I don't love *him*   (negation)
I love *her*   (displacement)
She loves *me*   (projection)

In every case you begin with a forbidden homosexual desire and you end with delusions, one of which is a jealous delusion.

I am only half serious about this, but it is a paradox of the whole approach that the steps are supposed to be taking the patient from the intolerable to the tolerable, when in fact it seems to me that the psychogenic 'solution' is much worse than the problem. The unconscious can perhaps be excused for taking such a disastrous path as paranoia or morbid jealousy, but why, given the painful position it reached, didn't it keep walking? If it is so ready to convert love to hate and hate to love, why not change your delusion to make your lover hate your rival, for example, and put your mind at ease? My answer to that is that jealousy may very well be jealousy and not converted love at all.

I must add one last ingredient to Freud's account – narcissism. According to Freud there are strong links between narcissism, or self-love, and morbid jealousy. For some reason he mentions this only in discussing female morbid jealousy. The idea of female narcissism was taken up with great vigour in one of the few modern monographs on sexual jealousy, Noel Lamare's *La Jalousie Passionnelle*. Narcissism is the theme around which Lamare builds an appalling diatribe against women, which I shall comment on in a moment.

Let us return briefly to the three mechanisms that are supposed to bridge the gap between latent homosexuality and various delusional states. Freud had formulated them prior to 1911 with the help of Carl Jung and Ferenczi, and he thought he saw confirmation of them in the Schreber case. I don't think Freud's logic is completely fanciful in terms of the content of Schreber's delusions, but it seems inadequate to explain the gross delusional state itself. If suppressed homosexuality is sufficient to cause paranoia and megalomania, how do we account for all the multitudes of conflicted, repressed (and stressed) homosexuals who are not in the least deluded and hallucinated?

This problem also applies to layer 2, projective jealousy. In particular cases one may find that excessively jealous persons have been unfaithful. Nearly half the adult population is unfaithful at one time or another. But what do we make of all the millions of unfaithful people who are not excessively jealous? Neither infidelity nor latent homosexuality is a sufficient cause for abnormal jealousy.

Unfortunately for the theory, homosexuality isn't even *necessary* for paranoia. Oversey writes from a psychodynamic standpoint. He observes that there are many non-homosexual people for whom homosexuality none the less represents a problem. We may become anxious and fearful about our possible homosexual tendencies when we have no erotic interest in members of our own sex. Males may become anxious about their inability to assert themselves or they become concerned about their overdependence on other men they consider more powerful or more competent. They falsely identify this as homosexuality in themselves, and Oversey classifies them as 'pseudo-homosexuals'. But even if we include these doubtful cases, casting our net as widely as possible, we still find only a small minority of paranoid patients showing homosexual preoccupations of any detectable sort. Oversey quotes a study by Klein and Horwitz, who searched case histories of paranoid patients looking for any evidence of homosexual feelings or homosexual anxiety:

The investigators classified as homosexual content not only erotic homosexual needs, feelings and conflicts, but also fears of being considered homosexual, fears of being or becoming homosexual and fears of homosexual attack. Their findings are extremely revealing. To begin with, such content was found in only one-fifth of the total group; furthermore, within this fraction, even at the height of the illness, most of the patients neither showed any behaviour of a homosexual nature nor expressed during treatment any erotic homosexual feelings, in spite of the fact that many of these patients were so disorganized that effective defense would seem impossible.

Since Oversey reports that anxiety and fear about homosexuality is more common than direct homosexual erotic attraction, the statistics here probably indicate no more homosexuality amongst this patient population than is found in the community at large. Of course there is no defence against the claim that if Freud had had the opportunity to examine these cases, he might have uncovered the latent homosexuality that he believed to be essential to the various paranoid states including pathological jealousy. The other possibility is, however, that Freud simply moved too far too fast, or in the wrong direction.

Freud applied the same logic that he developed in the case of male paranoia to the female case, and this too has come under critical attack on the basis of careful casework. Modlin selected five female cases of paranoia, including pathological jealousy, from a large pool of patients at the Menninger Clinic in the United States. They were free of schizophrenic or depressive symptoms, of drug or alcohol problems. None had a history of marital infidelity; all grew up in apparently stable homes. I shall be discussing these five cases later when I deal with delusional jealousy arising from life crises of one sort or another, but in the present context I simply want to quote Modlin's concluding remarks about Freud's theory. Modlin seriously considered the possibility that the deterioration of the women's relationships with their husbands and their desperate attempts to maintain or restore them had something to do with hidden homosexual desires.

However, the carefully obtained case histories of these patients and our extensive psychiatric examinations and psychological test batteries did not provide evidence of latent or disguised homosexual preoccupation.

Klaf came to a similar conclusion after a much larger survey of seventy-five female paranoia cases from the Maudsley Hospital in London. He found no significant difference between them and normal cases in their homosexual thoughts or experiences, and found that 83 per cent of their sexual delusions and hallucinations were heterosexual in content.

What does it matter? If I am so sceptical about Freud's theories of jealousy, why devote a whole chapter to the object of my scepticism? I think there are two reasons why it matters, one weak, one strong. The weak reason is that unless you have heard what Freud said, you will not understand why to this day certain ideas (including narcissism, paranoia and homosexuality) keep being repeated endlessly in the mainstream literature. A more serious reason relates to the impact these beliefs have on the victims of jealousy – both the jealous themselves and those they persecute and box in. I should therefore like to comment on the possibly maleficent effects the theory can have in the hands of the thoughtless and finally on the significant ideas that may none the less lie within it.

One particular problem with Freudian theory is that if it is wrong in its explanations, it is not simply failing to cure, but is piling disaster upon disaster. Perhaps my main motive in writing this book is to alert readers to the widespread habit of accusing jealous people of errors and character weaknesses that are said to 'cause' their jealousy. I mentioned earlier Lamare's 'analysis' of sexual jealousy in terms of narcissism. That work, still on sale in Paris in 1986, contains page after page of the most extravagant and fantastic abuse of women who are jealous: they are frigid or partially frigid, they are egoistic, preoccupied with menstruation and contraceptives, with masturbation, with passive eroticism. They have a horror of ageing, feel repugnance for pregnancy. They are clients of abortionists. They clothe themselves in a way that is more indiscreet than nudity. When they try to love, they can only pretend; they deceive others and themselves. They are unable to love their husbands and so are unable to love their children. Their milk is lacking or insufficient. When there *is* tenderness it is tyrannical. The children of such mothers are neurotic, psychoneurotic or even psychotic, and so on.

All of this is built on a theoretical infrastructure of infantile narcissism and homosexuality. What is so outrageous about this material is that it is a man writing about women (and an especially vulnerable group of women), accusing them of character faults that, even if they were true, spring not so much from infantile sexual abnormalities as from social attitudes to which men contribute at least as much as women.

I do not want to insist on sweetness and light where there is none, but if you are going to reduce every action in relentless detail to what Freud called 'the primitive, savage and evil impulses of mankind', it is helpful if you are right. Indeed I would go further than that and insist that we ask two questions before we launch into such an interpretation of people's behaviour: first, is it true; and second, if it is true, is it helpful?

Freud was described by H. Stuart Hughes as an 'ethical liberator'. It does not matter that your apparently innocent behaviour is reduced to what seem to be unclean or immature motives, because Freud himself, and Freudians in general, are supposed to be 'non-judgemental'. However, Freud himself found it hard to sustain a non-judgemental position. Hughes quotes a letter in which Freud writes, 'I have not found much "good" in the average human being. Most of them are, in my opinion, riff-raff.' And as Szasz documents, he was not above presiding over the character assassination of his critics by his disciples using the apparatus of his theories.

However, what Freud *thought* in this respect is not so relevant if the person on the receiving end of the interpretation has not yet reached the desired state of sublime moral calm. To tell a stammerer (as people did, quite erroneously) that they are so unconsciously aggressive that they bite off their words, or to tell a deluded person that, all evidence to the contrary, they are narcissistic and homosexual as well as deluded, seems to me to be like putting a devil on the left shoulder of a person who already has one on the right.

CHALLENGING THE HEGEMONY OF SEX

It is possible after all this to close on a positive note? Is there a phoenix to be resurrected? I think there is, but to do this, we must give the coals another stir. I want to discuss Freud's dependence on one unified instinct, one driving force in mental life – the sex instinct. (Admittedly Freud did propose *thanatos*, the death instinct, but this, too, was a 'blockbuster' instinct like the sex instinct.)

When I was discussing instinct theory in an earlier chapter I pointed out that in biology we no longer talk about a 'reproductive instinct' or a 'sex instinct'. Even explicitly sexual behaviour, that is, copulation, involves a complex set of nervous mechanisms organized in the spinal cord and the brain, which normally act in a co-ordinated way but which can be shown to be separable. The effects of specific drugs, damage to the nervous system or, in animals, experimental procedures, show that the system is organized more like a parliament than a dictatorship. Let me give one practical example. At the end of what Freud called the 'latency period', that is, at puberty, the romantic interest and the sexual performance of young adolescents rise, presumably under the influence of sex hormones. Under normal conditions that seems to be true. But, as Money and Ehrhardt report, in a small number of boys the hormone changes are substantially delayed (a condition simply called 'delayed puberty'). The bodily changes don't occur and sexual performance will be retarded, but the interest in members of the opposite sex, erotic imagery and romantic attachments may arise none the less. Similarly, early love affairs are uncommon amongst boys with *precocious* puberty, in spite of their physical maturity. In other words, these aspects of sexuality are normally co-ordinated, giving the impression that they depend on the same mechanism: it is only when one part of the system malfunctions that we discover that the basic systems are separable. They may be co-ordinated but they are not a unity.

This is not just a feature of sexual behaviour. All biological systems are like this. To explain why would involve a long digression into evolutionary theory, but let me sum it up by saying that our bodies and brains were not built to a preconceived plan, but have evolved in a haphazard way. François Jacob of the Pasteur Institute described it as a process of 'tinkering'. If we were motor cars, we would have evolved more like the old models that 'grew like Topsy', a new bit tacked on or adapted here or there, working in a fashion but not planned from the wheels up like a modern computer-designed car. Brenner, a molecular biologist from Cambridge, makes the same point:

I lost faith in the perfection of biological systems a long time ago and so it is not surprising that they just muddle through. Anything that is produced by evolution is bound to be a bit of a mess.

Although this is said in a joking way, it is absolutely fundamental to biology. Because evolution is unplanned, biology has a mass of basically happenstance intricacies to unravel. Behavioural science has a task several orders of magnitude larger, because it includes all the 'muddling through' of biological systems like the brain, plus the detail of culture and personal biography. It is because we are so far out in this area of particularities that a psychological theory built on the model of physics (or classical philosophy) is such an anachronism.

Freud had no idea about this 'opportunistic' process in evolution; it made sense to him to follow the intellectual habit of the time and trace everything back to a big central organizing principle – the sex instinct. What else could he have done? He might have thought to separate out several things that are often found in parent–child relations but which may not necessarily be all of a piece, such as attachment, affection, sexuality, allegiance, and authority. Freud tied these together under the control of sexuality, so that when he wanted to describe how attached children might become to their parents he spoke in the language of sex. The child wants to 'possess' the mother and/or the father. Deprivations and threats are sexual: penis envy and castration. Domination and submission relate to who is sexually active and who is passive, who 'enters' and who is 'entered'. What children object to and are traumatized by in the relations between their parents is sexual intercourse, the 'primal scene', not just problems of attention or neglect, affection or rejection, allegiance or hostility. I am not trying to deny infantile sexuality. I simply want to point out that in order to keep all the emotional processes between adults and children as basically sexual, in the genital, copulatory sense, Freud had to endow the child with innate ideas about sex, and was forced into an overuse of ideas like repression and unconscious symbolism.

To illustrate what I mean by the terms power, allegiance, authority and affection in family dynamics I can think of few better examples than the dramatic events in Ingmar Bergman's semi-autobiographical film *Fanny and Alexander*. It tells the story of a pair of children whose father unexpectedly dies and whose mother decides to marry the bishop who has comforted her during a period of emotional vulnerability. A terrible confrontation then occurs between the boy, Alexander, who battles on his own behalf and on that of his younger sister Fanny against the cold authoritarian they now have as a step-father. This collision involves all the ingredients I have specified: the dependency of the woman on the bishop, the attachment and affection between the children, their mother and other members of the family, the battle between the children and the adults over allegiance, and above all the power and authority of the new father. These are the forces in the drama and it would be farcical to suggest that it is played out simply in genital terms – to say that the boy was sexually jealous of the new step-father.

We can even trace these separate forces in Freud's personal life. With his fiancée he was clearly sexually jealous, he was out to exercise authority over his sisters, and later in dealing with his wife and her relatives he was preoccupied with allegiance.

A letter to Martha, his fiancée, displays sexual jealousy. After her engagement to Freud, Martha wrote a letter to a former admirer, an artist named Fritz Wahle, affirming their friendship. Freud had a stormy session with Fritz in which there was talk of shooting, tearing up of letters, stormy departures and tears on all sides and he then wrote to Martha:

When the memory of your letter to Fritz . . . comes back to me I lose all control of myself, and had I the power to destroy the whole world, ourselves included, to let it start all over again – even at the risk that it might not create Martha and myself – I would do so without hesitation.

This is clearly straight rivalrous rage. Freud also wrote about Fritz's profession:

I think there is a general enmity between artists and those engaged in the details of scientific work. We know that they possess in their art a master key to open with ease all female hearts.

Of course, it was Fritz's ability to open Martha's heart, not his particular occupation, that bothered Freud.

Freud's antagonism towards another 'dangerous rival', his wife's brother Eli, did not involve sexual jealousy, but simply power and allegiance. Eli and his mother expressed strong doubts about Freud's ability to support Martha, and Freud was in turn hostile to their orthodox Judaism. According to Ernest Jones, Freud made 'stern demands' of Martha:

She had to change her fondness for being on good terms with everybody, and always to take his side in his quarrel with her brother and mother. In fact she must recognize that she no longer belonged to them, but only to him . . . they were his enemies, so she should share his hatred of them. If she did not do this she did not really love him.

This is an example of frank wielding of power to secure conformity and allegiance. Freud's efforts to control his wife's personal relations with others persisted long after he had described his sexual relationship with her as 'amortized', as when he became upset at Martha's sociability at a dinner party.

The issue of universal sexuality in Freud's theory is a theme of almost every critic. It was a matter of far-reaching importance because his constant references to genital motivation in emotional life and the intellectual gymnastics he had to indulge in to tack it all together cost Freud the allegiance of many of his colleagues. It alienated his contemporary readers and continues to do so to this day. For a time the system was defended on the grounds that the sceptics themselves had sexual hang-ups and resisted the primacy and ubiquity of sex for this reason, but people are no longer prepared to acquiesce to that idea. For the quite unnecessary (and inappropriate) unification of the mental apparatus under the authority of the 'sex instinct' the price Freud paid was his basic credibility, and this was in an important sense a tragedy. Tying all the issues of attachment, affection and authority to sexuality, means that if sexuality is rejected so are all the others.

It is not that mainstream psychological theorists haven't talked about these issues, but they tend to be 'cool' theorists, whereas I think of psychoanalysts as 'hot'. By this I mean that power, allegiance, affection and attachment are not simply issues of who changes the baby, who makes decisions and who issues rebukes. They involve deeply felt emotions and powerful motivations. Taking sexuality out of the parent–child relation (which I do not want to do) would 'sanitize' it. Taking affection, attachment, allegiance and authority out of a family would reduce it to a puppet show. This is why people are continually attracted and repelled by Freudian thinking. It is like a store full of valuable objects but you can shop only dressed like Casanova.

One might say that if we remove sexuality from a dominant position in parent–child relations we remove everything that is distinctive about Freudian theory, for without sexuality what need is there for the elaborate mental apparatus of the unconscious, symbolism, defence mechanisms, etc., for which Freud is famous? After all, the other elements in family dynamics that I have listed are obvious, even banal. Who needs Freud to tell them about attachment, allegiance, and so on? But Freud did not simply say that (sexual) family dynamics existed, he brought them into competition with organic factors in the explanation of mental disturbance. So even if we 'demote' sexuality to just one of several important areas of family dynamics, as I am proposing, there is still this important idea: that it may be essential to explore the history of family emotional life, the attachments, allegiances and conflicts, to understand certain crises, disturbances and distortions. Let me illustrate this by two cases quoted by Malan.

One involved a drama student married to a man who indulged in what Malan calls 'enlightened infidelity'. Just how enlightened it was I leave you to judge:

She and her husband had an agreement that as long as they were open with one another they could do what they liked, and if they wished they could have extramarital relations. In complete accord with this, one evening her husband had told her that he was going to put their agreement into effect. The result had been that she was much more upset that she had imagined possible and her symptoms started shortly afterwards.

The drama student experienced a severe jealous panic attack, with 'sweating, trembling and awareness of her heart', and subsequently developed a fear of travelling on the subway. I don't want to try to find some symbolic significance for that any more than Malan does. Let me simply report that panic attacks of this sort often lead to phobias because patients begin feeling that another attack is imminent and quickly retreat from whatever situation they happen to be in. The panic itself may occur at the time of the provocation or some time after, depending perhaps on how long and how effectively the person can suppress their anxiety. The subsequent spread of the phobia seems to depend on the general state of anxiety the person remains in and on how able they are to identify the source of their anxiety. In extreme cases the patient may be completely confined to a house or even to a single room, and with severe anxiety about infidelity the jealous person may try to restrict the movements of their partners rather than themselves.

Let us now ask the question why, when the pact was implemented, did the young woman react so strongly? Is it necessary to go back to infantile sexual desires? I believe a good part of her reaction is predictable from the situation itself. First, anyone who forms a strong sexual and emotional attachment is a candidate for a strong jealous reaction when the provocation is so specific and remorseless. Second, the prior announcement gives the victim plenty of time to allow her imagination to play over the situation and her anxiety to grow. Throughout this time she is aware of her powerlessness, of her inability to protest or to express her anger and resentment, both because she has given a guarantee that she will not 'make waves', and also because the very person from whom she is likely to seek support is at that moment in bed with another woman. (Of course there is no reason in theory why all this should not be happening to a man, although it would be interesting to know how often women 'announce' their infidelity in such a way.)

The second case quoted by Malan deals with the consequences of jealousy rather than with its causes. A woman was divorced under somewhat paradoxical circumstances. She suspected her husband of infidelity and he in fact wanted to leave her, but she couldn't or wouldn't take action against him. The separation took place only when she eventually gave him reason to divorce *her*. He also took their son away from her under false pretences and instead of caring for him himself, left the boy with his grandparents. Again the wife failed to assert herself. She was a self-critical person, chronically self-effacing and non-competitive. Malan found that her fear of asserting herself was related to earlier experiences with jealousy. I say *with* jealousy rather than *of* jealousy, because although she was very jealous as a child, she became aware of this only from being told by her mother that she had tried

146

to kill her brother when he was a baby and had tried to suffocate a baby with a pillow when she was twelve years old. Such attributions can be massively destructive, of course, and seem to provide the explanation why, as an adult, the woman doubted her capacity to control herself should she ever allow her now quite justified resentment and jealousy to have its head. Once again the behaviour is difficult to fathom without looking back to emotional issues in the person's life, and once again this does not necessarily mean going back to early childhood, nor specifically to issues of sexuality.

THE POWER OF CIRCUMSTANTIAL DETAIL

I mentioned at the beginning of this chapter that we can evaluate theories in this area in two ways. First, we can ask if, on the whole, the patients show evidence of the experiences and predispositions that are alleged to cause their symptoms. Hence we asked whether paranoid people were in fact suppressed homosexuals and found strong reasons to doubt it. The second way we can convince ourselves of the validity of an interpretation is to ask if there is adequate circumstantial evidence to support it. I do not mean by this such things as dreams that subjects report after extensive therapeutic education, but well-attested details that come to light quite independently of the role of a therapist.

Docherty and Ellis quote three cases that seem impressive for exactly this reason: there are some surprising and puzzling aspects of the cases as they first presented themselves to the investigators that seem to match independently authenticated and potent events in the patients' biographies. Furthermore there is no need to make use of any intermediate symbolic steps to get from one to the other – the parallels are direct and literal.

ADOLESCENT TRAUMA AND GUILT RETURN

Docherty and Ellis first identify the nature of the jealous disorder in their three male patients, describing it as 'obsessive-delusional'. This means that it was not simply a case of excessive suspicion and vigilance, but the jealousy was plainly irrational and out of control. On the other hand the patients were not generally thought-disordered or hallucinated and could conduct their lives quite well outside their marriages.

Two of the three cases are more clear-cut than the third, so I shall concentrate on them. In both these cases the husband unjustly

147

accused his wife of sexual infidelity and then extended the accusations to other faults that were even more obviously false. One accused his sober wife of heavy drinking, the other accused his extremely dutiful wife of neglecting her household responsibilities. The therapists were puzzled by the specificity of these blatantly inaccurate allegations. On close inquiry it emerged that the descriptions of the infidelity, the drunkenness and the domestic negligence applied to the husbands' *mothers*. When they were young they had had to respond to calls from pubs and bars to collect their drunken mothers. Furthermore as early adolescents each had walked in on his mother engaged in sexual intercourse at home with a male drinking companion or a stranger. Both patients concealed this discovery from their fathers. This produced long-term emotional turmoil in them throughout adolescence. They felt shame and anger towards their mothers and intense disloyalty to their fathers (each of them had been more closely attached to his father than his mother).

Docherty and Ellis do not report details of therapy or its outcome in their paper. They do remark that cases such as these tend to be difficult to treat, but it goes without saying that there is a much greater chance of success if these background facts are known. Even if it does not prove easy to rid the man of his obsessions about his wife's infidelity, it does help to release the woman from the insurmountable task of meeting her husband's demands, since it is now obvious that these demands are not connected with her behaviour but with that of his parents.

Most of the papers I have mentioned, including that by Docherty and Ellis, are framed in psychodynamic language. What I have tried to do, following to some extent the lead of Malan, is to discuss the cases in common-sense terms, without continual reference to Oedipal reawakening, homosexual attachment to betrayed fathers, and so on. I have also tried to avoid an exclusive emphasis on infantile experience. I mentioned in an earlier chapter the case of a farmer who, after experiencing great emotional loss and humiliation as a result of the blatant sexual affairs of his first wife, killed his second wife because of a quite trivial transgression. That case bears certain resemblances to those of Docherty and Ellis, but of course the setting for the farmer's psychological drama was his first marriage, not adolescence or infancy. It seems sensible to me to look at every phase of a person's life to find events and predicaments that help to understand strong jealous reactions. By this account our family background and our early childhood simply represent one important closet in which to rummage.

Let me lay a little groundwork for the next chapter on pathological jealousy. A key issue that I have already mentioned is the difference between the *content* of people's madness and the *fact* of their madness. If we go back to the Schreber case, various writers have shown how links can be built between the facts of Schreber's life – his ambitions, his failures, his illustrious family, his childlessness, his father's bizarre treatment of the children, his views about God, etc. – and the contents of his complex delusional systems. However, do those links also explain the onset and persistence of his delusions and hallucinations? We feel that the conflicts and agonies of the man's life have something to do with the fact of his collapse, but the strategic weakness of the Freudian view in such cases is a failure to bridge that gap convincingly. This is linked to my point that Freudian theory is much more adept at working backwards from symptoms to hypothetical causes, but time and time again leaves us with the problem that those same 'causes' in thousands of other people do not produce the disorder in question. This issue is absolutely fundamental to the understanding of extreme jealousy.

With some of the cases we have reviewed, like those analysed by Malan for example, we may well feel satisfied that the predicament combined with the psychological history will bear the whole weight of explanation. In the case of the brooding farmer who killed his second wife, we might suspect some predisposing temperamental element, but his reaction does not leave our psychological imaginations gasping. Yet although the Docherty and Ellis cases illustrate the power of adolescent experiences to play havoc with marital trust and emotional control, the men's irrational, obsessive, delusional states seem to point to a significant shift in the mental mechanism. Between the traumas and emotional turmoil of the adolescents and the bizarre and intractable beliefs of the married men something seems to have 'flipped', just as it did on a more massive scale with Dr Schreber. Freud's mechanism of 'projection' may possibly describe what these men are doing, but it does not satisfactorily explain their fundamental incapacity to control their thoughts and monitor their own irrationality. In the next chapter we will deal in more detail with this collapse.

CHAPTER 8

Morbid or Pathological Jealousy

———————————— Q ————————————

THE DIFFICULT CAREER OF CARITAS

We are now going to discuss modern case studies involving abnormal jealousy – people who spy, shadow, snoop, make scenes, write malicious letters, throw stones, try to extract confessions, refuse their partners their right to free movement, deny the paternity of their children, and in the final case, stab and strangle. There is no item on this list that does not spread misery and pain. For this reason it is difficult not to cast the delusionally jealous person in the role of a monster, for what they are doing is in many cases monstrous. But they are *not* monsters. They are tragic figures. There is no happiness in it – readers who have had a severe bout of jealousy will know how racked and unhappy they can get, and so can glimpse the mental hell of people who, from no personal fault, find themselves in the continuous grip of such a passion. Sometimes they alternate between acute uncontrolled jealousy and periods of insight, and then, realizing what they are doing to the persons they love, they are tortured by remorse, depressed, often suicidal. Even then by abjectly begging forgiveness they frequently alienate sympathy almost as much as by prying and accusing.

Sometimes pathological jealousy has a sudden onset, sometimes it follows on a lifetime of suspiciousness and minor tyranny over those one loves. When a person's character changes suddenly it is easier for families to see that they are in the grip of some disorder and to sympathize, but it is almost impossible to be caring and sympathetic towards someone who has always been unpleasantly jealous, who deteriorates into an uncontrollable shrew or tyrant, even though they were no more responsible for their suspicious natures than they are now for their pathological jealousy.

After reading hundreds of cases and recognizing intellectually that these people are victims, I still cannot stop myself feeling hostile and indignant about what they do. On occasions their households take on the character of a detention centre or a torture chamber rather than a home. I think to be clear-headed and caring about these patients demands the mind of a saint, but it nevertheless has to be done. Having a strongly jealous nature or becoming an irrationally jealous person is no more a matter of personal fault than having six fingers on your hand or losing all your hair.

A complementary and equally seductive error fallen into even by the experts and professionals is the assumption that the victims somehow bring it on themselves, perhaps by how they treat the deluded person, perhaps by choosing them as partners in the first place, and even by simply being around and trying to cope. This mechanism is now familiar enough to be given the label of 'blaming the victim', and it has to be fought just as ruthlessly as blaming the suspicious and the deluded. It is obvious that we must take the most vigorous practical action to protect victims, yet finding fault with them is not only a common public reaction, but also used to be a disease of many social-science professionals. It had two roots: the folk belief that 'evil effects must spring from evil causes'; and the need of the professionals to favour 'causes' amenable to personal advice and secular preaching.

In raising this issue I am dipping my toe into the edge of a great ocean of social-ethical injustice that I don't have the time to explore – the mobilization of social credit and blame for virtues and vices that have nothing to do with the voluntary actions of the individuals concerned. When, by some at present obscure accident of heredity or life experience, or by a nervous system dysfunction, an uncontrollable mental disorder produces persecutory and violent behaviour towards innocent people, the infant justice is likely to be left exposed on a cold hillside and hatred sits by the hearth.

WHAT ARE DELUSIONS?

Shepherd maintains that the delusion we are dealing with is not a primary delusion of jealousy, but a delusion of infidelity, from which jealousy arises. Delusions have been described as unreasonable beliefs that are not abandoned when reasonable objections are raised. This sounds fair, but we have to face the fact that not all obstinately held unreasonable beliefs indicate 'mental disorder'. Mowat, who compiled the classic account of jealous murderers, points out that various persons have plenty of ideas that seem obviously unreasonable to their fellows, yet which are completely resistant to sensible objections. While we may call the ideas and the people 'crazy' in a half-joking way, we don't seriously consider them deluded. The same system of ideas that in one person is eccentric may be morbid in another. We would not classify as mad the members of groups who believe that it is possible in the right spiritual mood to float above the ground. There are people who think God made the White Cliffs of Dover from hundreds of metres of microscopic organisms to give the world a spurious look of antiquity. Both beliefs are easily challenged by what I personally would consider reasonable objections, but I don't think the believers are deluded, because their beliefs derive directly from their group membership. Yet if an individual came to tell me about floating in the air, or that he or she had discovered God's intentions in a limestone cliff, I'd think differently.

It is the personal reference and the private discovery that makes the difference. But delusions sometimes also lack the most elementary practical sense. Revitch describes a case where a man forbade his wife from going to the toilet in their house because of the lovers who spied on her there. Bleuler reports that one man believed his wife's backside was being heated by her lover from underneath the bed. Some jealousy-deluded people come to believe that adulterous intercourse is taking place right beside them while they sleep. Turbott describes a couple who took it in turns to have jealous delusions of this sort. The husband on awakening would inspect his wife's genitals for suspicious moistness. After a period on chlorpromazine therapy his symptoms receded, but she then accused *him* of adultery with his sister-in-law and detected moisture on *his* genitals, which she attributed to nocturnal visits to their bed.

As we shall see, pathological jealousy occasionally appears as a solitary delusion in an otherwise intact person, but more frequently it is part of a more general disorder. Amongst Mowat's jealous murderers or attempted murderers half the men and four of the seven women had delusions of poisoning and/or venereal disease, as well as their irrational belief in infidelity. Several of the remainder entertained other paranoid delusions. Indeed, only fifteen out of the sixty-two did not have some pattern of delusions outside the general area of infidelity, and two of those suffered hallucinations. Of course, since they were from an institution for the criminally insane (Broadmoor), these were all severe cases. But if we turn to Shepherd's eighty-one cases from the Bethlem Royal and Maudsley Hospitals in London in the 1950s, we still find high rates of delusions of other types. Of twenty-four paranoid patients several believed they were being poisoned, and there were all sorts of irrational beliefs about plots, spying, secret messages, intercepted telephone calls, and so on.

The other identifying feature of pathological jealousy is the extent and severity of the reaction. It is one thing to believe that a partner is meeting a lover in a shed, but another to wait up a tree with a can of petrol and try to incinerate them. But even this criterion is not altogether straightforward. 'Normal' spite can generate some weird and extraordinary acts. In a later chapter we shall encounter cases of people who take the most violent vindictive action after breaking up with their partners, often fuelled by disputes over child custody or property. Some develop intense hatred of the various parties involved, including not only their ex-partners, but also the courts that are making judgments against them, the lawyers who are losing their cases, and the police who are enforcing court orders. Sometimes this arises from a conflict of cultures – for example, a person from a country that gives almost exclusive rights to fathers, especially when a woman's adultery is involved, may act in a manner that seems quite deranged when a court respects the rights of the estranged wife – but this is exceptional. In the case studies there is a certain irrational flavour to much of the action that points clearly to mental instability. It is the watching, the following, the continual interrogations, the repetitive wrought-up public scenes, and the impression that things are out of control that points to delusional states, along with the implausibility of the cues that people attend to. To quote Mowat,

He may see a red flush on his wife's cheek, she may appear to be standing awkwardly, or sitting sideways on a chair, she has put on a clean dress, there is a cigarette-end in the fireplace . . . the jealous man [most of his murderers were men] sees a handkerchief on the floor, a wet cloth in the bathroom, newspapers in a ditch, and attaches to all the same import.

However, a deluded person may sometimes be so competent intellectually in all respects outside their delusion that nobody suspects that what they are saying about their partners is untrue. This arises directly from the nature of the delusion. Accusations of infidelity are not inherently implausible. If people tell you that stars of the opera are singing personally to them in the theatre, or that wires over the roadway caused their car accident by affecting their brains, you have little problem identifying an aberration, no matter how intact they are in other respects. But in the case of jealous accusations you can't even depend on other parties to testify truthfully. For this reason the literature is full of elaborate testimonies to the impeccable virtue of spouses and lovers. Some writers simply refuse to classify a person as deluded if the partner is in fact unfaithful. Mooney even reports a case described as irrational jealousy in the literature that was challenged after publication because new data came to light about a partner's conduct.

In a society and at a time when anything brutal and persecutory could be done by a spouse to an unfaithful partner (especially a woman) it might have been reasonable to reclassify a pathologically jealous person as sane simply by uncovering an act of infidelity by the partner. But with the rates of extra-marital affairs for both males and females rising, as they now are, this would abolish at a stroke 50 per cent of all cases! I want to discuss the practical problems that arise mainly in the early stages of detection of pathological jealousy by outsiders, because they tell us quite a lot about the problems of victims as well as the character of the deluded.

THE DEMORALIZATION OF VICTIMS

Severely jealous people may occasionally reduce their partners to a state so desperate and disordered that it is hard for outsiders to tell at first who is the patient and who is the victim. Shepherd reports the case of a woman who turned up in the hospital in London in a depressed state with slashed wrists. The staff discovered that her depressive husband, after a bout of drinking, had been interrogating her for several hours about her supposed infidelity. (His 'clues' about this were stains on her handkerchief and coat lining, and curtains drawn in the bedroom.) Shepherd follows this with a story of a second woman hospitalized for depression after a suicide attempt. She was pregnant (and didn't want to be) and had been subjected to the standard violent jealous attack that her husband had directed at her every time she became pregnant, which was why she was in the psychiatric observation unit and not her husband.

Sometimes the deluded husband actually arranges for his wife to be committed to a psychiatric institute, or tries to. In the case of the jealous husband who was worried about voyeurs inspecting his wife when she visited the toilet, the husband contacted Revitch because he wanted to have his 'mentally disturbed' wife certified insane. When Revitch arrived at the house he found the woman in a bad state. 'She broke the radio, tore his shirt, and lay motionless on the bed.' This, it transpired, was the result of the husband's jealous persecution, and it was only when the neighbours explained the situation, including the story about the ban on visits to the toilet at night, that he could identify who it was who was deranged.

When an accusation by a deluded person involves anti-social actions the issue is liable to become especially clouded. In another of Revitch's cases the woman was deluded and accused her husband of attacking her, as indeed he had, in response to continual irrational accusations of infidelity. Let me say quickly I am not supporting or excusing wife-bashing. Indeed, it is the very hostility we have towards a wife-basher that can make it difficult to get past this behaviour to the primary problem. Likewise allegations of incest with a parent, sibling or child, or an alleged affair with an in-law, can divert people's attention away from the actual state of affairs. Shepherd recounts a story of a woman who had a number of schizophrenic episodes. She abandoned her husband and went to stay with her parents, telling them tales of her husband's infidelity. When she accused him of sexually assaulting his own son (because she had seen a jar of vaseline in the room) her brothers contacted the police, evidently with the intention of having the husband arrested. It was the Scotland Yard police doctor who finally convinced them of the wife's irrationality.

Paranoid patients can sometimes make a lot of people see their version of things. The final example has erotomania as the major theme and jealousy as the minor. It involved an intelligent young woman I came into contact with, who developed an erotic obsession towards a married colleague in a school. She convinced both the security and cleaning staff that she was being victimized by the man's wife and colleagues, then a series of police officers, ambulance drivers, a magistrate or two, and the paramedical staff of the hospital where she was briefly confined several times. Even the principal of the school was for a time confused about the case. Yet all the while she represented an acute physical danger to the man, and especially to his wife, of whom she was intensely jealous. Over the many months that this continued the couple received more psychiatric treatment and medication than the girl. As it progressed this affair stirred up endless civil-liberties debates. When the girl was separated from her victims it took an acute observer to detect that she was anything but a practical, outgoing, pleasant individual with no place in a custodial institution.

At one time psychiatric hospitals accepted deluded people simply because they were deluded, as was recorded by Clouston, the superintendent of the Edinburgh Asylum, in 1887. Many of the delusions suffered by such people were benign. Recall Dr Schreber. Only by his eloquence and his social standing could he accomplish his release from an asylum in which he was incarcerated simply because he had a special agreement with God and a penchant for wearing women's jewellery. Naturally there are instances where some restriction is essential. Consider three of Clouston's patients:

D. T. D. was said to be killing his wife. I found a most respectable man, of first-rate business capacity . . . who was reputed by the world at large to be perfectly sane, making the most outrageous allegations about his wife . . . I have now in the asylum two quiet, rational-looking men, whose chief delusion is that their wives, both women of undoubted good character, have been unfaithful to them. Keep them off that and they are rational. On that subject they are utterly delusional and insane.

These are the classical monomanias, not as common as one might suppose, but found here and there through the literature. What do we do in their cases? Fortunately physical separation, simply keeping the partner out of the sight and hearing of the jealous person, reduces the risks in many cases, but there are difficulties if the person actively seeks out his or her partner. Also the problem may on some occasions recreate itself in the next relationship.

PATTERNS OF DISORDER

How common is pathological jealousy? Most of our case studies come from hospitals and clinics in Europe and North America. Searches of the records for cases with irrational and extreme jealousy as a major symptom seem to give a rate of about 2 to 5 per cent of the clinical population, so it is not a massively common disorder at this level of severity. It is less common amongst patients with brain damage. In Finland Achte, Hillborn and Aalberg examined the records of 3,552 military personnel with head wounds and found only forty-two cases of severe jealousy – a little over 1 per cent. If we turn to the criminally insane, that is, those who commit crimes of violence under the influence of irrational jealousy, the proportion is higher. In his report on English murderers or attempted murderers in Broadmoor Mowat found a rate of 12 to 15 per cent, three or four times higher than the rate among clinic and hospital patients. Tennant reports that on the whole people with psychiatric backgrounds are less likely to do anyone an injury compared with the general population, so morbid jealousy is considerably more dangerous than most mental illnesses.

But we must keep all this in perspective. If you work in the reception area of a hospital or clinic and encounter someone who is jealous and threatening, it should never be taken casually, but for the general population it doesn't rank as one of life's common perils. The incidence is probably higher in some countries than in others (in the United States, for example) but that has more to do with the prevalence of really effective weapons (guns) than the incidence of delusions. More significant is the frequency of serious irrational or semi-irrational jealousy within partnerships, which does not reach clinics and hospitals. It may be discussed with a doctor, police officer, magistrate, priest or marriage-guidance officer. The case studies sometimes mention severe jealousy in previous relationships, which was presumably both irrational and unreported. The combination of excessive jealousy and actual infidelity is especially risky for victims, since they are likely to try to cope alone – they may accept responsibility and be reluctant to seek help or escape from the situation.

Another theme in case studies is the difficulty that medical staff often have in convincing a person that their partner is deluded, even after the most horrific ordeals and a long history of harassment and restriction of movement. People often prefer to think that their partner is mistaken, and may get locked into endless attempts to provide final proof of fidelity and virtue. However not all victims adopt a charitable attitude towards their persecutors, even if they are convinced they are sane. Clouston tells the story of a female patient, 'quiet in manner, ladylike, and almost rational', who had her husband hauled before the church authorities for infecting her with syphilis. (It transpired she had a uterine tumour.) Her husband hated her to the day he died.

Where does pathological jealousy start, what does it look like, how does it progress? I shall deal with a series of diagnostic labels applied to the pathologically jealous: delusional, obsessive, phobic, depressed, and neurotic or character disordered, as well as with some of the traditional 'causes' such as alcoholism.

DELUSIONS AND OBSESSIONS

You may recall Shepherd's remark that the primary event in pathological jealousy is not a delusion of jealousy but a delusion of infidelity, from which jealousy springs. The delusion has the quality of a conviction, so when people spy, search and interrogate, they do not do so with any intention to prove themselves wrong, but to provide evidence for what they already 'know' to be true.

If Shepherd is correct, and the critical flaw in the patients' psychology is this mistaken or improperly arrived at conviction of infidelity, we are faced with an enigma: are there people (presumably unreported) who irrationally believe their partners to be unfaithful, but don't care about it, or think it funny, charming or 'about time', as normal people occasionally do? If you read old textbooks like those by Bleuler or Clouston, you will encounter cases of people who believe the doctors are misusing their correspondence, but still deliver it to them. There are people who believe their food is poisoned and say they know the poisoner, but neither smash up the kitchen nor attack the poisoner as you might expect. But the case studies on delusions of infidelity or irrational jealousy include only people who have strong unpleasant emotional reactions, inquisitorial (where they follow, spy, search, cross-examine), ruminative (where they brood and agonize) or confrontationist (where they accuse and attack). Perhaps it is fanciful to expect many people to treat infidelity, real or imagined, frivolously, but when one considers the range of reactions normally jealous persons display, the pathologically jealous do emphasize the negative, the violent and the antagonistic.

Even when patients react by increasing their sexual activity, it isn't usually by being seductive but by being demanding. There are only two cases I can recall in the literature showing a positive reaction to supposed infidelity. Both were women. One of Modlin's cases showed 'increased affection' and Shepherd reports that one woman suddenly took a new 'active pleasure' in sex. But before long the affection in the first turned to 'demands', then to shrill accusations, and in the Shepherd case the new pleasure turned to depression, with jealous thoughts that 'occupied most of her waking hours for many months'. One man increased his sexual activity outside the relationship, but only after his wife had fled from him, and his substitute activity involved visiting prostitutes and engaging in a dissolute existence in search of confirmation of his wife's supposed low life. He was miserable, suspicious and assaultive throughout.

As I said, all this could well be a product of the way the cases came to light, but I have reservations. I think that pathological jealousy extends beyond delusions of infidelity and involves also adverse reactions that are equally difficult to control. When a partner confesses, deluded people never 'make up' and go off to bed as normal people often do. They are likely to escalate their reactions. Buunk quotes Gelles:

And he would keep it up [so that] finally you would admit to anything in the world to get him to shut up. He would keep it up for five hours and not let me sleep. I would say, 'Yes! Yes! I did, are you glad?' . . . and then he would beat me.

Some patients have a clear idea about the supposed place, the time, the rival and the act, others have none of this to report. Sometimes the rival is quite a plausible candidate: a tradesperson, a lodger, a neighbour, a secretary, a colleague. In other cases the allegation is quite bizarre, involving unlikely relatives or multiple lovers. Occasionally other members of the family become incorporated into the delusion, especially children, who are sometimes seen as conspiring, carrying messages, etc. Also there may occasionally be retrospective delusions involving what are called 'pseudo-memories' – mistaken convictions about past events. The way in which the delusion can swamp all reason is shown by the patients described by Enoch, who in fact have never given any real thought to who the rival is and can give no details. The feeling of jealousy and the conviction of infidelity are real enough but the actual infidelity is not called up in imagery. There are those who have fantasies of sexual acts and those whose belief is quite disembodied and theoretical. The cases described by Docherty and Ellis in Chapter 7, in which the patient's mother was a model for their delusions about their wives, suggest that the content of delusions, when they are concrete and specific, may occasionally be of some real significance to the case.

Obsessions

Is pathological jealousy like an obsession in the technical sense? There is a (sometimes fuzzy) distinction between a delusion and an obsession. Obsessions are recurring unwanted thoughts or feelings. Victims frequently work to block them out, perhaps by trying to stop all thought, or by repeating things to themselves. Sometimes they take action, like checking something over and over because they can't get rid of a thought of incompleteness or omission, washing incessantly because of a thought that they are contaminated. They may keep quite still because of a thought that movement will do harm.

Obsessive thoughts are often felt to be imposed, to be intrusive; they are often highly repetitive, recurring unchanged over and over. Hoaken quotes cases of delusional jealousy that have this quality, but more often it is more *integral* to the person, more part of their own thinking, and usually more elaborate and *productive*. I mean by this that the delusion, like many paranoid ideas, develops and motivates new thoughts and actions. So people will seek confirmation, interpret, confront, interrogate, force confessions, demand promises, and so on. It does not have the quality of a cracked record, which is the stereotype of the obsession.

Insight

Many people, especially the depressives that we will shortly be discussing, have periods of insight when they realize their ideas are not true and their actions are irrational. Others may be dimly aware even while they are acting out their jealousy that it is not sensible. I interviewed a middle-aged man a few years ago who described how be began at one time to worry about his wife's fidelity. As he approached the house he found himself turning off the car engine and the lights and allowing the car to coast into the driveway. He then burst into the house precipitously. One night he went to the back of the house, climbed the steps on tiptoe and dramatically flung open the rear door. His wife was simply standing by the stove in an apron and looked at him with considerable curiosity. Fortunately he quickly got this sort of behaviour under control, partly as a result of some changes in his feelings of security in other areas.

This informant reported that even when he was doing these things, some part of him knew they were absurd. He said that he knew that it was not the situations that were creating the jealousy but the jealousy creating the situations. In the literature this question of detachment is very variable. Some people never seem to doubt their convictions, others go through intervals of painful lucidity, and others exist in a twilight state, half insightful but under a compulsion to feel and act as they do. Herceg describes an interesting case of this simultaneous insight and obsessive thought and action:

she was accusing her husband every night of philandering, in foul language, which was not at all in keeping with her otherwise ladylike behaviour. She was never free of obsessive thoughts of him having relationships with other women, which no amount of reasoning, explanation, or pointing out the illogicality of her arguments could resolve . . . *Yet at the same time she had full insight into the objective unreality of her accusations* and knew that her husband had no free time on his hands . . . The patient felt degraded and humiliated by her behaviour.

Of course the big difference between the jealous delusion and common obsessions is the depth of the delusion. When someone strips the bed and searches for hairs and examines underwear for semen stains, as this woman did, she is not doing so hoping there will be none, just the reverse. People do not spy for reassurance, they do not question to elicit denial. If people had irrational thoughts about *evidence* of infidelity, one could fight it by reference to other evidence. But deluded patients rarely listen to contrary evidence or they argue it away. Most writers say it is a waste of time to dispute, and often partners simply bring down more violence and abuse by trying to meet the deluded persons on their own grounds. Unfortunately delusional jealousy has no aim that can be satisfied. It is not as if when the deluded persons have found their proof, or forced a confession, they are content. Passionate jealousy is not interested in closure and tranquillity. If victims deny, they are lying, if they confess they are guilty.

Late last century there developed two schools of thought about the invulnerability of delusional ideas. The Swiss, Bleuler, supported the idea of a strong intrusive conviction growing upwards like a volcano from the sea. The Frenchman, Janet, saw the problem as a failure of critical abilities, like the ocean receding and leaving the peak exposed. Of course the two processes could occur together for some psychological or organic reason.

The difficulty about the Janet theory is that a deterioration in general critical ability would be expected to produce widespread intellectual deterioration, while most of these cases involve either a monomania – a single delusion – or a cluster of related delusions (like jealousy, poisoning and venereal disease, for example). It seems much more plausible that an idea or an emotional mechanism should become abnormally strong and intrusive and as a consequence is simply impervious to objections.

Normal jealousy is always rather like this, as is love, anger, grief, disappointment, regret, suspicion, hatred. Once they have started they do seem to rumble on their way for a time before you can apply the brake of reason to them. If the process is exaggerated, people are either distracted from considering evidence properly, or if they do, contrary conclusions simply 'bounce off'. It is a dramatic process to witness. I remember going over a letter with a woman line by line examining each sentence for the hostile message she believed it contained. At first it was difficult to get her to concentrate, simply because she was so emotionally worked up about it, but when she did, she seemed to follow my logic right up to the point where it contradicted her belief, and after a split second of doubt, she simply dropped the whole process and reaffirmed that the letter was hostile.

Sometimes the force of an objection will make a limited impact, and as a result we get secondary or accessory delusions. 'How can my partner be making love in the bed right beside me without me waking?' 'Not only are they meeting in the bed, they are drugging me.' I do not suggest that *all* the delusions of poisoning, etc., arise in this way. Some come from a heightened sensitivity to bodily upsets (stomach pain, chest constriction). Occasionally there are hallucinations – taste and smell are the most common in the case studies – which lead either to further suspicions about sexual activity or belief in drugging or poisoning. At this level of disorder we are dealing with a psychotic disturbance that combines delusions with thought disorder – the volcano *and* the receding ocean – and very likely with a biochemical problem in the brain. I am not ruling out a specific organic basis for delusions themselves. That would be rash, considering the limited state of knowledge of the phenomena. But at least with frank psychoses, there is a considerable body of data about specific organic brain dysfunction.

Phobia-like Reactions

Just as the primary delusion (of a lover in the bed for example) can spread cognitively to a secondary delusion (like drugging), so the fear and anxiety can spread, with the result that the disorder begins to resemble a phobia. This spreading anxiety is often the source of the extraordinary web of restrictions a jealous person may progressively impose on a partner.

A young woman described to me how irrational anger arose in her when her husband braked his car at a pedestrian crossing to allow a young woman to cross. She dragged her husband from a hospital clinic after a blood test when a nurse offered to put a small dressing on his arm. 'That feeling [of jealous panic] now comes back whenever I see a Band-aid.' At home she censored everything her husband saw or read, vetting all the TV programmes, tearing pictures from magazines. Her disorder was delusional in the sense that she was convinced of her husband's unfaithful intentions, and strongly fearful of all the situations in which his intentions might be activated. She was quite insightful about it except when panic struck, and what she feared most, intellectually, was that she would see her husband talking to a woman, would lose control, leave and never come back to him.

Depression is the most common symptom associated with delusional or obsessive jealousy. Mooney (whose excellent article is worth reading by anyone seriously interested in pathological jealousy) assessed the rate at 66 per cent. That is to say, two thirds of a hospital and clinic population of morbidly jealous people are seriously depressed at one point or another in the progress of their disorder.

Clinical depression can be a long-term state, or can come as an acute reaction to local problems. Long-term (endogenous) depression may express itself as mood swings (usually downwards but occasionally up) that don't seem related to life stresses. Acute depression is the sort of thing that occasionally hits people when their jobs are failing (or disappearing), they lose a close friend or their lives generally deal them a foul blow. It is termed 'reactive' depression for that reason – it is a reaction to ill-fortune, and the victim can either be dull, lethargic and despairing, or wound-up and agitated. In many if not most of the jealousy cases the depression is reactive and the person is agitated rather than inert. There are frequent reports of loss of appetite, difficulty in sleeping and worry about health (chest constriction, headaches, gastric pain). The person is likely to be moody and irritable, with family arguments and crying spells. Often people lose interest in their jobs and responsibilities. (Many people reading all this may think, 'Ah, that's me!' or 'That's George. My God, agitated reactive depression!' But there are literally millions of people who get irritable, anxious or depressed in this world, who are neither clinically abnormal nor likely to break out into delusional jealousy.)

Under the category 'depressives' in the case studies there will be no reports of hallucinations, or delusions (like voices in the head, or signals coming through the bathroom plumbing.) This isn't because the two things are incompatible, but simply because if those symptoms appear, the case is quickly transferred to the 'paranoid' category. But depressed people can be highly irrational, especially in pursuit of clues to infidelity. Just like the paranoid patients they may pick up minor clues, snoop, examine clothing, interpret changes in routine as significant evidence, etc.

Also, although their mood may be very low, they do not necessarily just mooch about ruminating to themselves, especially those who end up in hospitals and clinics. They are not as dangerously violent as some paranoid cases (most of Mowat's murderers were paranoid) but there are plenty of activists. Their jealous delusions can make them extremely aggressive. They may enforce restrictions on the comings and goings of their partners, argue with them or attack them. Since violence normally occurs in the context of an argument, it tends to be a bare-handed physical attack like an attempt to strangle. They are not so likely to launch a premeditated attack and for this reason do not figure so prominently in the 'murderer' group.

Another characteristic that might seem unlikely in a depressed person is an actual *increase* in sexual demands. Several authors report this. Todd and Dewhurst, who wrote a good specialist article on the course of such cases, describe a man (their 'Case 7') who intended to keep his wife pregnant and demanded frequent sexual relations 'to satisfy her lust' (that is, the lust he *attributed* to her). Shepherd reports the following case:

About one year before the patient was seen his wife had developed gynaeco-logical symptoms which eventually necessitated an amputation of the cervix. At the same time she began to take an interest in another man, though no intimacy occurred. The marital relationship began to suffer and the wife's operation provided her with a strong reason for continence. The patient became increasingly depressed and moody; he lost interest in his children and the home and began to act in a jealous manner; he became more violent in his demands for physical relations and questioned his wife persistently about her reaction during intercourse, and her feelings for the other man. He took to watching his wife while she slept and then waking her to accuse her of erotic dreams. He frequently stated he felt lost and hopeless and often threatened suicide . . . He admitted he had always been a possessive person but that only in the previous year had he become dominated by his feelings of jealousy, which were accompanied by depression.

Modlin, working at the Menninger Clinic, describes a case of a woman whose husband, a professor of nuclear physics, was always being called away unpredictably on classified assignments:

She became, in turn, curious, irritated, depressed and complaining, then suspicious. After a brief period of increased affection and sexual demanding-ness, she withdrew, seemed subdued, then became angry and accusatory. She decided her husband was having an affair with his secretary and berated him in screaming scenes. On two occasions she eluded security measures . . . and appeared in her husband's office 'to catch him in his philandering'.

This case, which began as agitated depression and developed into morbid jealousy, progressed into an elaborate paranoia.

Although sexual difficulties, especially in the partner, frequently precipitate these reactions, the depression can arise from other sources. Seeman mentions illness, ageing and career setbacks as fac-tors that cause lowered self-esteem and depression and have provided the background for irrational jealousy. Herceg mentions failing eyesight. Just how central the depression is to the jealousy is hard to say, but it is an important issue. Todd and Dewhurst describe cases of sexual difficulties that give rise directly to delusions of infidelity without a major involvement of depression. Sokoloff, whose extraordinary cases often sound like sensational B-grade movie plots, describes how jealousy developed in a woman whose husband was almost impotent due to a spinal cord injury. Not only did this woman make angry accusations, but she also began to bring young women into the house: 'I wanted to prove to myself that he is unfaithful to me.' Cobb and Marks describe cases where the depression was successfully treated but the irrational jealousy persisted.

Depression as a Consequence of Delusions

It is vital to document the time-course of these cases. In a great number depression clearly *follows* the abnormal jealousy. Evidently the guilt, the drama of confrontation, the violence and the general chaos in the family lead to severe depressive reactions and suicidal thoughts or intentions. For those who have periods of lucidity and see the irrationality and injustice of their conduct, this is almost inevitable. There are more than a dozen examples of severe depression in the aftermath of jealousy in Shepherd's material, including many who initially developed paranoid problems. More than half of Mowat's murderers or attempted murderers were suicidal, nineteen of the sixty-two prior to the assassination attempt and twenty-three after. Since the murderer's attack is always the culmination of a longer history of delusions (five or six years on average) the 'prior' suicidal ideas could just as well have followed the delusions as preceded them.

Causal Links in Depressive Cases

We tend to think of causation in linear terms, like a train going from A to B to C, whereas we should sometimes be thinking in terms of forks, going from handle to prongs, with causes producing a number of effects. It is not improbable, for instance, that the traumas of daily life – fear of pregnancy, illnesses, work problems, spouses becoming exhausted, impotent or rejecting, worries about impotence or failing interest within oneself – can produce anxious depression. One or another of these events may simultaneously activate our fears about infidelity, which, under the influence of our general depression and agitation, can grow explosively into delusional jealousy.

Sometimes the 'trigger' is an independent event: workmates speculating about their partner's promiscuity (Todd and Dewhurst), or a spouse coming home late (Enoch), or a partner who suddenly appears more seductively dressed (Docherty and Ellis). It is clear that jealousy is not a mechanism that needs to be driven reluctantly into action. It has a capacity to motivate a search and an active process of interpretation. The mystery is why in certain individuals it needs so little provocation and once started becomes so obsessive, violent and resistant to reason.

Predispositions

One obvious explanation could be that, either because of earlier life events or because of some temperamental or 'dispositional' factor, the irrationally jealous have always been jealous and suspicious – their noses always sniffing for fumes of faithlessness. This is so obvious an idea that we might be tempted simply to accept it immediately. It resembles the theory that when a neat, clean and careful person has a nervous breakdown, they will naturally become an obsessive-compulsive, checking things endlessly or washing their hands a hundred times a day. But that seemingly obvious 'fact' about careful personalities and obsessive patients is incorrect; as Carr shows, the two things are *not* related, and this warns us to step cautiously in the case of normal and irrational jealousy.

What does the evidence tell us about this relationship? Surprisingly some of the major studies do not provide the basic data. Vauhkonen carried out an extraordinarily detailed study of fifty-four jealously deluded patients from Helsinki. He seems to have measured every conceivable thing about the patients and their spouses: their family characteristics, child rearing, jobs, birth order, IQ, age at first intercourse, etc. He documents whether they were stingy, talkative, obstinate or easily offended, but as far as I could discover doesn't say whether they were normally jealous!

Mooney pulled together data from five major studies that *did* provide the information (Jaspers, Langfeldt, Shepherd, Todd and Dewhurst and his own) – 138 cases in all. He found patients *without* a prior jealous predisposition were in a clear majority: seventy-eight to fifty-nine. We don't know of course how this compares with the normal population in the various countries where the studies were conducted, but it clearly contradicts the idea that delusional jealousy *necessarily* grows from strong but 'normal' jealous sensitivity. (It is also worth noting that there were twice as many men as women in

166

these samples, remembering that men's early jealousy is more likely to be expressed outwardly.)

Is it possible, however, that there is a more complex relationship, that a prior jealous predisposition may form a background for one type of case rather than another? Jaspers divides the pathologically jealous into two classes, those who develop slowly and those who 'flip' unexpectedly into a strong delusional state – the 'ramp' versus the 'step'. The theory is that the gradual developers, those with a personality disorder, will be those with a prior history of jealousy, and the psychotic ones (those who become depressed and paranoid) will not. Mooney, who reports Jaspers' theory, provides clear figures on his own cases, but they give no support to the theory. After examining the various other studies I have to conclude either that the diagnostic categories (depressive, paranoid, personality problem) are rather slippery, or that there is nothing to support Jaspers' theory.

PERSONALITY DISORDERS

I have so far restricted my treatment of pathological jealousy to the major systematic forms – delusions of a paranoid or obsessive kind, or those associated with depression. However, the literature includes many cases that are termed 'inadequate personality', or 'psychopathic personality', 'immature', 'sensitive', 'neurotic traits', etc. All these cases have the central jealous delusion, but don't fit the major psychiatric categories. They are very diverse, and in some instances I doubt if anyone would see them as abnormal except for the jealousy. They include one or two apparently 'gung-ho' confident people, one or two who practised body-building and self-improvement, even one who was a (frustrated) sexual athlete of sorts. But many had been somewhat isolated, rootless, with irregular employment records, difficulties during army service, and so on. At one moment I find myself thinking that this is just a cross-section of ordinary humanity, randomly struck down with a strange disorder, and at another that this is a group that is clearly at risk of *some* disorder. They obviously need help to get them through their crises, but on balance I doubt if most of them could be 'remade' by a therapist, short of totally rebuilding their lives.

MONOMANIA

Mairet, a French professor of psychiatry, included pure cases of delusional jealousy in a category called *monomanie* (monomania). There were no hallucinations or thought disorder that might indicate

167

schizophrenic problems. There were no secondary or parallel delusions like persecution, poisoning or imaginary diseases. There was no severe depression and the personalities of the jealous individuals were not especially inadequate or neurotic. This is pure delusional jealousy, not in principle unlike the cases of persecutory paranoia that sometimes afflict otherwise intact persons. Although we don't have any details, Clouston's 'two quiet rational-looking men' seem rather like this – basically reasonable people with one fixed delusion. Among the published case studies it seems rare. Some writers absorb it into the 'inadequate personality' category, the jealousy itself constituting the inadequacy, I suppose.

It is clear that pathological jealousy does vary in form – whether or not there is a specified rival, whether the deluded person has fantasies, how bizarre the accusations are, how episodic it is, how much insight the person enjoys – yet there is really no clear reason to see the jealous delusion as distinctly different in each case. Nobody to my knowledge has detected any systematic variation in the form of jealousy according to the category of patient. The most obvious variability is in those accessory matters I have listed, which follow the logic of the accompanying disorder. If a depression deepens and lifts, the jealousy may come and go. If the patient is severely disturbed, the content of the delusion may be correspondingly bizarre. Yet overall there seems to be more consistency in pathological jealousy than in normal jealousy, perhaps because it tends to be so strong and raw. What is needed is some effort to locate cases of persistent jealousy that are clearly irrational yet benign, just to establish whether jealous delusions need be consistently negative and antagonistic, as they seem to be from the published studies.

ALCOHOL

While we are dealing with popular theories, let us look at the issue of alcoholism. There is a long-standing idea, which still occasionally surfaces in the literature, that pathological jealousy is closely linked to alcoholism. Shepherd traces the idea back to Krafft-Ebing, although it may well be older. In 1891 Krafft-Ebing made the rather ambiguous remark that he found only four patients among 'thousands' who had delusions of jealousy without alcohol problems. Even if we reasonably assume that the 'thousands' were all his patients and not just the jealous ones, the claim was quite extreme and has *not* been supported by later research. Shepherd himself had only five patients out of eighty-one for whom alcohol was the primary problem, although it was mentioned as an accessory before and after the fact in several others. The figures for heavy drinking vary across the studies from 8 per cent in Langfeldt's Norwegian group, to 16 per cent in Kala and Kala's sample from India. When we look at jealous killings, alcohol is involved in a third to half the cases. Yet according to Virkkunen, drinking amongst jealous murderers is no higher than amongst murderers in general, which suggests that it may play its role not as a cause of pathology, but rather in affecting how the pathological mental state expresses itself in action.

Although alcoholism is no longer seen as an important primary cause of morbid jealousy, drinking appears at various points in the development of the disorder. If a man drinks heavily he may lose his sexual vigour, and may also be rejected by his partner because he is so unappealing. In other words, alcohol joins illness, ageing, failing eyesight, and a whole range of things that might make a partner unhappy or make the jealous person think he or she is unhappy and rejected. From this, as I said, may come ruminations and speculations about the 'real' reason for the difficulty, that is, irrational beliefs about infidelity.

It is possible that a steady alcohol diet could contribute to that failure of critical ability that seems to characterize deluded patients, but I don't think this is a key issue because the failure is so often quite specific. People have a critical 'blind spot' rather than generalized confusion. The case material more often refers to the immediate effects of being drunk – accusations after returning from the hotel or after drinking bouts (either with or without the partner). And, as I said, quite a bit of lethal violence takes place when people are drunk.

In understanding the role of alcohol, it is important to know *when* it plays its part, because, like depression, heavy drinking often occurs in the aftermath of delusional jealousy, as a reaction to conflict or remorse, and not necessarily before it, as a cause. Of course there can be a round of accusations, drinking and more confrontation, or, as in one of Shepherd's cases (p. 705), drinking, jealousy and more drinking. But all this has to be kept in perspective. Alcohol is no longer regarded as the key to irrational jealousy, and in the majority of cases it doesn't even figure as a significant contributing cause.

AGE DISCREPANCIES AND JEALOUSY

Before turning to the general issue of therapy, let me drive a stake through another old phantom, the idea that extreme jealousy arises from big age discrepancies between partners. Todd and Dewhurst quote Geoffrey Chaucer and Robert Burton (*The Anatomy of Melancholy*) to the effect that an older husband will be abnormally jealous of a young wife. When he was sixty-three Cervantes published a mildly amusing moral tale on the same theme, 'The Jealous Estramaduran'.

The idea is consistent with the theory that pathological jealousy can be triggered by a person's concern about their declining sexual performance. However, the evidence in Mowat indicates that the decline in a *partner*'s sexual interest or performance is a more likely precursor to depression and jealousy, which suggests that the younger partner might be the pathologically jealous one. It is doubtless just a coincidence, but in the one case where relationships between a couple were affected by an age difference (in Vauhkonen) it was the younger partner who developed the delusions.

RESUMÉ

What a triumph it would be to be able to extract from the archaeology of delusional jealousy the plans of its foundations. I do not believe that the cases are simply a miscellany, the arbitrary pulling of filing cards from clinic case records just because the word 'jealousy' appears on them. There is too much of a sameness to the accounts, whether from India, Finland, England or North America. I could not safely assert, however, that pathological or delusional jealousy is one clinical entity. But just as there is a real phenomenon to be explained in the paranoia of conspiracy and persecutions, so I feel that there is a breakdown in functioning in morbid jealousy that can't be explained simply in terms of the conditions that precipitate it. We encountered the same problem when discussing Freud's theories. There are too many people encountering stressful life events of similar kinds and not becoming delusionally jealous. Those events themselves are not sufficient reason for the delusion.

Many of our complex emotions are like minor madnesses. Although love, grief, humour, pity and so on are shaped, suppressed or amplified by culture and by personal life events, at the heart of each there is, in my belief, one or sometimes several abstract core mechanisms in our organic make-up. Sometimes the output from such a mechanism is excessive, simply because of the conditions of life of the individual, but sometimes it seems to me to be like a car with a jammed throttle – it is often hard to unjam and is capable of doing great damage if you stay in its path.

CHAPTER 9

A Mini-chapter on Therapy

———————— Q ————————

THERAPY

Although in this book I sometimes seem to be tackling half the social sciences' major problems – biology, psychopathology, cultural anthropology, etc. – I have no intention of embroiling myself in long debates about therapy. As far as my personal, lay opinions go, I would generally favour short, pragmatic therapy to long, deep therapy, and I think that management of the social relations between people is at least as important as the exploration of their psyches.

I shall concentrate on those few issues in the literature that seem specific to jealousy. Most therapy practised and written about in cases of severe or pathological jealousy is simply therapy that is appropriate to the poor sexual and personal relations that often prevail; the poor self-esteem, guilt and anxiety that is produced; and, in the more serious cases, the depression, phobias and psychotic states that are associated with the severe jealousy. Delusional states themselves have always had a reputation for resisting treatment. Fortunately they sometimes lift spontaneously, especially if they have been precipitated by some episodic event like a pregnancy. If Enoch is correct in his remark that 'the purer the form, usually the more lasting the illness', we can only draw comfort from the fact that pure cases of irrational jealousy are in a minority.

BRINGING THE JEALOUSY TO LIGHT

In serious cases the top priority is to get the problem out in the open and to get help. If someone finds that jealousy of their partner is resulting in continual aggressive encounters, or in weeks and months of unpleasant brooding and ill-temper, constant recriminations, or restrictions on their autonomy and free movement, then the problem has to be faced, and the sooner the better.

It is not uncommon for seriously jealous people (and not just deluded ones) to place more and more restrictions on their partners, demanding they give up their jobs, stopping them from going out, refusing to allow them to have a car or to use it, restricting their finances, objecting to contact with their friends or even their neighbours, censoring their mail, confiscating their magazines, forbidding them to dress in ways that are seen as provocative, and so on. Much of this control is practised by men, but it is not all one-sided. While men may exercise physical and financial power more directly, both men and women can achieve similar effects through a series of what seem at the time small concessions. Consider this account from Morgan, where the man

> consented to a censorship of all magazines, which his wife would look at first. He had to shop with her under her direction with his head held erect, so that he might not gaze down at magazine covers or around at other women in shops . . . To placate his wife he did not argue, but the submissive behaviour could be and was interpreted as a further admission of guilt. More accusations followed, leading to a reinforcement of the jealous ideas, rather than the hoped-for reduction.

The paradox of this situation is, as Morgan implies, that the jealous person is no less jealous and unhappy with a boxed-in partner than with a free one; indeed the amount of conflict is often directly related to the closeness of the physical contact.

Surely, one asks, can't this problem be solved by simple rebellion? But in my experience the absurdity of the whole scenario often does not hit people until they actually sit down and begin to describe it all. Then we face the issue of how the inevitable and necessary showdown is to be accomplished. It is clear from the case studies that if a reasonable *modus vivendi* cannot be achieved, the parties must consider separation, especially when aggressive, delusional conduct is involved.

There is an unhappy irony that the more punishment is meted out to a domestic victim, especially a wife, the more difficult it may be to escape the situation. First, there is the problem of physical danger, the escalated violence that may follow any rebellion. Second, contemplating a showdown raises a series of anxieties about ending up with a 'failed marriage', the stigma of deserting, or the even crueller and more unjust stigma of being tagged a 'battered wife'. Finally, there is the problem I mentioned earlier of not wanting to accept that one's spouse or partner is mentally unstable. Because so much of our self-esteem is associated with our choice of partner, all these identifications can be highly threatening.

Outside help is indispensable, and this help is needed for both parties. There is an agreement that the jealous person has to get support, both from the partner (if he or she can continue to offer any assurances of positive feelings) and from a third party who, though firm, is never dismissive of the problem. Just how tough people have to be depends on how tough the jealous person is.

If a separation is inevitable, therapeutic help will need to be most intensive to cope with the practical problems, the guilt and the possible backlash. Two statistics are of interest here. Amongst families where homicide occurs, four out of every five cases involve the husband killing the wife, and one half of these occur either after a separation *or during the process of moving out*.

Even when a separation does not occur, active management is essential. Revitch makes the useful comment that the partner of the jealous person can benefit from an active campaign to strengthen outside interests and to gain social and economic independence. Therapists have to be realistic about the future of these cases. Mooney provides figures on long-term treatment results from a number of studies and found a *worsening* in one third of cases. Admittedly most of these data came from studies conducted before the regular use of chemotherapy, but even when this is introduced, many patients simply refuse to continue on drug programmes. So providing partners with alternative sources of social support and, particularly for women, an independent income if they don't have one will not only help them with the confidence and assertiveness they need, but may provide some sort of safety net should the situation become unmanageable. I am not suggesting that these are the only circumstances under which women should acquire economic independence, of course, but rather that the vulnerability of a dependent woman is particularly dramatized by this predicament.

WEATHERING THE STORM

For a couple who remain together and try to cope with regular, escalating face-to-face brawls, it has been suggested that they pay careful attention to exactly what transpires. Instead of trying to sort out the situation during therapy sessions, they should keep an informal diary, documenting what seems to trigger the conflict, whether there are any advance warnings, and especially what it is that seems to accelerate the escalation process. With the help of an outsider it may then be possible to develop evasive strategies or to get out of the situation before it gets out of control. Some normal families evolve these strategies informally to handle repetitive disputes. In fact it is sometimes the children who first recognize the danger signals from the drift of a conversation or a tone of voice in their parents, and quietly excuse themselves, or, even better, alert the adults.

The most specific advice about the management of frankly delusional jealousy in a clinic or hospital setting comes in two papers by Modlin. What he recommends may seem anomalous to therapists raised on non-directive sympathetic listening and above all on deep interpretation and 'insight'. He simply outlaws the expression of the irrational ideas, telling the patients that what they are tempted to say about their partner's infidelity is not socially acceptable, and that they are not to say it. He encourages and amplifies any glimmerings of insight and doubt. Modlin is flatly against interpreting the false ideas; the therapist 'does not, at any time, push the patient towards insight through exploration of psychodynamics or interpretations'. No expressive psychotherapy. Shore up the partner to be consistent and firm. Make sure no relatives undermine the campaign by lending a sympathetic ear. In parallel with this, undertake a vigorous programme of outside activity and try to raise the patient's self-esteem in every area. Modlin also points out that demoralization and passivity of the spouse (in his cases the husband) actually compounds the problem, because the woman's irrational accusations have effectively deprived her of the firm support she needs. So therapeutic efforts to support the victims of pathological jealousy by making them more assertive and restoring their self-confidence should in the end help both partners. In his 1964 article Modlin provides examples of the tactics used to build up the self-assurance of the patients in areas outside the pathology.

The policy of deflecting attention away from the delusions is supported by Cobb and Marks:

. . . direct stimulation of jealous thoughts by exposure in fantasy or *in vivo* were reported as being anxiety provoking and unproductive. More general methods not aimed at jealous symptoms but at assertive training, clear definition of marital roles and sex therapy were also found to be helpful.

So far we have treated the situation as though the partner is never at fault, but this cannot always be assumed. In a case described by Teismann we encounter a strongly jealous husband in his early fifties, demoralized, drinking heavily and making homicidal and suicidal threats. Originally the therapy was designed to rid him of these reactions by displays of affection, reassurances and humour, but in the end the therapy succeeded in bringing to an end the well-advertised affair the woman was having with a slightly younger man in a patently unsuccessful attempt to practise an 'open marriage'.

Do we also need therapy for the therapist? Beltz describes an extraordinary chronicle of domestic and emotional chaos in a group of families in 'therapy'. Presumably the therapist was sympathetic, at least at the beginning, about open sexual exploration amongst the couples. The text is interspersed with meticulously drawn diagrams showing the state of play. More and more arrows show an avalanche of new liaisons growing month by month, until the final picture looks like the Paris Métro. As Beltz himself admits, the end result of the therapeutic process was complete disarray. Over the five-year period three of the five key partnerships ended in divorce and 'one additional divorce was not unlikely'.

Before I comment on the substantial literature on therapy for normal to moderate jealousy, I cannot resist recounting the therapy of another era. Mairet, writing in 1908, sympathized with women trapped with irrationally jealous men. It was not possible to have husbands committed to an institution if they were simply jealously deluded, and at that time divorces could not be had on the grounds of mental illness of a spouse. Mairet recommended that doctors give these women sympathetic moral support and five grammes of bromide salts a day. These chemicals were intended for the husband's food, introduced partly into the normal daily fare and partly into *plats particuliers*, special dishes prepared for the purpose. Bromide salts were supposed to be sexual pacifiers. (There were always tales in the army of food laced with bromide to calm the troops from the waist down.) Five grammes is a substantial sedative dose. Although Mairet was not in a position to know this, bromide is a cumulative poison, producing skin eruptions in about a quarter of cases, and according to Goodman and Gilman, 'almost every type of organic or functional neurological disease'. Mairet distinguished *monomanie* (pure delusional jealousy) from irrational jealousy plus thoughts of persecution – *folie*. He warned doctors that the bromide strategy had to be carried out with the utmost secrecy, because a husband who discovered what was going on was almost certain to promote himself from simple *monomanie* to persecutory *folie*. Mairet's heart may have been well placed, but professorial and medical ethics in 1908 seem somewhat rubbery.

The literature on therapy for normal or moderate jealousy is extensive. It is a difficult area to write about because so much depends on the experience, personal manner and informal skills of those practising it. The reporting is sometimes very general and has a distinctive tone – I think of it as the therapeutic *vie en rose*. Articles on therapy with couples sometimes read like prospectuses. One misses the sharper documentation and candour of the classic case studies of Shepherd. It is partly an American–European difference, but more significantly a social science–medical contrast. The medical tradition sees a failed outcome as a product of a persistent disease process, whereas lack of success in personal therapy advertises defects in the product, that is, the therapist and the therapy.

Since much of the material is common to all personal or family therapy, I shall again concentrate on matters directly tied to jealousy. The case studies are drawn from Constantine, Blood and Blood, Daher and Cohen, and Morris (who worked with lesbian couples). It is not possible to make up a composite formula from these sources because the approaches differ. For instance, the Bloods began their weekend workshop with a series of point-blank extended statements made by participants to partners and lovers (or proxy lovers if the real ones were not present). Daher and Cohen spent the first of their six 90-minute sessions easing the people into the situation with a cool cognitive exploration of the topic. Everyone seems to agree on who should participate. All three members of a triangle is regarded as ideal, the partners next, the lovers least useful. It is clearly undesirable to identify a certain individual as the one under 'treatment' and the others as the therapist's helpers. The jealous partner is probably the natural 'patient', especially if the workshop has a liberated image. A strong effort has to be made to balance the scales at the outset, and to make it clear that there is no doctrinaire policy and no 'patient'. Each triangle should aim at its own resolution, compromise or contract.

The Constantines have a particularly well worked-up strategy, a little of which I shall describe. They suggest that early in the process participants 'clarify their boundaries'. This means they make clear what they can tolerate (or think they can) and what are their most sensitive concerns. In the case of a jealous partner this means what invasions are the most threatening – their house, their children, nights spent away, intrusions on special places or activities, disclosure, unpredictability, neglect of certain significant personal or family events, affectionate intimacy, explicit sex, exposure of the affair to others (such as parents), public appearance of the lovers together, and so on. Constantine suggests that the question can be put in this form: 'What are you afraid of? What bad or unpleasant outcomes might you fantasize as a result of your partner's other relationship?'

On the other side there will presumably be statements about what the 'lovers' hope to achieve or preserve. (Our treatment of the problem of disclosure suggests that it might be unwise to make this very detailed or too comparative in emphasis!) The discussion also takes in what, if anything, the jealous partner has to gain from the involvement of a third party (a topic that might in reality be dealt with in no time at all).

As Francis points out, there is no way to tell in advance what participants will get particularly exercised about. It is rare in my experience for couples to have broached the question of jealousy, let alone to have a relatively uninterrupted exposé of their various points of view. Indeed many people will not have worked over the topic in any detail even in their own minds. It is also clear why this sort of revelation might be best conducted in the company of other people with similar problems, and why participants should not try to impose a group ideology.

Nor should one assume that all will be magically resolved. If the process is searching, there will be groups with plainly irreconcilable priorities (or maybe they don't come to workshops). It is doubtless necessary to keep in mind that here, as in many predicaments, the job is not so much to find a happy outcome, as to choose the best from a set of less than perfect alternatives.

There must be opportunities also to test out solutions. Blood and Blood report that one woman suggested she be told in advance when her husband was to be with another woman and should 'know where she could reach him in an emergency'. From one or two of the case studies described in this book we can see that she could conceivably miscalculate the type of emergency that might ensue and end up having a serious crisis. 'Contracts' are not magical documents and people should be able to return and rework them, or do so in another context once the basic situation has been explored.

I won't describe the various games and rituals various authors say they find useful, such as miming, role reversal, etc. They are described (occasionally a little sketchily) in the various books and papers. For anyone thinking of participating in a workshop, my advice would be to do some consumer research. It probably won't be easy to contact people who have participated in the group you are considering joining but you should interview the person directing the therapy. For anyone wanting to start a workshop, an apprenticeship would seem highly desirable, rather than working book in hand. The history of the encounter group movement provided by Lieberman, Yalom and Miles warns us that unless workshops are well managed and follow strict ground rules (about ganging up, for example), they are potentially quite destructive. Finally it is possible that some people trying to enrol in a workshop are simply in the wrong place. If one projects one's mind back to the case material in the last chapter, it is hard to visualize how some of those people could benefit from, much less contribute to, a weekend jealousy workshop. It is obviously not just a matter of printing a prospectus, hiring a room and making sure the urn is switched on.

CHAPTER 10

Summing Up: Sexual Politics in Triangles

—————————— Q ——————————

Let us begin this final chapter with a list of incidents that recall some of the madness of pathological jealousy. They come from *Woman versus Woman* by Shirley Eskapa and they reflect not madness, but the beginning of a sort of ruthless sanity:

Larry always wore striped ties. His wife had fallen into the habit of noting the direction of the stripe in his tie in the mornings. She realized his tie had been retied during the day.

Paul bought a very trendy overcoat with a hood. His wife's 'immediate instinct' was that 'he'd got it bad for a very young girl'.

Mark and his wife used to read the astrology charts together. She saw him read a new sign, smile and say nothing.

Victor became a Beethoven fanatic. His wife guessed the other woman was a music lover.

Each of these dawning suspicions of infidelity was accurate and introduced a wife to jealousy and to the problem of what to do: to ignore, to brood, to explode or to devise a plan to rescue the partnership: woman versus woman.

The fifth book I had read on 'affairs' in the space of a week, *Woman versus Woman* was the one that broadened my thinking most radically, partly because of the startling things that some women did to fight back. To give just one example: when a mother of four discovered that her husband had set up house with a young woman in their London flat, she packed the four children, their dog and a box of food in a taxi and sent them to the address with this note:

Dear Patrick,

By the time you receive this I will be on my way to Los Angeles. Like you, I am following a thing that's bigger than me.

Clive needs extra attention to be given to his Latin. Laura has to have her anti-allergy shots every day this week. Simon, as you may or may not remember, is not yet old enough to go to school.

Amanda is fairly capable, as you know, and has kindly offered
to help Anne [the girlfriend] with the washing up. I'm told that
Anne has given up work, so I know you won't be burdened with
a babysitting problem, if only because you now have live-in help.
  Simon may be allergic to dog hair and so to Bruce [the dog].
But Dr Sanderson will let you know the test results as soon as he
has them.
  Much love,
  Sarah
P.S. In case you have forgotten, they are on holiday.

The real difference between *Woman versus Woman* and the other
books is that it is directed not only to the triumphs of new emotional
constructions but back towards the disarray of the old. In so doing,
it makes us more thoughtful about the politics of jealousy.

Not every author of the recent books about 'affairs' is female, but
most of them are, and the case studies are predominantly about
women. They are kept women, old women, opportunistic women,
career women, battered women, bored women, sexually deprived
women. There are married women and single women, mistresses of
long standing and proponents of the one-night affair. There are single
affairs, serial affairs and multiple affairs, occasionally of such number
and frequency of connection one wonders how the participants had
time to keep abreast of the outside world or open a can of cat food.

Most of these books are celebratory of the freedom and initiative
of the 'new woman'. They document the rise in the number of women
who take lovers and the decline in the average age when this occurs.
They herald the time when women will demand, and secure, the
same variety and satisfaction in intimacy and erotic adventure that
so many men have for so long regarded as their prerogative. In such
company *Woman versus Woman* is like a boiler suit at a garden party.
It points out that not every romantic initiative is for the better for all
concerned, and that condemning the jealous and telling them to
rejoice at the new world may be like asking people to remove their
hats for the benefit of a mugger with a club.

How do we make sense of these contrasts of direction? Each book
has a certain moral and ideological position. Each attracts a certain
type of informant. Each tries, as every author must, to keep a sort of
coherence. Some authors even display a sense of betrayal when one
of their informants makes a miscalculation, stepping from the shore
into some leaky sexual boat, for instance, or finding that a fast new
boat is a slow one after all. We are all, both as writers and people,

victims of a certain irreducible perversity in the world. I now want to tackle the problems of human relations, passions and ideology, and decision-making under conditions of uncertainty and emotional stress.

TRIANGLES

The jealousy we have been concerned with throughout much of this book is that between partners and intruders – the jealous triangle. Although these triangles are often complicated by additional relationships – extra lovers, lovers' spouses, offspring, even dogs – we will confine ourselves to the two standard orthodox triads. Let's call the partners 'husband' and 'wife', just to avoid having to keep saying 'male partner' and 'female partner', but remembering that they don't have to be married. And we will call the intruder the 'lover'. So the first triangle is the wife with a male lover, and the second, the husband with a female lover.

If we leave aside the possibility that at the end of it all there may simply be three older, wiser (or more bruised), independent participants, there are three possible outcomes for each triangle. In triangle 1 the wife and husband can separate and the wife retain her relation with her lover; the lover can leave (or be cast off or out) and the original partnership can continue in whatever state it finds itself; or the triangle can continue. There are two ways in which it can continue: as an open marriage (or free-love relationship); more often, as a clandestine relationship, whether quite concealed, denied or unacknowledged. Persisting secret relationships have been described by Wolfe as 'playing around' and by Denholtz as 'having it both ways'.

In support of each outcome there is an ideology – a mixture of belief, wish and moral attitude – and each ideology defines jealousy in a different way. To take one example, there is the very familiar ideology connected with the idea of open marriage, according to which multiple sexual attachments make for health and happiness, exclusivity equals possessiveness, honesty and disclosure are necessary, concealment is evil. This ideology conceives of jealousy as a hang-up or a hangover arising from 'bad conditioning'. It is the ideology of *romantic permissiveness*, an expression that emphasizes the supposed ease with which possessiveness and jealousy can be discounted or eradicated. Some supporters of sexual freedom and candour take jealousy more seriously, like the Keristas, who took elaborate pains to suppress and evade it.

The term 'ideology', strictly speaking, refers to the beliefs and attitudes of a group, so we can speak of the ideology of the Keristas or the Mormons, the French existentialists or the Russian nihilists. But any particular individual is likely to have a variety of often contradictory beliefs and attitudes: an ideology of secure family life, an ideology of 'personal growth and self-actualization' and a more ruthless ideology of dog-eat-dog and devil-take-the-hindmost. What we often do is to pick up the ideological weapon that best fits our current case.

Ideology isn't just a matter of moral attitudes – it even applies to matters of fact, of belief. So when one is in the arms of one's lover, the philosophy of love-is-all and this-is-my-chance-for-happiness may prevail. At the same time jealousy may be seen as unreasonable (a question of attitude) and actually unlikely (a question of belief). Sometimes these special-purpose beliefs are quite creative, and we can then speak of wishful thinking or rationalization rather than ideology (as in the cases of men who propose to their wives that their girl-friends move in with them).

The Social Texture of Jealousy

Not all ideologies are hostile to jealousy. Indeed, there is a sense in which society expects it. Wagner comments on the strange status of *non-jealousy*. Pinta even speaks of 'pathological tolerance'. According to Wagner, jealousy may be a crime, but if so, it is a 'natural' crime. Non-jealousy, that is, genuine indifference to real provocation, is also a transgression of a sort, but it is not a normal crime. One can apologize for being jealous, and one's apology performs the function of helping to restore normal relations. But it is difficult to apologize convincingly for not showing jealousy. Absence of jealousy, Wagner says, simply puts one outside the social order. It isn't a mistake, it is a defect. This is because jealousy is a signal that exclusive affiliation is socially valued. We condemn the robber and so assert the value of property. We act embarrassed at rudeness and so assert the importance of propriety. We are jealous of intrusion and so assert the value of exclusive love. Jealousy is in this sense the other side of sexual affirmation. (I would not argue that jealousy is *necessary* for sexual affirmation, any more than I would say that robbery was necessary for the existence of property.)

There has been continual pressure to condemn the jealous, and jealous persons themselves tend to conceal their jealousy. Do these facts suggest that our society abhors jealousy in all the settings in which it might appear? Obviously not. Review the course of heterosexual attachment through all its traditional stages in Western society: acquaintance, courtship, betrothal, marriage, honeymoon, early wedlock, child-bearing, child-caring (early parenthood), marital stress and break-up, separation, divorce and post-divorce. Now consider the possibility of intrusion into the relationship between a couple at each stage. Davis identified intrusions at the earliest stages as 'rivalry' and at the later stages as 'trespass'. In fact the situation has a finer texture. Jealousy is prescribed at some points, and proscribed at others; one could almost draw a graph of the rise and fall of its legitimacy. Imagine a husband or wife who did not resent sexual intrusions during their honeymoon, or during late pregnancy. One can expect not just jealousy but moral outrage. Yet is jealousy acceptable after a divorce? Could one always expect sympathy over one's jealousy in early courtship? Furthermore, society treats jealousy differently according to other measures of the participants: consider an old man with a young wife, or an old woman with a young lover. Neither can depend on sympathy if an intruder succeeds in alienating their partner's affections. To take it one step further, what if the old man were Picasso or Hemingway, or the old woman were Edith Piaf or Dietrich? Here status and dominance modulate age just as age modulates the impact of the marital situation.

The cuckold, the object of scorn and derision, is the person who, in forming an alliance, has stretched or defied the rules of propriety about sexual affiliation – the foolish, the old, the poseur, the braggart. When attachments are asymmetrical according to some calculus of sexual or social worth, jealousy is not to be taken seriously. So, although in general one could hardly say that modern Western society celebrates jealousy, it certainly doesn't extend a uniform blanket of intolerance towards it. The jealous may all be treated like pigs, but the squeals of some seem to sound more plaintive than others.

Failures of Empathy

People often activate an ideology that doesn't fit all sides of a case. They do this as a result of a sort of blindness to others' points of view. This failure of empathy is a chronic problem in human relations, but may become especially acute when we are emotionally involved or emotionally aroused. It is sometimes difficult, for example, to recognize that one's own feelings are not unique. Personally I think this is one of the charms of human existence, to feel that you are in untrodden territory when you are actually in tram-tracks, but it has its costs. Salamon had this to say about the 'kept women' she interviewed:

183

My female respondents generally presented their particular relationships as the exceptional case. They implied that their unique circumstances, whatever they may have been, warranted their behaviour. They were not particularly tolerant of others in the same position.

This applies precisely to jealousy. As I said in Chapter 1, people see jealousy as potent and irrepressible in themselves, but immature and easily modifiable in others.

I should add that perhaps the greatest barrier to realistic empathy is that between male and female. I read Eskapa's anecdote about the four children, the dog, the hamper and the note arriving by taxi at the husband's love-nest with great amusement, but not with the falling about and crows of triumphant delight with which some of my female colleagues greeted it. (I am sure, of course, they were right.) I think Lee's important insight that women are regularly subjected to fierce adverse prejudice is true. She labels them a very 'out' out-group. But I think there is a sense in which both men and women form in-groups, and members of each find it more difficult to recognize the predicaments of the other. As a result they can apply quite different ideological viewpoints to exactly the same emotional predicament.

This 'bifocal vision' is nowhere more blatant than in the moral outrage of the previously unfaithful. An idealist might suppose that the experience of having affairs oneself might instil some tolerance, but this isn't so. Time and again after a big scene with walk-outs, throw-outs and drama the unfaithful person discovers (often from their suddenly talkative friends) that all this jealousy, hurt and moral heat comes from a partner who earlier had their own unannounced affairs. The clockwork of jealousy does not seem to be housed in the same cabinet as the scales of justice. It is because of this independence of jealousy and justice that we get only limited relief from the pains of jealousy in thinking about our own exploits.

The Clandestine Affair

Perhaps the biggest revolution in recent writing about adult sexual relations has been the swing away from advocating 'open marriages' towards recognizing the potentialities of continuing secret affairs. This is the brand of permissiveness that many feminist writers now advocate, and it seems to represent an implicit acknowledgement of the power of jealousy. After all, the concealment and deceit that mark off the clandestine affair from the open marriage are hardly adopted for their own sakes, and the literature is full of dramatic accounts of what happened when partners disclosed their affairs, or of explanations of why they did not.

We have been over this ground in the chapter on pacts and arrangements, but it might be worthwhile to reiterate the point in the context of the secret affair. First a comment from Wolfe's book from one who didn't tell: 'My husband is the kind of man I can share everything with. All my thoughts and feelings, except of course about this.' What happens when people *do* tell? Adulterers' standard advice seems to be, 'Don't.' Strean reports:

Nearly three quarters of the married men and women interviewed by Morton Hunt (1969) who found out about their partner's affairs experienced negative emotions ranging from 'paralyzing fright to fulminating rage, including jealousy, humiliation and overwhelming depression. Their behaviour ran the gamut from total passivity to violent action . . . some men smashed furniture, beat their wives, and threatened to kill their wives' lovers; women sometimes did similar things, though more often they threw tantrums, wept hysterically, or threatened to kill themselves.'

According to Strean, mendacity and concealment have even been elevated to a Christian virtue under such circumstances:

Bishop Pike in *You and the New Morality* (1967) argues that when two lovers have decided to embark on an affair, they have a responsibility to lie about it for the sake of their mates. He contends that once a primary ethical decision has been made in a particular way, more often than not secondary ethical responsibilities are entailed.

It seems that in this respect the Bishop and Jean-Paul Sartre converged on the same conclusion! In an interview with Madeleine Chapsal, Pauline Reage commented on the same support for deceit coming from Catholic clergy in France:

There is the familiar advice of confessors who say to a tearful wife, 'No, you do not have the *right* to tell your husband that you have deceived him. You do not have the *right* to jeopardize your home. Consider your children's future. If you confess, you risk a separation and you cannot have that because of the children. You must hold your tongue.' 'But father, that is lying.' 'Then lie.'

TACTICS

The decision by a partner to conceal an affair and so 'have it both ways' is of course moral, but it is also tactical. If a partner makes a discovery, a person has a more difficult task if he or she wants to retain her relationship. In many cases the matter is simply out of control. A female informant said: 'My husband walked out to his car. He went to a friend of his for a talk. Then he went to our lawyer, and began arrangements for a divorce.' But sometimes there is time and scope for negotiation. Bouts of jealousy may be furious, but they need not necessarily last for ever. The partner has to assess whether he or she is interested in a rescue operation, if so there are at least two issues to be faced. First, how should one handle the likely demands for more detail from a partner, and second, how should one react to the anger and hostility that has been provoked by what is already known.

On the first issue the general opinion is in line with everything else about disclosure. No matter how seemingly calm the request is, don't get into a inquisitorial session. Proust in *Swann in Love* describes the process with excruciating accuracy: how the jealous person asks one question and gets an unpredicted or oblique reply that opens up new agonies of doubt, or even sudden exasperated candour that devastates them. It is difficult to see how it can help anyone. In dealing with anger and righteous indignation, we can easily pull from our ideological box the philosophy of permissiveness: the obscenity of sexual possessiveness, the immaturity of the jealous, etc. Even if you were to believe all this, you might be wise, again, to hold your tongue for the time being. Of course if recriminations come served with every meal, as well they may, then it makes sense to counter them; in fact at that point it is essential. But a discussion of the future seems more promising than a minute scrutiny of the past or a confrontation over ideologies.

I am preaching cool pragmatism, and it isn't everyone's style. There are domestic quietists who would keep brushing up the fallen plaster through an earthquake, and those who leap into a brawl with a minimum of premeditation. But at least we should recognize that jealousy is jealousy, not just a silly attitude, that it is sometimes to be expected, that it may well subside, and that a defence that mobilizes a questionable (or even reasonable) ideology to belittle the victim may be as counter-productive as it is unjust.

Let me quote a case from Salamon: a woman was attached to and dependent on a lawyer thirty years her senior. She was not married to him, but she had a son by him and the lawyer accepted financial responsibility for both her and the child. Subsequently her career took her (and the child) to another city, where her lover continued to help support her and visited her regularly. She then fell in love with a young man. When they decided to marry she flew back to break the news to her old lover. She had two things to report about his reaction: at first 'he came unhinged' but after the crisis subsided he handled the situation 'logically and reasonably' as he always had. You might wonder why the woman put herself through the ordeal, or why she showed patience with the 'unhinging'. But she stuck with her intention to remarry and parted on civilized terms from a person she had deeply cared for. If she had adopted the view that such jealousy betrayed a sick mind, she would doubtless have contaminated the years of good relations they had enjoyed with the rancour of their separation.

Practical Accounting

When the triangle breaks up and a partnership and a household looks like being dismantled, the situation is particularly vexed. As I said in an earlier chapter, when people form a family and household, both may invest a lot of effort, daily preoccupations and future plans in it. The ideology of romantic permissiveness either floats in a cloud above all this or regards it (with a certain justice) as a trap, but the elaborate physical paraphernalia and the heavy investment of care and effort in a family in Western society are social facts that will hardly evaporate in the heat of someone's falling in love. There is none the less something vaguely indecent nowadays about jealous partners, particularly men, referring to this 'investment' aspect of their personal agony, and I imagine that a lot of public talk (as opposed to private resentment) is shifted sideways, on to the issue of children, for example, if there are any. (Alternatively it may be shifted out of the house or apartment into the lawyer's office, where the jealous bitterness may translate itself into a toughly fought partition of the couple's physical resources among the man, the woman and the legal professionals.) Such activity mobilizes the ideology of duty and betrayal, and what the Chinese call 'bourgeois right' – the feeling that you should be able to take out from an enterprise at least what you think you put in.

These issues of justice and equity do not exhaust the factors at work, as we see in the phenomenon of 'spoiling'. A couple of examples will explain what I mean. Recently a man in a Sydney suburb hired a bulldozer and reduced to powdery rubble the house he was supposed to divide with his wife. Another man destroyed just *half* the house, presumably the half with 'hers' written on it. Although in Australia, where I am writing this book, much of the adversarial heat has been taken out of the property issue by more advanced family law legislation, it does not completely cool the passions. The nexus between love and giving, and between hating and taking away, means that one cannot say, 'Here ends jealousy and there begins practical resentment.'

When we turn to the second triangle, the male partner with a lover, there are some important changes in tone. The clandestine triangle could now be said to be the *man* 'having it both ways'. In 1975 Lake and Hills wrote:

There can be no doubt that the lives of a very large proportion of married men and women are being enriched and made more meaningful by secret sexual relationships.

They extend their congratulations to both sexes, but over the next ten years of writing, there seems to be less cheering for the man. There is not quite so much emphasis on what a healthy sexually liberating event it is for him. Even the 'open marriage' changes its flavour when the man initiates it. As I commented earlier, there is a whiff of retribution in the air when, for instance, a man suggests 'swinging' and then cracks up with jealousy.

There is no mystery about all this: the worm turns. The double standard is doubling back on the patriarch. The old, well-founded morality of the betrayed and bitter wife with the bewildered children is being re-written by the new moralists, and they are now well armed with data on battering, abuse and neglect. The feminist stance on woman as victim has its feet planted firmly in reality and the benign male philanderer is not on any of the banners.

The Women in the Triangle

There are two other changes to the scene. One is the altered picture of what was once the scarlet woman, the 'floozie', the home-wrecker; the other is the attitude towards the jealous or potentially jealous female partner. Let us begin with the partner.

One of the earliest documents I read dealing with jealousy in women was by Latymer. He wrote:

One of the most hideous, most selfish sentiments that too often accompanies love is jealousy . . . jealousy is the crime of cruelty. Hatred, not love, is its motive force. Moreover jealousy is the only villainy that produces its own pabulum [nutrition] . . . jealousy engenders temptation. It is not only the father of murder, but the father of adultery . . . Perfect love must always be the abnegation of jealousy.

What was that all about? It is a warning to spouses from a Christian moralist not to be jealous of their partner's infidelity because being jealous will render the partner unfaithful. It was the statement that first prompted me to wonder whether someone ought to give a bit of moral and political support to the jealous.

There is, of course, a grain of sense in Latymer. The great dilemma of the jealous is how to fight back without jeopardizing the relationship by making oneself more unattractive. This is the dilemma that Eskapa addresses herself to, and her answer (or rather the answer of the women she interviewed) is two-fold: do not simply let fly indiscriminately at your faithless partner, but don't let the energy of your reasonable hurt and indignation turn inwards or dissipate. Above all, don't be put off by the thought that you are just an irrational, jealous woman. If you want your relationship to survive, take action. If you are a woman, avoid what all the empirical research suggests is the more typical reaction – depression, self-blame, unexpressed anger. Exploit the one thing that women do better, turning to friends. If you need to conciliate, conciliate. If you are the victim of a stupid dream, shatter it. There is no fixed formula and no guarantee of success.

Perhaps it was not the original intention, but the lessons of *Woman versus Woman* are just as relevant to men who don't want to see their relationship with their partner, wife or children disintegrate without putting up a fight. People do some pretty drastic things when they are jealous, and the self-righteousness they feel may conceal from them how strategically useless as well as damaging they may be. I have never agreed with Hibbard (who follows the philosophy of Albert Ellis) that jealousy is 'self-induced misery' and that what a person does outside our presence doesn't matter. But I do agree that hurt and outrage ought not completely to displace a little constructive thought.

When we turn to the 'other woman', we find that the 'floozie' has gone. Richardson's 'new other woman' has taken her place. She has her supporters and advisers, some congratulating her, some warning. I have referred several times to Salamon's *The Kept Woman*, which is based on Ph.D. research about women given financial support by men to whom they are not married. Salamon by no means approves of the conduct of all of them, but observes that there are many stable and loving relationships between men and such 'kept' lovers. Let me concentrate on the question of exclusivity and jealousy in these relationships. Salamon's case studies reveal the existence of pacts of fidelity between the man and his female protégée, and show that the latter's jealousy may be more active towards outsiders than towards the patron's wife. This attitude may not develop immediately. Affairs commonly progress from acquaintanceship (in working situations, often a sense of camaraderie) to sudden sexual involvement, and then, in spite of all intentions, to attachment and loving intimacy. This process will normally be accompanied by a growing expectation of exclusivity and jealousy at transgressions.

Denholtz cites an interesting case in which a woman was prepared to tolerate what would seem quite unacceptable jealous conduct from her married lover. He was a university administrator or something similar (normally occupations are adjusted a little to protect anonymity) and was twenty years her senior. In spite of his age, his evident urbanity and his professional superiority, he was very jealous – systematically and deep-seatedly jealous. He had his girl-friend followed, confronted her with evidence of another lover and extracted promises of better behaviour. She, thirty-three years old, ambitious and energetic, hardly gives the impression of a pathological victim. Yet instead of severing relations, as one might expect, with this lover who had her shadowed, she agreed to maintain fidelity within their mutual infidelity. We can only assume that she did some reckoning, asking whether she could reasonably expect to find another interesting, satisfying and devoted lover who took a constructive interest in her career and who would share her not only with her husband and children, but with other lovers as well.

The younger unmarried woman in this situation is perhaps the one who will encounter the most difficulties. Richardson documents the predicament. She is likely to have trouble with everyone – her family, who see the relationship as one without a future, and very likely immoral; her colleagues, who may suspect she is exploitative; her feminist friends (if she has any), who regard her as both exploited and betraying the cause. Richardson does not condemn the 'new other woman' out of hand. She documents how, from a demographic point of view, there is a certain inevitability about the situation. It arises from the imbalance in numbers of unmarried males and females of a certain age. She sees the relationship in some ways as a sign of emancipation, but identifies some of the same dependency and lack of autonomy of women as in traditional relationships. It is the woman who so often waits to be beckoned by the married man.

How does the 'other woman' cope with sexual jealousy towards the wife? Denial is prominent. Salamon reports that about 60 per cent of the hundreds of women she interviewed were convinced that their married lovers had no sexual relations with their wives, in spite of sharing a bed with them, and some reported shock when they discovered by chance that they were wrong. When she works with her lover the woman may have plenty of opportunity to build a close cooperative relationship with the man and may recognize that she is much more privileged than the wife in this respect. But when they do *not* have this contact, when their lives are compartmentalized, to use Richardson's term, episodes of jealousy, loss and exclusion can occur, especially on birthdays, Christmas and so on. One female lover told Lake and Hills:

I wanted to be his official wife. I was very proud of him . . . it disturbed me that she could go anywhere with him and be accepted as though he was hers . . . When one loves a man one wishes to be seen with him officially. The little things matter – being accepted as family, being able to phone him at work, being with him at Christmas and birthdays. It mattered so little to her, and too much to me.

WHEN THINGS COME UNSTUCK

I now want to deal with the problem of 'lashing out'. Although I am going to discuss hatred and vindictiveness in women, women are far less physically aggressive than men, and far more often the victims. What I want to bring out is that when women *do* behave aggressively, either physically or symbolically, other women are often their targets.

When an extramarital relationship breaks down, the female lover may have little to lose by letting her jealousy and resentment show. But consider this vignette from Eskapa: 'Sheila mailed Henry's underpants to his wife.' It may be amusing to some in a macabre way, but it is vindictive. In my view, the spite was quite incorrectly addressed. Eskapa relates how one rejected woman took action against her ex-lover directly. During a final act of seduction she mutilated his body, but she didn't seem to feel the job was complete until she visited her 'rival' to ensure the wife knew how the damage had been inflicted. What about the growth of sisterly feeling? Eskapa again:

Many wives, hoping to appeal to the Other Woman for the sympathy they are sure she must feel, are shocked when they find hatred instead. The unexpectedness of the hatred leaves many wives bewildered, shocked and wounded to the point of derangement.

191

Can it be that when women cease blaming themselves, their next target is likely to be another woman? Men obviously don't have such problems and will regularly attack across the sexual frontier. In fact one might almost claim that the mystery of why some jealous people attack partners and some attack rivals can largely be resolved by saying that the target for aggression is most likely to be the woman: men attack their partners and women attack their rivals. I discovered that I had been anticipated in this view by Marcuse (1950), who recognized that the sort of love, or the style or motivation of the rival is not necessarily a key issue, but rather that women tend to be magnets for hostility whether partners or rivals. This does not hold as a blanket generalization. There are plenty of women who blame their husbands. One woman who was enraged by the discovery of her husband's regular infidelity while on interstate business trips said to me, 'Who *she* is doesn't matter to me. It's not her I blame.' It may be significant that she did not regard the woman as a serious threat to the relationship, and she did not fear losing her husband by confronting him.

There are two possible explanations of why women are so often targets. The first is the obvious fact that men have the power and you don't attack power. This concrete circumstance may be translated into and amplified by ideology. Although the enlightened avant garde may identify women, whether partners and lovers, as heroines and/or victims, many women in this predicament may still be in the grip of an ideology that makes them not just competitors but despised enemies.

The second explanation is relevant when it is the female partner who attacks the other woman. There is more to this than just power; in most cases the very point of the attack is to win back the man. Eskapa retells a story from James and Kedgley of a Viennese woman who plastered the city with poster-sized photographs of her rival, naked, with a caption proclaiming the woman's adultery. Why not the *man's* photograph? Eventually the wife ended up back in her husband's arms, and that would hardly have happened if she had chosen him as a full-frontal public pin-up.

Women may be quite defensive about the man, as Eskapa reports: 'Many wives whose husbands are involved with the Other Woman would rather not hear a word against their husbands, and frequently defend them from criticism.' The anonymity of the rival makes it easier to cast her in the role of the 'intrusive bitch'. That we are dealing here with personal dynamics and social constructions is obvious from the discrepancies between what research tells us are the typical histories of affairs between men and women, and the beliefs that jealous partners develop.

Eskapa's solution is to try to bring the two women together in the hope that they will come to recognize one another as human beings rather than as hostile stereotypes. Sometimes it happens successfully by accident, but a meeting that identifies them from the start as rivals is unlikely to be a success. Being friends and known to one another *in advance* is little help. Both the survey research and the case studies show that a friend who becomes a rival provokes the most powerful jealousy. Nor can we draw much comfort from the research in social psychology on prejudice. While it is true that contact between strangers can reduce prejudice if they meet as neutrals on neutral ground, contact between people in conflict seems more likely to inflame their antagonism.

We seem driven to the conclusion that the safest course is either abstinence from affairs (desirable, perhaps, but hardly a likely development, given the trends) or discretion (that is, concealment and very likely some degree of deceit). If the rivals can be got together, there is a (remote) chance of mutual understanding, and a distinct chance that one will leave the field, or be driven out. Whether a realignment can be achieved without undue rancour or vindictiveness does seem to depend on controlling the mobilization of ideologies, and this in turn requires that we be realistic about jealousy. Having an affair while denying the risk of jealousy is hardly sensible. It is like walking around on a dark night on a lawn littered with garden rakes. Sooner or later one will hit us in the face.

PASSION AND IDEOLOGY

The principal theme of this chapter has been that sexual triangles can either persist or disintegrate. People can move on or retreat. In the process we can expect passion. Passion has senders and receivers and both recruit ideologies. Reason says we should be watchful of the alliance between passion and ideology and try to see through the smoke of fury in order to consider long-term interests – our own and hopefully those of the other parties involved. Playing out the conflict in a social vacuum is a poor way to proceed, and the social vacuum itself can be created by our own guilt and reticence, or by blame or trivialization by others.

It may not be strictly correct from a technical point of view to have been talking about the various systems of beliefs and values as separate ideologies, because they often fit together as complementary ideas within a society's system of thought: family duty versus pleasure, commitment versus freedom, etc. But rather than complicating the discussion with academic reservations, I have simply stretched the term 'ideology' a little. The main thing I want to avoid is making it seem that the justifications people give for what they are thinking and doing about jealousy are rationalizations, that is, their personal, unique psychological interventions. In fact they are part of our cultural system. They are in our literature, in our legal system, in the media, in sermons, in advice to the love-lorn. We talk and gossip and argue about them. It is largely from these sources that they come into our heads ready to be drawn upon.

And as I said at the end of the chapter on the anthropology of jealousy, these ideological systems – these beliefs and values of society – did not themselves originate in a few great minds. Modest minds and great minds grow in the soil of history and culture. In talking about possible changes in social attitudes to the emotions, Lillian Rubin comments: 'to think about mass psychological change without changes to the social institutions within which we live and grow is to give in to fantasy'. We are not talking about bloody revolution, but the shape of the practical circumstances of life. The books that are being written now about 'affairs', and the things they say about jealousy, for example, are related to such issues as these: changes in the levels of women's employment, especially perhaps for the middle-class women who write the books, who are interviewed and who read them; changes in overall affluence that result in single people, even those with children, being able to contemplate independent lives; and contraception.

What complicates the situation is that these changes, though massive, are uneven and incomplete, and the ideological changes often outrun the practical realities. The practical realities include the fact that few women with dependent children can easily become free souls or be left without penalty by free-soul husbands. That is why we get a backlash, like Eskapa's trenchant *Woman versus Woman*. Furthermore, all the economic and ideological changes in the world will not abolish the reality of love and attachment, of emotional and practical investment. That is why we get the refreshing candour of Sally Vincent: '. . . *my* man at *my* table eating *my* egg . . .' and the marvellous eloquent debunking by Karen Durbin: '. . . the sweetly promiscuous hippie chicks in their granny dresses . . .'

From all these sources emerges a strange conflict of views on jealousy. On the one hand there is the happening itself, or rather the happenings, for it almost always comes as a cluster of reactions. These are in my view partly biological, partly due to personal history, but at the same time heavily cultural in what provokes them and how they manifest themselves. On the other hand there is the way we *think* about jealousy. This is a product of how in reality we experience it (through our 'bifocals', to be sure). But it is also a product of the complex and sometimes contradictory social beliefs about jealousy. When it occurs in a young man who picks up an attractive but mobile country girl as an ornament to his ego, we think one thing. When it appears in a woman whose lover has used her bedroom to entertain the opposition, we think another. It may involve worries about an attractive partner's breezier social life, or terror of a replay of one's mother's drunken infidelity to one's father. It may manifest itself as a catastrophe in the life of a mother of three small children stuck in a suburban apartment, or an 'unhinging' in a 50-year-old patron of a 'kept woman'.

Each of these situations differs from the others, and each of us will see them somewhat differently. It might seem from this that jealousy is a floating world, a tissue of relativity and point of view. But as all of us know who have experienced jealousy or have seen it in others, it may be variable and contingent, but it is also real, unpleasant and sometimes devastating as a personal event. Furthermore, it can leave lasting traces of its presence in the tentativeness and fright that people exhibit when they feel themselves drifting into emotional intimacy and dependency. This capacity both to bite and to bruise is responsible for the broader impact of jealousy. Jealousy goes beyond a personal experience. It is a potent social force, like a sleeping serpent whose capacity to uncoil and sting affects all our emotional plans and ultimately shapes the whole geography of our social arrangements as well as our affectionate voyaging.

References

—————————— Q ——————————

CHAPTER ONE: MY LOVER'S LOVER IS MY ENEMY

Bringle, R. G. and Buunk, B. (1985) Jealousy and social behavior, Ch. 10 in Shaver, P. (ed.) *Self, Situations, and Social Behavior. Review of Personality and Social Psychology*. Beverly Hills, Calif.: Sage Publications, pp.241–64.

Davis, K. (1936) Jealousy and sexual property. *Social Forces*, **14**, 395–405.

Dawkins, R. (1976) *The Selfish Gene*. Oxford: Oxford University Press.

Dunn, J. (1985) *Sisters and Brothers*. Cambridge, Mass.: Harvard University Press.

Dunn, J. and Kendrick, C. (1982) *Siblings: Love, Envy and Understanding*. London: Grant McIntyre.

Durbin, K. (1973) On sexual jealousy. *The Village Voice*, October 18. Reprinted in Clanton, G. and Smith, L. G. (1977) *Jealousy*. Englewood Cliffs, NJ: Prentice-Hall, pp.36–45.

Foster, G. M. (1972) The anatomy of envy: a study of symbolic behaviour. *Current Anthropology*, **13**, 165–202.

Foster, S. (1927) A study of the personality make-up and social setting of fifty jealous children. *Mental Hygiene*, **11**, 53–77.

Gazzaniga, M. S. and Le Doux, J. E. (1978) *The Integrated Mind*. New York: Plenum.

Gazzaniga, M. S. (1985) *The Social Brain: Discovering the Networks of the Mind*. New York: Basic Books.

Gordon, H. W. and Sperry, R. W. (1969) Lateralization of olfactory perception in the surgically separated hemispheres of man. *Neuropsychologia*, **7**, 111–20.

Hoyland, J. (1973) Jealousy: the injured lover's private hell, the tyrant of the mind. *The Living Daylights*, pp. 14–22 (reprinted from *Spare Rib*, London).

Huxley, A. (1955) *Point Counter Point*. Harmondsworth, Middlesex: Penguin Books.

Laclos C. de (1782) *Les Liaisons Dangereuses*. Trans. Adlington, R. (1957) *Dangerous Acquaintances*. Norfolk, Conn.: New Horizons Books.

Linton, R. (1939) Marquesan culture. Ch. 5 in Kardiner, A. (ed.) *The Individual and His Society*. New York: Columbia University Press.

Milton, J. (1971) *An analysis of embarrassment*. M.Sc. Thesis, University of New South Wales, Australia.

Mitford, N. (1957) *Voltaire in Love*. Harmondsworth, Middlesex: Penguin Books.

Peele, S. and Brodsky, A. (1975) *Love and Addiction*. New York: Taplinger Publishing Company.

Schachter, S. (1964) The interaction of cognitive and emotional determinants of emotional states. In Leiderman, P. H. and Shapiro, D. (eds.) *Psychobiological Approaches to Social Behavior*. Stanford, Calif.: Stanford University Press.

Schoeck, H. (1969) *Envy: A Theory of Social Behaviour* (trans. Glery, M. and Ross, B.). New York: Harcourt, Brace and World.

Seeman, M. V. (1979) Pathological jealousy. *Psychiatry*, **42**, 351–61.

Sokoloff, B. (1948) *Jealousy: A Psychological Study*. London: Carroll and Nicholson.

Tellenbach, H. (1974) On the nature of jealousy. *Journal of Phenomenological Psychology*, **4**, 461–8.

Vincent, S. (1970) Sexual jealousy. *Nova Magazine*, 47–9.

Wagner, J. (1976) Jealousy, extended intimacies and sexual affirmation. *ETC, Journal of General Semantics*, **33**, 269–88.

Weitman, S. R. (1973) Intimacies: notes toward a theory of social inclusion and exclusion. In Birenbaum, A. and Segarin, E. (eds.) *People in Places: The Sociology of the Familiar*. New York: Praeger.

Whitehurst, R. N. (1975) Violently jealous husbands. Ch. 7 in Gordon, S. (ed.) *Sexuality and Contemporary Marriage*. New York: Halstead Press, pp. 75–85.

Wisdom, J. O. (1976) Jealousy in a twelve-month-old boy. *International Journal of Psycho-analysis*, **3**, 365–8.

CHAPTER TWO: LOVE AND JEALOUS REACTIONS

Ainsworth, M. D. S., Blehar, M. C., Waters, E. and Wall, S. (1978) *Patterns of Attachment: A Psychological Study of the Strange Situation*. Hillsdale, NJ: Erlbaum.

Bailey, F. G. (1983) *The Tactical Uses of Passion: An Essay on Power, Reason and Reality*. Ithaca, NY: Cornell University Press.

Beauvoir, S. de (1972) *The Second Sex*. Harmondsworth, Middlesex: Penguin Books.

Berscheid, E. and Fei, J. (1977) Romantic love and sexual jealousy. Ch. 9 in Clanton, G. and Smith, L. G. (eds.) *Jealousy*. Englewood Cliffs, NJ: Prentice-Hall, pp. 101–9.

Bowen, E. (1936) *The House in Paris*. New York: Vintage Books.

Bringle, R. G. and Buunk, B. (1985) Jealousy and social behavior, Ch. 10 in Shaver, P. (ed.) *Self, Situations, and Social Behavior. Review of Personality and Social Psychology*. Beverly Hills, Calif.: Sage Publications, pp.241–64.

Bryson, J. B. (1976) The nature of sexual jealousy: an exploratory study. Paper presented at the meeting of the American Psychological Association, Washington, DC.

Burns, A. (1984) Perceived causes of marriage breakdown and conditions of life. *Journal of Marriage and the Family*, **46**, 551–62.

Burns, A. (1986) Why do women continue to marry? Ch. 13 in Grieve, N. and Burns, A. (eds.) *Australian Women: New Feminist Perspectives*. Melbourne: Oxford University Press, pp. 210–32.

Clanton, G. and Smith, L. G. (eds.) (1977) *Jealousy*. Englewood Cliffs, NJ: Prentice-Hall.

Darroch, S. J. (1976) *Ottoline: The Life of Lady Ottoline Morrell*. London: Chatto and Windus.

Eibl-Eiblesfeldt, I. (1970) *Ethology: The Biology of Behavior*. New York: Holt, Rinehart and Winston.

Ernst, K. J. (1972) *Situational aspects of jealousy*. MA (Qual.) Thesis, University of New South Wales, Australia.

Freud, E. L. (1960) *Letters of Sigmund Freud*. New York: Basic Books.

Freud, S. (1922) Certain neurotic mechanisms in jealousy, paranoia and homosexuality. In Freud, S. *Collected Papers*, Vol. 2, pp. 232–43. London: Hogarth Press.

Freud, S. (1930) *Group Psychology and the Analysis of the Ego*. London: Hogarth Press and the Institute of Psycho-analysis.

Fromm, E. (1956) *The Art of Loving*. New York: Harper and Row.

Hatfield, E., Traupmann, J. and Walster, G. W. (1979) Equity and extramarital sex. In Cook, M. and Wilson, G. (eds.) *Love and Attraction*. Oxford: Pergamon, pp. 323–34.

Hendrick, C. and Hendrick, S. (1986) A theory and method of love. *Journal of Personality and Social Psychology*, **50**, 392–402.

Hoyland, J. (1973) Jealousy: the injured lover's private hell, the tyrant of the mind. *The Living Daylights*, pp. 14–22 (reprinted from *Spare Rib*, London).

Jones, E. (1948) *Papers on Psychoanalysis*, London: Maresfield Reprints.

Kierkegaard, S. (1922) *Stadien auf dem Lobensweg*. Jena: E. Diederichte. Quoted in Tellenbach, H. (1974) On the nature of jealousy. *Journal of Phenomenological Psychology*, **4**, 461–8.

Lee, J. A. (1977) A typology of styles of loving. *Personality and Social Psychology Bulletin*, **3**, 173–82.

Maslow, A. H. (1970) *Motivation and Personality*. New York: Harper and Row.

Mauss, M. (1954) *The Gift: Forms and Functions of Exchange in Archaic Societies* (trans. E. N. Gunnison). Glencoe, Ill.: Free Press.

Mead, M. (1931) Jealousy: primitive and civilized. Ch. 3 in Schmalhausen, S. D. and Calverton, V. F. *Women's Coming of Age*. New York: Horace Liveright, pp. 35–48.

Morris, V. (1982) Helping lesbian couples cope with jealousy. *Women and Therapy*, **1**, 27–34.

Pines, A. and Aronson, E. (1983) Antecedents, correlates and consequences of sexual jealousy. *Journal of Personality*, 51, 108–36.

Pitt-Rivers, J. (1973) The kith and the kin. Ch. 7 in Goody, J. (ed.) *The Character of Kinship*. Cambridge: Cambridge University Press, pp. 89–105.

Reich, I. O. (1970) *Wilhelm Reich: A Personal Biography*. New York: Avon.

Reik, T. (1957) *Of Love and Lust*. New York: Farrar, Straus and Cudahay.

Robbe-Grillet, A. (1965) *Jealousy*. New York: Grove Press.

Rubin, Z. (1970) Measurement of romantic love. *Journal of Personality and Social Psychology*, **16**, 265–73.

Russell, B. (1929) *Marriage and Morals*. London: Allen and Unwin.

Shaver, P., Hazan, C. and Bradshaw, D. (1987) Infant-caretaker attachment and adult romantic love: similarities and differences, continuities and discontinuities. In Sternberg, R. and Barnes, M. (eds.) *Anatomy of Love*. New Haven, Conn.: Yale University Press.

Shettel-Neuber, J., Bryson, J. B. and Young, L. E. (1978) Physical attractiveness of the 'other person' and jealousy. *Personality and Social Psychology Bulletin*, **4**, 612–15.

Sternberg, R. J. (1986) A triangular theory of love. *Psychological Review*, **93**, 119–35.

Swenson, C. M. (1972) The behavior of love. Ch. 8 in Otto, M. A. (ed.) *Love Today*. New York: Delta, pp. 86–101.

Tennov, D. (1979) *Love and Limerence*. New York: Stein and Day.

Tolstoy, L. N. (1968) *The Kreutzer Sonata*. In Tolstoy, L. N., *The Complete Works*, Vol. 18. New York: AMS Press.

Tolstoy, S. A. (1929) *The Countess Tolstoy's Later Diary, 1891–7*. London: Gollancz.

van Sommers, P. (1986) Male and female body and brain: the biology of sexual differentiation. Ch. 5 in Grieve, N. and Burns, A. (eds.) *Australian Women: New Feminist Perspectives*. Melbourne: Oxford University Press, pp. 70–89.

Walster, E. and Walster, G. W. (1978) *A New Look at Love*. Reading, Mass.: Addison-Wesley.

Weitman, S. R. (1973) Intimacies: notes toward a theory of social inclusion and exclusion. In Birenbaum, A. and Segarin, E. (eds.) *People in Places: The Sociology of the Familiar*. New York: Praeger.

White, G. L. (1980) Inducing jealousy: a power perspective. *Personality and Social Psychology Bulletin*, **6**, 222–7.

Zajonc, R. B. (1980) Feeling and thinking: preferences need no inferences. *American Psychologist*, **35**, 151–75.

CHAPTER THREE: PACTS AND ARRANGEMENTS

Armstrong, J. (1976) *The Novel of Adultery*. London: Macmillan.

Bartell, G. D. (1970) Group sex among mid-Americans. *Journal of Sex Research*, **6**, 113–30.

Beauvoir, S. de (1943) *L'Invitée*. Trans. Moyse, Y. and Senhouse, R. (1984) *She Came to Stay*. London: Fontana.

Beauvoir, S. de (1962) *The Prime of Life*. London: André Deutsch and Weidenfeld and Nicolson.

Beauvoir, S. de (1964) *Force of Circumstance*. New York: G. P. Putnam.

Bok, S. (1979) *Lying: Moral Choice in Public and Private Life*. New York: Vintage Books.

Carden, M. L. (1971) *Oneida, Utopian Community to Modern Corporation*. New York: Harper Torchbooks.

Edwards, A. (1981) *Sonya: The Life of Countess Tolstoy*. New York: Simon and Schuster.

Evans, M. (1985) *Simone de Beauvoir: A Feminist Mandarin*. London: Tavistock.

Freeman, L. and Strean, H. S. (1981) *Freud and Women*. New York: Frederick Ungar.

Gilmartin, B. G. (1977) Jealousy among the swingers. In Clanton, G. and Smith, L. G. (eds.) *Jealousy*. Englewood Cliffs, NJ: Prentice-Hall, pp. 152–8.

Kinsey, A., Pomeroy, W. and Martin, C. (1948) *Sexual Behavior in the Human Male*. Philadelphia: Saunders.

Laclos, C. de (1782) *Les Liaisons Dangereuses*. Trans. Aldington, R. (1957) *Dangerous Acquaintances*. Norfolk, Conn.: New Horizons Books.

Linton, R. (1939) Marquesan culture. Ch. 5 in Kardiner, A. (ed.) *The Individual and His Society*. New York: Columbia University Press.

Madsen, A. (1977) *Hearts and Minds: The Common Journey of Simone de Beauvoir and J. P. Sartre*, New York: Morrow.

Murdoch, G. P. (1949) *Social Structure*. New York: Free Press.

Nietzsche, F. (1932) *Thus Spake Zarathustra. A Book for All and None* (trans. T. Common). London: Allen and Unwin.

Peters, H. F. (1962) *My Sister, My Spouse: A Biography of Lou Andreas-Salomé*. New York: Norton.

Pines, A. and Aronson, E. (1981) Polyfidelity: an alternative lifestyle without jealousy. *Alternative Lifestyles*, 4, 373–92.

Smith, J. R. and Smith, L. G. (1970) Co-marital sex and the sexual freedom movement. *Journal of Sex Research*, 6, 131–42.

Whitmarsh, A. (1981) *Simone de Beauvoir and the Limits of Commitment*. Cambridge: Cambridge University Press.

Young, K. (1954) *Isn't One Wife Enough?* Westport, Conn.: Greenwood Press.

CHAPTER FOUR: JEALOUS INSTINCTS?

Chimbos, P. D. (1978) *Marital Violence: A Study of Interspouse Homicide*. San Francisco: R and E Research Associates. Quoted in Daly, Wilson and Weghorst (1982).

Daly, M., Wilson, M. and Weghorst, S. J. (1982) Male sexual jealousy. *Ethology and Sociobiology*, 3, 1–27.

De Vore, I. and Morris, S. (1977) The new science of genetic self-interest. *Psychology Today*, 11, 42–51.

Dickemann, M. (1979) The ecology of mating systems in hypergynous dowry societies. *Social Science Information*, 18, 163–95.

Dickemann, M. (1981) Paternal confidence and dowry competition: a biocultural analysis of Purdah. Ch. 25 in Alexander, R. D. and Tinkle, D. W. (eds.) *Natural Selection and Social Behavior: Recent Research and New Theory*, New York: Chiron Press, pp. 417–38.

Ghiglieri, M. P. (1984) *The Chimpanzees of Kibale Forest: A Field Study of Ecology and Social Structure*. New York: Columbia University Press.

Hosken, F. P. (1982) *The Hosken Report: Genital and Sexual Mutilation of Females*, revised edition. Lexington, Md.: Women's International Network News.

McDougall, W. (1910) *An Introduction to Social Psychology*. London: Methuen.

Morris, S. (1977) A man in the middle. *Psychology Today*, **11**, 44–5.

CHAPTER FIVE: THE ANTHROPOLOGY OF JEALOUSY

Clark, A. and van Sommers, P. (1961) Contradictory demands in family relations and adjustment to school and home. *Human Relations*, **14**, 97–112.

Dickemann, M. (1981) Paternal confidence and dowry competition: a biocultural analysis of Purdah. Ch. 25 in Alexander, R. D. and Tinkle, D. W. (eds.) *Natural Selection and Social Behavior: Recent Research and New Theory*. New York: Chiron Press, pp. 417–38.

Fox, R. (1967) *Kinship and Marriage*. Harmondsworth, Middlesex: Penguin Books.

Fox, R. (1975) Primate kin and human kinship. In Fox, R. (ed.) *Biosocial Anthropology*. New York: Wiley, pp. 9–35.

Gough, K. (1961) Nayar: central Kerala. Ch. 6 in Schneider, D. M. and Gough, K. (eds.) *Matrilineal Kinship*. Berkeley: University of California Press, pp. 298–384.

Harris, M. (1980) *Cultural Materialism: The Struggle for a Science of Culture*. New York: Vintage Books.

Hiatt, L. R. (1980) Polyandry in Sri Lanka: a test case for parental investment theory. *Man*, **15**, 583–602.

Hupka, R. B. (1981) Cultural determinants of jealousy. *Alternative Lifestyles*, **4**, 310–56.

Levinger, G. (1966) Sources of marital dissatisfaction among applicants for divorce. *American Journal of Orthopsychiatry*, **36**, 803–7.

Lévi-Strauss, C. (1969) *The Elementary Structures of Kinship*. London: Eyre and Spottiswoode.

Macintyre, M. (1986) Female autonomy in a matrilineal society. Ch. 15 in Grieve, N. and Burns, A. *Australian Women: New Feminist Perspectives*. Melbourne: Oxford University Press, pp. 248–56.

Meggitt, M. J. (1965) *The Lineage System of the Mae-Enga of New Guinea*. Edinburgh: Oliver and Boyd.

Murdoch, G. P. (1949) *Social Structure*. New York: Free Press.

Wolf, E. R. (1982) *Europe and the People Without History*. Berkeley: University of California Press.

CHAPTER SIX: SOCIETIES OF HONOUR AND SHAME

Abou-Zeid, A. (1965) Honour and shame amongst the Bedouins of Egypt. In Peristiany, *Honour and Shame*, pp. 243–60.

Antoun, R. T. (1968) On the modesty of women in Arab muslim villages. *American Anthropologist*, **70**, 671–97.

Bourdieu, P. (1965) The sentiment of honour in Kabyle society. In Peristiany, *Honour and Shame*, pp. 190–242.

Campbell, J. K. (1964) *Honour, Family and Patronage*. Oxford: Clarendon Press.

Campbell, J. K. (1965) Honour and the devil. In Peristiany, *Honour and Shame*, pp. 171–90.

Chiva, I. (1977) Social organization, traditional economy and customary law in Corsica: outline of a plan of analysis. In Pitt-Rivers, J. (ed.) *Mediterranean Countrymen*, Westport, Conn.: Greenwood Press, pp. 97–112.

Cutileiro, J. (1971) *A Portuguese Rural Society*. Oxford: Clarendon Press.

Davis, J. (1969) Honour and politics in Pisticci. *Proceedings of the Royal Anthropological Institute*, 69–81.

Davis, J. (1977) *People of the Mediterranean: An Essay in Comparative Social Anthropology*. London: Routledge and Kegan Paul.

Denich, B. S. (1974) Sex and power in the Balkans. In Rosaldo, M. Z. and Lamphere, L. (eds.) *Women, Culture and Society*. Stanford, Calif.: Stanford University Press, pp. 241–61.

Elias, N. (1978) *The Civilizing Process: The History of Manners*. Oxford: Blackwell.

Elwin, V. (1943) *Maria Murder and Suicide*. London: Oxford University Press.

Gilsenan, M. (1976). Lying, honor and contradiction. In Kapferer, B. (ed.) *Transactions and Meaning*. Philadelphia: Institute for the Study of Human Issues, pp. 191–219.

Meeker, M. E. (1976) Meaning and society in the Near East: examples from the Black Sea and the Levantine Arabs (I and II). *International Journal of Middle Eastern Studies*, **7**, 243–70, 383–422.

Meeker, M. E. (1979) *Literature and Violence in North Arabia*. New York: Cambridge University Press.

Peristiany, J. G. (ed.) (1965) *Honour and Shame: The Values of Mediterranean Society*. London: Weidenfeld and Nicolson.

Peristiany, J. G. (1965) Honour and shame in a Cypriot Highland village. In Peristiany, *Honour and Shame*, pp. 171–190.

Pitt-Rivers, J. (1965) Honour and social status. In Peristiany, *Honour and Shame*, pp. 19–78.

Quaife, G. R. (1979) *Wanton Wenches and Wayward Wives: Peasants and Illicit Sex in Early Seventeenth-century England*. London: Croom Helm.

Schneider, J. (1971) Of vigilance and virgins: honor, shame and access to resources in Mediterranean societies. *Ethnology*, **10**, 1–24.

Schneider, J. and Schneider, P. (1976) *Culture and Political Economy in Western Sicily*. New York: Academic Press.

Segalen, M. (1983) *Love and Power in the Peasant Family*. Oxford: Blackwell.

Silverman, S. F. (1975) The life crisis as a clue to social function: the case of Italy. In Reiter, R. R. (ed.) *Towards an Anthropology of Women*. New York: Monthly Review Press, pp. 309–21.

Silverman, S. F. (1975) *Three Bells of Civilization*. New York: Columbia University Press.

Wollstonecraft, M. (1792) *A Vindication of the Rights of Woman*. London.

CHAPTER SEVEN: FREUD AND JEALOUSY

Brenner, S., quoted in Lewin, R. (1984).

Carden, M. L. (1971) *Oneida, Utopian Community to Modern Corporation*. New York: Harper Torchbooks.

Docherty, J. P. and Ellis, J. (1976) A new concept and finding in morbid jealousy. *American Journal of Psychiatry*, **133**, 679–83.

Fenichel, O. (1931) Specific forms of the Oedipus complex. Ch. 22 in *The Collected Papers of Otto Fenichel*. New York: Norton.

Freud, S. (1911) Psycho-analytic notes upon an autobiographical account of a case of paranoia (dementia paranoides). In Freud, S. (1948) *Collected Papers*, Vol. 3, pp. 387–470. London: Hogarth Press.

Freud, S. (1915) A case of paranoia running counter to psychoanalytic theory of the disease. In Freud, S. (1948) *Collected Papers*, Vol. 2, pp. 150–61. London: Hogarth Press.

Freud, S. (1922) Certain neurotic mechanisms in jealousy, paranoia and homosexuality. In Freud, S. (1948) *Collected Papers*, Vol. 2, pp. 232–43. London: Hogarth Press.

Hughes, H. S. (1979) *Consciousness and Society: The Reorientation of European Social Thought 1890–1930*. Brighton, Sussex: Harvester.

Jacob, F. (1977) Evolution and tinkering. *Science*, **196**, 1,161–6.

Jones, E. (1930) Jealousy. Ch. 16 in Jones, E. (1948) *Papers on Psychoanalysis*, 5th edition. London: Maresfield Reprints, pp. 325–40.

Jones, E. (1953–7) *The Life and Work of Sigmund Freud*. New York: Basic Books.

Klaf, F. S. (1961) Female homosexuality and paranoid schizophrenia. *Archives of General Psychiatry*, **4**, 84–6.

Klein, H. R. and Horwitz, W. A. (1949) Psychosexual factors in paranoid phenomena. *American Journal of Psychiatry*, **105**, 697–701.

Lamare, N. (1967) *La Jalousie Passionnelle*. Paris: Buchet/Chastel.

Lewin, R. (1984) Why is development so illogical? *Science*, **224**, 1,327–9.

Macalpine, I. and Hunter, R. A. (1953) The Schreber case. *Psychoanalytic Quarterly*, **22**, 328–71.

Macalpine, I. and Hunter, R. A. (1955) *Daniel Paul Schreber: Memoirs of my Nervous Disease*. London: Dawson.

Mairet, A. (1908) *La Jalousie: Étude Psychophysiologique, Clinique et Medicolégale*. Montpellier: Coulet.

Malan, D. H. (1979) *Individual Psychotherapy and the Science of Psychodynamics*. London: Butterworths.

Modlin, H. C. (1963) Psychodynamics and management of paranoid states in women. *Archives of General Psychiatry*, **8**, 263–8.

Money, J. and Ehrhardt, A. A. (1972) *Man and Woman, Boy and Girl*. Baltimore, MD: Johns Hopkins University Press.

Niederland, W. G. (1974) *The Schreber Case: Psychoanalytic Profile of a Paranoid Personality*. New York: Quadrangle, New York Times Book Co.

Oversey, L. (1955) Pseudo-homosexuality, the paranoid mechanism and paranoia. *Psychiatry*, **18**, 163–73.

Szasz, T. (1977) *Karl Kraus and the Soul Doctors*. London: Routledge and Kegan Paul.

CHAPTER EIGHT: MORBID OR PATHOLOGICAL JEALOUSY

Achte, K. A., Hillborn, E. and Aalberg, V. (1967) *Report from the Rehabilitation Institute for Brain Injured Veterans in Finland*, Vol. 1. Helsinki: Kirjapaino Yrjö Levikoski, Ky.

Bleuler, E. (1950) *Dementia Praecox or the Group of Schizophrenias*. New York: International Universities Press.

Carr, A. T. (1974) Compulsive neurosis – a review of the literature. *Psychological Bulletin*, **81**, 311–17.

Cervantes, M. de (1894) The jealous Estramaduran. In *The Exemplary Novels of Miguel de Cervantes*. London: Bell.

Clouston, T. S. (1898) *Clinical Lectures on Mental Disease*, 5th edition. London: Churchill.

Cobb, J. P. and Marks, I. M. (1979) Morbid jealousy featuring as obsessive compulsive neurosis: treatment by behavioural psychotherapy. *British Journal of Psychiatry*, **134**, 301–5.

Docherty, J. P. and Ellis, J. (1976) A new concept and finding in morbid jealousy. *American Journal of Psychiatry*, **133**, 679–83.

Enoch, M. D. (1980) Sexual jealousy. *British Journal of Sexual Medicine*, **7**, 30–4.

Gelles, R. J. (1974) *The Violent Home*. Beverly Hills, Calif.: Sage. Quoted in Buunk, B. (1986) Husband's jealousy. Ch. 5 in Lewis, R. A. and Salt, R. E. (eds.) *Men in Families*. Beverly Hills: Sage, pp. 87–114.

Herceg, N. (1976) Successful use of thiothixene in two cases of pathological jealousy. *Medical Journal of Australia*, **1**, 569–70.

Hoaken, P. C. (1976) Jealousy as a symptom of psychiatric disorder. *Australian and New Zealand Journal of Psychiatry*. **10**, 47–51.

Jaspers, K. (1910) Eifersuchtswahn. Ein Beitrag zur Frage: 'Entwicklung einer Personlichkeit' oder 'Prozess'? *Z. ges. Neurol. Psychiat.* **1**, 567–637. Quoted in Mooney, H. B. (1965) Pathological jealousy and psychochemotherapy. *British Journal of Psychiatry*, **111**, 1,023–42.

Kala, A. K. and Kala, R. (1981) Psychotic jealousy: a phenomenological study. *Indian Journal of Psychiatry*, **23**, 237–41.

Krafft-Ebing, R. (1891) Über Eifersuchtswahn beim Manne. *Jahrb. f. Psychiatrie*, **10**, 221. Quoted in Shepherd, M. (1961).

Langfeldt, G. (1963) The erotic jealousy syndrome. *Journal of Neuropsychiatry*, **3**, 317–21.

Mairet, A. (1908) *La Jalousie: Etude Psychophysiologique, Clinique et Medicolégale*. Montpellier; Coulet.

Modlin, H. C. (1963) Psychodynamics and management of paranoid states in women. *Archives of General Psychiatry*, **8**, 263–8.

Mooney, H. B. (1965) Pathological jealousy and psychochemotherapy. *British Journal of Psychiatry*, **111**, 1,023–42.

Mowat, R. R. (1966) *Morbid Jealousy and Murder*. London: Tavistock.

Revitch, E. (1960) Diagnosis and disposition of paranoid marital partner. *Diseases of the Nervous System*, **21** (Feb. suppl.), 117–18.

Seeman, M. V. (1979) Pathological jealousy. *Psychiatry*, **42**, 351–61.

Shepherd, M. (1961) Morbid jealousy: some clinical and social aspects of a psychiatric syndrome. *Journal of Mental Science*, **107**, 687–753.

Sokoloff, B. (1948) *Jealousy: A Psychological Study*. London: Carroll and Nicholson.

Tennant, T. G. (1975) The dangerous offender. *Contemporary Psychiatry*. Special Publication No. 9.

Todd, J. and Dewhurst, K. (1955) The Othello syndrome. *Journal of Nervous and Mental Diseases*, **122**, 367–76.

Turbott, J. (1981) Morbid jealousy: an unusual presentation with the reciprocal appearance of psychopathology in either spouse. *Australian and New Zealand Journal of Psychiatry*, **15**, 164–7.

Vauhkonen, K. (1968) On the pathogenesis of morbid jealousy. *Acta Psychiatrica Scandinavica*, Supplement 202. Copenhagen: Munksgaard.

Virkkunen, M. (1974) Alcohol as a factor precipitating aggression and conflict behaviour leading to homicide. *British Journal of Addiction*, **69**, 149–54.

CHAPTER NINE: A MINI-CHAPTER ON THERAPY

Beltz, S. E. (1969) Five-year effects of altered marital contracts (a behavioral analysis of couples). In Neubeck, G. (ed.) *Extramarital Relations*. Englewood Cliffs, NJ: Prentice-Hall, pp. 162–89.

Blood, R. and Blood, M. (1977) Jealousy workshops. Ch. 19 in Clanton, G. and Smith, L. G. (eds.) *Jealousy*. Englewood Cliffs, NJ: Prentice-Hall, pp. 199–207.

Cobb, J. P. and Marks, I. M. (1979) Morbid jealousy featuring as obsessive compulsive neurosis: treatment by behavioural psychotherapy. *British Journal of Psychiatry*, **134**, 301–5.

Constantine, L. L. (1976). Jealousy: from theory to intervention. In Olson, D. H. L. (ed.) *Treating Relationships*. Lake Mills, Ia.: Graphic Publishers.

Constantine, L. L. and Constantine, J. M. (1974) Sexual aspects of multilateral relations. In Smith, J. R. and Smith, L. G. (eds.) *Beyond Monogamy: Recent Studies of Sexual Alternatives in Marriage*, Baltimore, MD: Johns Hopkins University Press, pp. 269–90.

Daher, D. M. and Cohen, M. (1979) Jealousy workshop: a conceptual base and format. *Personnel and Guidance Journal*, **57**, 480–2.

Enoch, M. D. (1980) Sexual jealousy. *British Journal of Sexual Medicine*, **7**, 30–4.

Francis, J. L. (1977) Towards the management of heterosexual jealousy. *Journal of Marriage and Family Counselling*, **3**, 61–9.

Goodman, L. S. and Gilman, A. (1958) *The Pharmacological Basis of Therapeutics*, 2nd edition. New York: Macmillan.

Lieberman, M. A., Yalom, I. D. and Miles, M. (1973) *Encounter Groups: First Facts*. New York: Basic Books.

Mairet, A. (1908) *La Jalousie: Étude Psychophysiologique, Clinique et Medicolégale*. Montpellier: Coulet.

Modlin, H. C. (1963) Psychodynamics and management of paranoid states in women. *Archives of General Psychiatry*, **8**, 263–8.

Modlin, H. C. (1964) Therapeutic management of paranoid states. *Current Psychiatric Therapies*, Vol. IV. Orlando, FA: Grune and Stratton, pp. 108–12.

Mooney, H. B. (1965) Pathological jealousy and psychochemotherapy. *British Journal of Psychiatry*, **111**, 1,023–42.

Morgan, D. H. (1975) The psychotherapy of jealousy. *Psychother. Psychosom.*, **25**, 43–7.

Morris, V. (1982) Helping lesbian couples cope with jealousy. *Women and Therapy*, **1**, 27–34.

Revitch, E. (1960) Diagnosis and disposition of paranoid marital partner. *Diseases of the Nervous System*, **21** (Feb. suppl.), 117–18.

Teismann, M. W. (1979) Jealousy: systematic problem-solving therapy with couples. *Family Process*, **18**, 151–60.

CHAPTER TEN: SUMMING UP: SEXUAL POLITICS IN TRIANGLES

Chapsal, M. (1977) *La Jalousie: Jeanne Moreau, Régine Deforges, Pauline Réage, Nadine Trintignant, Sonia Rykiel, Michèle Montrelay*. Paris: Gallimard.

Davis, K. (1936) Jealousy and sexual property. *Social Forces*, **14**, 395–405.

Denholtz, E. (1983) *Having it Both Ways: A Report on Married Women with Lovers*. New York: Bantam.

Durbin, K. (1973) On sexual jealousy. *The Village Voice*, October 18. Reprinted in Clanton, G. and Smith, L. G. (eds.) *Jealousy*. Englewood Cliffs, NJ: Prentice-Hall, pp. 36–45.

Eskapa, S. (1984) *Woman versus Woman: The Extra-marital Affair*. Danbury, Conn.: Watts (Franklin).

Hibbard, R. W. (1975) A rational approach to treating jealousy. *Rational Living*, **10**, 25–7.

Hunt, M. (1969) *The Affair*. Bergenfield, N.J.: The New American Library. Quoted in Strean, H. (1980).

James, W. and Kedgley, S. J. (1973) *The Mistress*. London: Abelard-Schuman. Quoted in Eskapa, S. (1984).

Lake, T. and Hills, A. (1979) *Affairs: The Anatomy of Extra-marital Relationships*. London: Open Books.

Latymer, F. B. T. C–N. (1915) *Ventures in Thought*. London: John Lane.

Lee, A. (1985) The foreigner within the walls. Paper presented to the Australian Institute of Criminology, Canberra, Australia.

Marcuse, M. (1950) Zur Psychologie der Eifersucht und der Psychopathologie ihres Fehlens. *Psyche*, **3**, 759–77. Quoted in Vauhkonen, K. (1968) On the pathogenesis of morbid jealousy. *Acta Psychiatrica Scandinavica*, Supplement 202. Copenhagen: Munksgaard.

Pike, J. A. (1967) *You and the New Morality*. New York: Harper and Row.

Pinta, E. R. (1978) Pathological tolerance. *American Journal of Psychiatry*, **135**, 698–701.

Proust, M. (1957) *Swann's Way*. Harmondsworth, Middlesex: Penguin Books.

Richardson, L. (1986) Another world. *Psychology Today*, **20**, 22–7.

Rubin, L. B. (1983) *Intimate Strangers: Men and Women Together*. New York: Harper and Row.

Salamon, E. (1984) *The Kept Woman: Mistresses in the 1980s*. London: Orbis

Strean, H. S. (1980) *The Extramarital Affair*. New York: Free Press.

Vincent, S. (1970) Sexual jealousy. *Nova Magazine*, 47–9.

Wagner, J. (1976) Jealousy, extended intimacies and sexual affirmation. *ETC, Journal of General Semantics*, **33**, 269–88.

Wolfe, L. (1975) *Playing Around: Women and Extra-marital Sex*. New York: William Morrow.

Index

———————— Q ————————

childhood jealousy, 9–13, 35
Chimbos, P. D., 86, 200
chimpanzees, 81–2, 101
Chiva, I., 125, 202
chlorpromazine, 152
clandestine affairs, 184–5
Clanton, G., 39, 196, 198, 200, 205, 206
Clark, A., 99, 201
Clouston, T. S., 155–6, 157, 158, 168, 204
Cobb, J. P., 165, 174, 204, 205
Cohen, M., 176, 205
companionate love, 30
complex emotions, 4, 6
connivance at infidelity, 19, 52–3, 103
Constantine, J. M., 176–7, 205
Constantine, L. L., 176–7, 205
control, loss of, 18–22
Cutileiro, J., 122–3, 202

Daher, D. M., 176, 205
Daly, M., 87–90, 94, 200
Dangerous Acquaintances, 52, 200
Darroch, S. J., 32, 198
Davis, J., 117, 123, 202
Davis, K., 8, 16–18, 183, 196, 206
Dawkins, R., 13, 196
deficiency love, 23
delayed puberty, 142
delusions, 130, 131–2, 135–8, 149, 150, 151–67
    of infidelity, 151, 157–9, 161
    of poisoning, 152–3, 161, 168
    of venereal disease, 152–3, 161, 162
    productivity of, 159–60
    secondary delusions, 162
Denholtz, E., 181, 190, 206
denial, 191
Denich, B. S., 126, 202
depression, 158, 160, 163–6, 168
    agitated, 163
    endogenous, 163
    frequency, 163
    reactive, 163
    subsequent to jealousy, 165
devaluation of partners, 43
De Vore, 1, 84, 90, 200

Dewhurst, K., 164, 165, 166, 169–70, 205
Dickemann, M., 90–93, 200, 201
disclosure, 33, 58–61, 184–5, 186
Docherty, J. P., 147–9, 159, 166, 203, 204
Dowson, E., 54
Duna, 109–10
Dunn, J., 9–12, 196
Durbin, K., 3, 194–5, 196, 206

economics of access, 13–16
Edwards, A., 59, 60, 200
Ehrhardt, A. A., 143, 203
Eibl-Eiblesfeldt, 1, 25, 198
Elias, N., 124, 202
Ellis, A., 189
Ellis, J., 147–9, 159, 166, 203, 204
Elwin, V., 116, 202
empathy, 183–4
Enoch, M. D., 159, 166, 171, 204, 205
envy, 1, 16, 46
equity theory, 27–8, 51
Ernst, K. J., viii, 36–7, 41, 198
Eskapa, S., 179–80, 184, 189, 191, 192, 194, 206
essentialist theories, 6–7
Euripides, viii
Evans, M., 56, 58, 200
evasion of jealousy, 79
evolution, opportunitistic nature of, 142–3
exclusion, 46–7
exclusivity, 15–16, 28
exogamy, 25, 81, 101–2

family structure, 96
fear of dependency, 43
Fei, J., 43, 197
'female circumcision', 88
Fenichel, O., 129, 133, 203
Ferenczi, S., 138
fictitious marriages, 62, 65
Flechsig, P., 136
Force of Circumstance, 57, 199
Foster, G. M., 16, 196
Foster, S., 9–10, 196
Fox, R., 97, 100, 101, 104, 105, 201
Francis, J. L., 177, 205
freedom, 55–8

213